Modern Scholarship on European History

HENRY A. TURNER, JR.,
Editor

THE
REFORMATION
IN MEDIEVAL
PERSPECTIVE

THE
REFORMATION
IN MEDIEVAL
PERSPECTIVE

Edited with an Introduction by
STEVEN E. OZMENT

CHICAGO
Quadrangle Books
1971

Library of Congress Catalog Card Number: 72-152100

SBN Cloth 8129-0194-0   SBN Paper 8129-6166-8

PREFACE

A WESTERN VISITOR to the Far East would not expect his hosts to speak the languages, practice the customs and in every way maintain the values of the western world. Another culture has its own unique and inalienable logic, which it surrenders only at the price of some self-distortion. It is the visitor who must make adjustments, some major and perhaps even painful, if true discovery and understanding are to occur.

The same is true of a past epoch of history. It too has its own languages, customs, and values. We do not so much compliment and make germane the past as insult and distort it if we demand that it give account of itself exclusively in and on our modern terms. Indeed, the study of the past can be as thoroughly subjugated and exploited for the sake of a shallow standard of relevance as can a foreign people in the name of a hollow promise of freedom. And when this happens the hard and valuable lessons of the past are smothered beneath the pleasant but insubstantial wishes of the present.

When we approach a way of life which differs from our own, the most difficult thing for us, as Alexandre Koyré points out in his essay on Paracelsus, is not so much to learn the unknown as to suspend the known. "Sometimes it is necessary not only to forget the truths which have become integral parts of our own thought but in fact to adopt certain modes and categories of reasoning or, at least, certain metaphysical principles which, for the people of a past age, were as valuable and as sure bases of reasoning and research as are for us the principles of mathematical physics and the fundamentals of astronomy."

This is a difficult but most important truth for us to remember

today. The will to tolerate, respect, and finally even relish difference
is as much a *sine qua non* of the study of the past as it is of good
interpersonal and intercultural relations. Historical study is a craft
to be mastered by those who would know more than one life style.

This volume attempts to practice what it preaches. It not only
places the Reformation in dialogue with its own historical past, but
it does so by bringing together essays by eight authors representing
almost as many cultures. Two were born in Russia, two in Germany,
two in Holland, one in France, and one in the United States. Most
of them have held teaching positions in more than one country.

Four of the essays focus on Martin Luther. This emphasis on
Luther in essays dealing with personalities results from the understandable fact that contemporary Luther scholarship has taken the
lead in placing the Reformation in medieval perspective. Greater
ecumenicity could have been practiced in this regard only at some
sacrifice of quality. It is to be expected, however, that the coming
generation of late medieval and Reformation scholars will remedy this
situation.

Six of the essays appear for the first time in English. Save for the
footnotes of one essay, the translations have been made by Miss
Joyce Irwin, Miss Janet Coleman and Mr. James J. Heaney. Miss
Coleman and Mr. Heaney are Ph.D. candidates at Yale University, as
is also Miss Irwin, who teaches history at the University of Georgia.
While the final formulations remain my responsibility, these young
scholars labored skillfully in difficult material to produce what I trust
the reader will agree are highly readable as well as accurate
translations.

In addition to individual introductions to the essays, I have ap-
pended a list of "Bibliographical Sources and Surveys of the Reformation," to enable the reader to bring himself up to date quickly and
comprehensively on trends in the various areas of Reformation studies.

S.E.O.

Branford, Connecticut
March 1971

ACKNOWLEDGMENTS

THE EDITOR wishes to express his appreciation to the following for permission to translate and/or to publish the essays included in this volume: the editors of the *Deutsche Vierteljahrsschrift für Literaturwissenschaft und Geistesgeschichte* and the Max Niemeyer Verlag for Gerhard Ritter, "Romantische und revolutionäre Elemente in der deutschen Theologie am Vorabend der Reformation"; the editors of the *Archiv für Reformationsgeschichte* and Professor Bernd Moeller for Bernd Moeller, "Frömmigkeit in Deutschland um 1500"; Professor František Graus for František Graus, "La crise du Moyen Age et l'hussitisme"; the editors of *Franziskanische Studien* and the Dietrich-Coelde Verlag for Paul Vignaux, "Sur Luther et Ockham"; the editors of the *Harvard Theological Review* for Heiko A. Oberman, "Facientibus quod in se est Deus non denegat gratiam: Robert Holcot, O.P. and the Beginnings of Luther's Theology," and Steven E. Ozment, "Homo Viator: Luther and Late Medieval Theology"; N. V. Boekhandel & Drukkerij, voorheen E. J. Brill for R. R. Post, "The Windesheimers After c. 1485: Confrontation with the Reformation and Humanism"; L'Association Marc Bloch and Mrs. Alexandre Koyré for Alexandre Koyré, "Paracelse"; and Professor Heiko A. Oberman for Heiko A. Oberman, "Simul gemitus et raptus: Luther and Mysticism."

ABBREVIATIONS

(USED IN THE TEXT)

ARG	*Archiv für Reformationsgeschichte*
HThR	*Harvard Theological Review*
PL or *MPL*	*Patrologia Latina,* ed. J. P. Migne (Paris, 1844–1890)
WA	*D. Martin Luthers Werke: Kritische Gesamtausgabe* (Weimar, 1883–)
WA Br.	*D. Martin Luthers Werke: Briefwechsel* (Weimar, 1930–)
WA Tr.	*D. Martin Luthers Werke: Tischreden* (Weimar, 1912–)
ZKG	*Zeitschrift für Kirchengeschichte*
ZSTh	*Zeitschrift für systematische Theologie*
ZThK	*Zeitschrift für Theologie und Kirche*

CONTENTS

THE
REFORMATION
IN MEDIEVAL
PERSPECTIVE

Introduction

In his masterly history of Christian philosophy in the Middle Ages, Etienne Gilson drew rather negative conclusions about the intellectual fiber of Europe on the eve of the Reformation. Compared with its noble beginning in high Scholasticism, particularly the achievement of Thomas Aquinas, the late Middle Ages, by the time it had run its course, was an essay in "speculative lassitude" and "doctrinal confusion." [1] Gilson was not surprised to find that the leader of the Protestant Reformation was the man who proclaimed: "The whole of Aristotle is to theology as darkness is to light." [2]

If Gilson is the most prominent intellectual historian who has assessed the late Middle Ages exclusively from its point of departure in high Scholasticism, Joseph Lortz, church historian and a director of the Institute for European History at the University of Mainz, can be said to be the most prominent intellectual historian to have assessed the late Middle Ages exclusively from its point of destination, the Protestant Reformation. [3] Of various evaluations of the late Middle Ages written with an eye to the Reformation, none has been more impressive in scope, persistent in influence, and challenging in assessment than Lortz's two-volume study of *The Reformation in Germany* (1939-1940). [4] It places the Reformation squarely in the perspective of the late Middle Ages and takes an unambiguous position on all

3

major controversial issues. It is a necessary introduction and a fitting foil for modern efforts to set the Reformation in medieval perspective.

The standard by which Gilson measured the thought of the late Middle Ages was the delicate balance between reason (philosophy, the State) and revelation (theology, the Church) which he felt Thomas Aquinas had achieved in fact and which all high scholastics applauded in principle if not in every particular. Although the conclusions of Gilson and Lortz are not dissimilar, the latter's yardstick for assessing the late Middle Ages is not an ideal synthesis of reason and revelation. Rather, it is the havoc which he feels was wreaked on western civilization by the Protestant Reformation,[5] a revolt which, in his opinion, supplanted the basic medieval commitments (*Grundhaltungen*) to objectivity, respect for tradition, and the clerical Church.

> Seen as a religious and ecclesiastical event the Reformation is the denial of the visible Church, rooted and grounded in the objective teaching authority and in the sacramental priesthood; and it is the acceptance of a religion of conscience erected upon the judgment of the individual with regard to the biblical word. That is to say: along these two lines of its development, the Reformation replaced the basic medieval attitudes of objectivism, traditionalism, and clericalism by those of subjectivism, spiritualism, and laicism.[6]

As he looks at the late Middle Ages, Lortz is especially sensitive to those ideas, events, movements, alliances, and personages which promoted, directly or indirectly, consciously or unconsciously, the conditions requisite for the overthrow of these basic medieval commitments. In order that the Reformation should occur—its *Grundvoraussetzung*—a question had to be posed: is the papal Church the true, authoritative representative of Christendom? Lortz sees this doubt about the objective validity of the institutional Church being raised throughout the late Middle Ages by such diverse men and movements as Philip the Fair, the Spiritual Franciscans, nominalism, William of Occam, Marsilius of Padua, The Waldensians and Cathari, the conciliarists, John Wyclif, John Huss and the widespread Hussite revolt in fifteenth century Bohemia.[7]

The objective authority of the medieval Church suffered decisively, Lortz feels, in the struggle between Philip the Fair and Boniface VIII. "After this confrontation the specifically medieval papacy no longer existed." [8] Here he sees the genesis of the modern autonomous state to which ecclesiastical interests must be subordinated. William of Occam

and Marsilius of Padua become the chief theoreticians for this step—
a calamitous one, according to Lortz—in the direction of Machiavelli.[9]
In the various estates of Germany this larger development triumphed
in what Lortz describes as a nationalistic "egoism," which, by en-
couraging the breakdown of centralized authority within the Empire,
consolidated political power sufficiently for effective revolt.[10]

Lortz uses the term "humanism" to characterize the general tenor
of intellectual life on the eve of the Reformation. Humanists returned to ancient literary sources and, by so doing, encouraged openness to new thoughts and experiences—radically new thoughts and
experiences.[11] Revolutionary movements, of course, must have such
openness to succeed. And because it fostered such openness, Lortz
considers the spirit of humanism to be the *conditio sine qua non* of
the Reformation." [12]

He also sees the writings of Joachim of Flora as influential in this
process of conditioning men for the new. In the closing decades of
the fifteenth century Joachite apocalypticism was especially in evidence.[13] Joachim had prophesied a future Age of the Spirit which
would supplant the present Age of the Son. Such teaching admon-
ished men to be prepared for something better, and thus became an
ally of the program launched by the humanists. They taught men to
seek the ideal in the past, Joachim expected it in the immediate
future, but both approaches undermined contemporary institutions
by stressing their penultimate and imperfect, if not downright corrupt, character.[14]

The spirit of humanism is betrayed for Lortz in a paradigmatic
way by Pico della Mirandola, who argued in his *Oration on the Dignity of Man* that every man has been created, as it were, formless,
so that he may choose to be exactly what he wishes. Man is the
creature who legislates by free volition what he will be. His nature
is not fixed. Among German humanists and theologians this was
expressed in terms of dedication to and expectation of the truly
novel.[15]

Together with the demand for new thoughts and experiences, humanists launched very effective, albeit often exaggerated, critical
satires against popes, scholastics, monks, and clerics.[16] In these attacks
the traditional and institutional was ridiculed, according to Lortz, by
a predominantly "worldly, naturalistic, anthropocentric" concept of
freedom.[17] "Renaissance and humanism became the first classical period
of criticism in Europe" [18]—a preview of greater doubts to come.[19]

On the eve of the Reformation Lortz finds humanists busy harvest-

ing the fruits of their work. They exposed the Donation of Con-
stantine as a forgery and demonstrated the lack of historical justification for other precedents of ecclesiastical authority. They pointed out
discrepancies between the official Latin Bible and the original texts.
Lortz sees the bold realism of Machiavelli as a typical product of the
critical humanist spirit which held nothing immune from the most
uncompromising analysis.[20] In Germany the humanists were not only
especially fierce in their criticism of traditional habits and values; they
were also more closely in touch with the people than were humanists
in Italy, who by and large gravitated to the universities, thus circum-
scribing their sphere of influence.[21]

What humanists accomplished by devastating vernacular satire Lortz
sees achieved in the nominalism of William of Occam by the philosophical separation of faith and knowledge.[22] Humanism and nominalism introduced profound doubt and skepticism into late medieval
society.

Lortz finds religious life on the eve of the Reformation no less
hostile to the traditional medieval commitments. The teachings of
John Huss were widespread among the people and, in Lortz's judgment, prepared the way for practically all of Luther's ideas.[23] The
fires of religious fervor were fanned by legitimate social discontent,
but they were also fed by the ideal of poverty in the Bible, now
increasingly available in the vernacular, and by apocalypticism.[24]

In searching for the causes of the agitation and deterioration of
religious life on the eve of the Reformation, Lortz does not mince
words about the Renaissance papacy. "To a significant degree the
Renaissance curia presents an acute secularization, which primitive and
early Christendom would have called anti-Christian (widerchrist-
lich)." [25] Among legitimate grievances Lortz points to the pastors'
utter neglect of residency requirements. In Germany, for example, it
is reported that only 7 percent of the parishes had pastors in resi-
dence. The Emperor Maximilian, certainly no particular friend of
the working man, is reported by Lortz to have lamented that the
papacy took a hundred times as many gulden out of Germany as he
did.[26]

Economically exploited and religiously adrift, the German people
were, in a very concrete pastoral sense, sheep without shepherds.[27]
Since the nobility were the recipients of significant ecclesiastical ap-
pointments, the church hierarchy in Germany was often populated
by the theologically inept and uninterested, who were, quite understandably, despised by the people. Lortz sees this situation as creating

hostility toward traditional religious forms and producing an enormous spiritual proletariat—large numbers of lower clergy and priests who were neither firmly located, indoctrinated, nor disciplined.[28]

Piety developed unchecked by the Church. It was a piety which, if not overtly hostile to dogma, was at least uninterested in precise doctrinal definition. Although much that was wholesome persisted, aberrations appeared which cast suspicion upon the substance of heightened religious fervor—aberrations such as witchcraft, superstition, the desire for miracles and visions, occult philosophy, astrology, cabala, magic, and ardent interest in relics and pilgrimages to holy places.[29] Such aberrations, in Lortz's judgment, tended to overshadow the sacramental life of the Church and often infiltrated and corrupted it.

On the eve of the Reformation, then, religious piety, so well exemplified in the *Devotio moderna,* evidenced the strong tendency to "relax the objective and universal in favor of the peripheral and individual." [30] As Lortz summarizes:

> . . . the inwardness we find in pre-Reformation piety bore, in a significant measure, a subjectivist colouring. It bore the mark of privacy, of the personal and also of the moralistic. This piety comprises the most intense striving for salvation by the individual soul. It is the prayer and endeavour of this soul that are central. The objective Church with its objective holiness was solidly affirmed, as were the sacraments and the holy sacrifice of the mass. Nonetheless, the piety of that time to some extent diverted the individual—often considerably—from the objectivity of the liturgical-sacramental organism of the risen Lord and from the mediation of the special priesthood, thus leading him away from the realm of the great sacrificial community of prayer and sacraments.[31]

When all the pieces are put in place, Lortz sees the late Middle Ages culminating in a relativization of traditional, objective, doctrinal Christianity—a relativization aided and abetted by late medieval humanism, nominalism, and mysticism.[32] Erasmus becomes its most eloquent representative—Erasmus who teaches that peace is more important than doctrinal truth and pleads for a relativistic *via media* which can affirm without deciding.[33]

Lortz, in almost verbatim agreement with Gilson's assessment of the journey's end, concludes that "theological unclarity" within the late medieval Church makes the coming of the Reformation comprehensible. It was "vagueness" about religious truth and authority that permitted Erasmus to go unaccused and allowed the young Luther to establish a firm beachhead before the peril he represented was recognized. This vagueness and lack of clarity prepared the soil during the late Middle Ages so that the Reformation was able to take root and thrive.[34]

When doubts arise about the validity of given social institutions, be they even so ancient and honored as the medieval Christian Church, they can and do carry destructive consequences in their wake. The doubts and questions, however, can be legitimate ones, formulated in the most reasonable as well as most critical way, intended to build up and renew as well as to tear down, set forth by those who would be reformers as well as revolutionaries, and developed so as. to preserve the old as well as to introduce the radically new. If it is true that doubting questions can undermine social institutions, it is also true that such questions cease only when the will to reform these institutions has ceased.

The essays collected in this volume vigorously debate the nature of the contribution of the late Middle Ages to the Reformation and provide the reader with abundant bibliographical resources for further pursuit of the problems considered. In each of the major areas emphasized by Lortz, the essays mark the direction of modern research on the Reformation. This is done, at times, by disagreement with Lortz's particular assessment, and at times by amiable concurrence. To the extent, however, that these essays may be said to speak as one, they depict the late medieval critics of the Church and the commanding figures of the Reformation as speaking as much out of their medieval past as against it, opposing Scripture with Scripture, canon with canon, and tradition with tradition. The Reformation emerges as being as much the product of progressive reform as of gradual disintegration, the climax—intellectually and institutionally— of a broadly based late medieval quest for a new objectivity rather than a bald triumph of anticlerical subjectivism in the midst of establishmentarian corruption and confusion.

NOTES

1. *History of Christian Philosophy in the Middle Ages* (New York, 1955), pp. 470ff., 528ff.
2. See the pointed discussion in *Reason and Revelation in the Middle Ages* (New York, 1938), p. 93.
3. Neither we nor Lortz mean to suggest that the late Middle Ages had only

one point of destination or that the Protestant Reformation is the only reform movement which peaks in the 16th century. On 16th century Catholic reform in medieval perspective, see especially P. Janelle, *The Catholic Reformation* (Milwaukee, 1949); H. Jedin, *A History of the Council of Trent*, I–II (St. Louis, 1957); R. M. Douglas, *Jacopo Sadoleto 1477–1547: Humanist and Reformer* (Cambridge, Mass., 1959); E. Iserloh, *Reform der Kirche bei Nikolaus von Kues* (Wiesbaden, 1965); H. A. Oberman, "Das tridentinische Rechtfertigungsdekret im Lichte spätmittelalterlicher Theologie," *ZThK* (1964), pp. 251ff.; and J. W. O'Malley, *Giles of Viterbo on Church and Reform* (Leiden, 1968). For pointed comments on variety within the Protestant Reformation, see especially G. H. Williams, *The Radical Reformation* (Philadelphia, 1962); *Spiritual and Anabaptist Writers*, ed. G. H. Williams and A. M. Mergal (Philadelphia, 1957); and my own forthcoming article in *ARG*, "Mysticism and Dissent in the 16th Century: The Assessment of the *Theologia Deutsch* from Martin Luther to Valentin Weigel." A popular synthetic volume, which distinguishes late medieval, Humanist, Protestant, Radical and Roman Catholic reform, is *Reformers in Profile: Advocates of Reform 1300–1600*, ed. B. A. Gerrish (Philadelphia, 1967).

4. Lortz's study has gone through four German editions (Freiburg, 1962 [4]) since its first appearance in 1939–40. It has recently been translated into English by Ronald Walls (London and New York, 1968). There is a small popular statement of its major theses: *Wie kam es zur Reformation?* (Einsiedeln, 1955[3]), which has also been translated into English—an excerpted translation appears in *The Reformation: Material or Spiritual?*, ed. L. W. Spitz (Boston, 1962), pp. 56ff., and the full text under the title *How the Reformation Came* (New York, 1964). Recent historical studies with conclusions similar to those of Lortz are Robert E. McNally, *Reform of the Church: Crisis and Criticism in Historical Perspective* (New York, 1963) and Christopher Dawson, *The Dividing of Christendom* (1965). Lortz's influence is also evident in recent Catholic Luther studies; Jared Wicks, *Man Yearning for Grace: Luther's Early Spiritual Teaching* (Washington, 1969) and Harry J. McSorley, *Luther: Right or Wrong?* (New York, 1969). On the other hand, there is the irenic placement of the Reformation in medieval perspective by John P. Dolan, *History of the Reformation: A Conciliatory Assessment of Opposite Views* (New York, 1965). Matching Dolan's conciliatory historical study is the still more conciliatory theological study by Otto H. Pesch, *Die Theologie der Rechtfertigung bei Martin Luther und Thomas von Aquin* (Mainz, 1967). Pesch not only sets aside Lortz's criticism of Luther's "subjectivism," but even maintains that Luther's theology marks no "Neuland" forbidden the Catholic theologian. *Ibid.*, pp. 919, 950.

5. "Of all the many factors that could be named as contributing to the de-Christianization of Europe, none is as important a single cause as the Reformation, or more precisely, the split in Christendom opened through the Reformation." *How the Reformation Came*, p. 18.

6. *Die Reformation in Deutschland*, I (Freiburg, 1962), 10=*The Reformation in Germany*, I (London and New York, 1968), 11. In subsequent references I will give first the German and, second, the English reference under Lortz, separated by a slash. In larger citations I have generally followed the Walls translation.

7. Lortz, pp. 13/14f.

8. Lortz, pp. 21/23. This confrontation can be followed in Brian Tierney, *The Crisis of Church and State 1050–1300* (Englewood Cliffs, N. J., 1964), 172–192. The secondary discussion is brought together in *Philip the Fair and Boniface VIII: State vs. Papacy,* ed. Charles T. Wood (New York, 1967).

9. Lortz, pp. 21f./23f. For more recent and moderate views of Occam's political ideas, which clearly distinguish him from the "Erastian" notions of Marsilius, see especially P. Boehner, "Ockham's Political Ideas," *The Review of Politics* IV (1943), 462–487, and A. Hamman, "La doctrine de l'Eglise et de l'Etat d'après le *Breviloquium* d'Occam," in *Franziskanische Studien* 32=*Wilhelm Ockham: Aufsätze zu seiner Philosophie und Theologie* (Münster, 1950), p. 140: Occam takes "la position moyenne," between those who would subordinate Church to State and those who would absorb the State into the Church.

10. Lortz, pp. 36/40.

11. Lortz, pp. 48f./54–56.

12. Lortz, 49/56. On the continuing debate over the definition of this slippery term, see the impressive collection of articles in the recent *Humanismus,* ed. Hans Oppermann, *Wege der Forschung,* XVII (Darmstadt, 1970).

13. We are brought up to date on Joachimism by Morton Bloomfield, "Joachim of Flora: A Critical Survey of His Canon, Teachings, Sources, Biography and Influence," *Traditio* 13 (1957), 249–309; and Marjorie Reeves, *The Influence of Prophecy in the Later Middle Ages: A Study in Joachimism* (Oxford, 1969). Relevant also is the recent study by Gordon Leff which is not unsympathetic to Lortz's overall assessment of the late Middle Ages, *Heresy in the Later Middle Ages: The Relation of Heterodoxy to Dissent c. 1250–c. 1450* (Manchester, 1967).

14. Lortz, pp. 49f./56f.

15. Lortz, pp. 50f./57f.

16. Lortz, pp. 54/61.

17. Lortz, pp. 56/63.

18. Lortz, pp. 57/64.

19. The continuing debate on whether the Renaissance was "medieval" or "modern," Christian or pagan, is brought together in *The Renaissance: Medieval or Modern,* ed. Karl H. Dannenfeldt (Boston, 1959). Much more positive assessments of the intentions of German humanists are Bernd Moeller, "Die deutschen Humanisten und die Anfänge der Reformation," *ZKG* 70 (1959), 46–61, and Lewis W. Spitz, *The Religious Renaissance of the German Humanists* (Cambridge, Mass., 1963), esp. pp. 274ff.

20. Lortz, pp. 57/64.

21. Lortz, pp. 57f./65.

22. Lortz, pp. 60/68. For detailed assessment of Occam and nominalism as determining factors in Luther's existential and theological outlook, see Lortz, pp. 172ff./195ff. The major monographs on this problem are Bengt Hägglund, *Theologie und Philosophie bei Luther und in der occamistischen Tradition: Luthers Stellung zu der Theorie der doppelten Wahrheit* (Lund, 1955); Erwin Iserloh, *Gnade und Eucharistie in der philosophischen Theologie des Wilhelm von Ockham: Ihre Bedeutung für die Ursachen der Reformation* (Wiesbaden, 1956); and, most recently, Helmar Junghans, *Ockham im Lichte der neueren Forschung* (Berlin, 1968). Also relevant is Gerhard Ritter, *Studien zur Spätscholastik,* I–II (Heidelberg, 1921–22).

23. Lortz, pp. 69/79. Cf. the recent judgment of Matthew Spinka, *John Hus'*

Concept of the Church (Princeton, 1966), p. 385: Huss has the "basic elements" of the Reformation. On Luther's view of Huss see Jaroslav Pelikan, "Luther's Attitude Toward John Huss," *Concordia Theological Monthly* 19 (1948), 747–763. On the Catholic reassessment of Huss, see Paul de Vooght, *L'hérésie de Jean Huss* (Louvain, 1960) and "Jean Huss et ses juges," in *Das Konzil von Konstanz. Festschrift für Hermann Schäufele,* ed. A. Franzen and W. Mueller (Freiburg i. Br., 1964), pp. 152–173.

24. Lortz, pp. 70ff./80ff. Herbert Grundmann brings the research on late medieval religious movements up to date in his recent historical-bibliographical survey: *Ketzergeschichte des Mittelalters* (Göttingen, 1967 2).

25. Lortz, pp. 75/85.

26. Lortz, pp. 77/87. The best documentation of the economic grievances of Germany at the outbreak of the Reformation is Luther's own *Address to the Christian Nobility of the German Nation* (1520). The secondary literature on the economic situation of the late Middle Ages is surveyed by František Graus, "Das Spätmittelalter als Krisenzeit: Ein Literaturbericht als Zwischenbilanz," *Mediaevalia Bohemica,* Supplementum 1 (1969).

27. Lortz, pp. 82f./94.

28. Lortz, pp. 83–87/94–98.

29. Lortz, pp. 100f./113f.

30. Lortz, pp. 121/137f.

31. Lortz, pp. 119/136.

32. Lortz, pp. 126/144.

33. Lortz, pp. 127ff./144ff. "With Erasmus—not with Luther—the destructive domination of the purely individual conscience appeared upon the scene of modern history." Lortz, pp. 128/146. Cf. the recent *Luther, Erasmus and the Reformation: A Catholic-Protestant Reappraisal,* ed. John C. Olin (New York, 1969).

34. Lortz, pp. 138/157. Later Lortz summarizes: "The Reformation is incomprehensible apart from this theological vagueness. Without it, the radical ideas expressed by Luther in 1517 would have encountered a general repulse from theologians and the decisive majority of public authorities, and would have died away before even taking root." Lortz, pp. 204/233.

PART ONE

ON THE
EVE
OF THE
REFORMATION

1

GERHARD RITTER

Romantic and Revolutionary Elements in German Theology on the Eve of the Reformation *

[TRANSLATED BY JOYCE IRWIN]

Gerhard Ritter (1888–1967), late Professor of Modern History at the University of Freiburg (since 1925), and editor of the Archiv für Reformationsgeschichte (since 1938), produced biographical studies of Luther, Karl Stein, Frederick the Great, Bismarck, and Carl Goerdeler. Master of Reformation and Modern History, Ritter's earliest major publication was the three-volume Studien zur Spätscholastik (1921–1927). One by-product of the research for this impressive project was "Romantic and Revolutionary Elements in German Theology on the Eve of the Reformation." The article explores the positive contributions already made to European intellectual history by German sources before the "Wittenberg Reformation." The conclusions are twofold. On the one hand, Ritter finds that fifteenth century German theology, embracing the philosophical achievement of Ockham and the conciliar movement, was more conservative than revolutionary, inclined to restore the purity of the old rather than to institute the fundamentally new. On the other hand, however, in the wider Germanic circles of the Netherlands reform theology of Johann von Wesel, Wessel Gansfort, and Pupper von Goch, the situation was quite different. Here Ritter sees not only a much needed scholastic

* A revised and expanded version of a lecture to the German historical convention in Breslau, October 8, 1926, printed in *Deutsche Vierteljahrsschrift für Literaturwissenschaft und Geistesgeschichte* V (1927), 342-380.

*base for the protest of German piety against Rome, but also ideas
which anticipate Luther. On such issues as indulgences, the priesthood, and the Eucharist, Ritter finds striking affinities between Luther
and these theologians, especially Wessel Gansfort, whom he considers
more revolutionary than the Ockhamists. Although they do not go
as far as does the Lutheran Reformation, these Dutch theologians indicate a second, indigenous form of German piety, which both prepared the way for the Reformation and remained a unique achievement
in its own right. As Ritter summarizes: "German life in the age of
the Reformation was rich enough to allow a second, original form
of German piety rebelling against Rome to bloom beside the Lutheran
Reformation." The article raises a tantalizing question, whether this
second form of German piety, with its derivation from medieval
mysticism and its openness to the practical bon sens of Humanism,
did not determine more of the post-Reformation course of German
intellectual history than did the Reformation itself.*

I. Formulation of the question: Was the Reformation a revolutionary
action of scholastically trained theologians? Were there already revolutionary elements in the German theology of the fifteenth century?

II. German scholastic theology of the fifteenth century. Diversion
of Ockhamist criticism of dogma and the church to dogmatically
and politically safe tracks. The unworldliness of German scholastic
theologians. The romantic-restorative character of their criticism of
the church.

III. The exceptional appearance of revolutionary ideas in the wider
circle of German theology of the fifteenth century: analysis of
Netherlands-Middle Rhine reform theology (Joh. Wesel, Joh. Pupper
[von Goch], Wessel Gansfort). The origins of their criticism in
the religious movement among the laity.

IV. The figure of Wessel Gansfort and his central significance for
reform theology of the Netherlands. His relationship to the humanistic movement.

V. The effect and more general historical significance of Netherlands-Middle Rhine reform theology.

I

The ecclesiastical revolution of the sixteenth century broke out and succeeded particularly in Germany, which had not outgrown the ecclesiastical traditions of the Middle Ages either inwardly or outwardly as much as had other countries of the Romanic-Germanic cultural circle. How this was possible is a question which will continue to elicit new formulations of historical problems from very different angles. But no matter how much economic, sociological, legal-historical, political, and religious-historical factual material the political historian may marshal in order to grasp the external aspects of this phenomenon, he will not be able to penetrate its essence unless he ventures onto its slippery surface, where he may easily (as I am well aware) slip and fall, or wander far from his original starting-point. Certainly Luther's action, by virtue of its spiritual origin as well as its most genuine intention, was something far more than an event in theology or the history of dogma, and something fundamentally different.

We have reason to assert this emphatically, against certain recent theological interpretations of Luther, and we rejoice in the confirmation which such a view receives from the thoughtful "Luther Fragments," recently published, of the young Ranke. Certainly the effect of Luther's preaching, in its nature and especially in its level, was most strongly determined by the fact that Luther the scholastic, after endless attempts, successfully countered the theological doctrine of Catholicism with a new system of fixed theological concepts (at first complete only in a few central questions). Only in this way was it possible to shake to its foundations the firmly established structure of the ancient church. The church history of the later Middle Ages abundantly illustrates this. Every reform movement had prospects of real success only to the extent that it succeeded in piercing the ancient church's thick network of dogmatic traditions with the weapons of ecclesiastical learning. The German Reformation made particular use of these weapons—if not exclusively, then at least more willingly than in any other country— and in this respect it was much more one-sided than the reform movements elsewhere. In England and Bohemia the ecclesiastical rebellion of the Wycliffites was entangled from the very beginning—and increasingly as time progressed—in political, national, and social undertakings and movements, but in Germany the Reformation, originally the work of a sequestered mendicant monk, was entrusted mostly to the hands of completely apolitical theologians, and remained so. As long as Luther remained its authoritative spokesman, it could never become seriously politicized.

Even in its later stages, when Lutheran theologians were encouraged or put under pressure by the politics of their princes and lords, as often as not they flatly or obstinately thwarted the princely designs. The fact that their preaching was taken much more seriously than the heretical ideas of the numerous popular movements which had surged against the ancient church since the fourteenth century is to be attributed not to the favor of worldly powers but to their own theological education. And this had a definite background. Luther himself had considered his doctorate of theology a substantiation of his right to criticize Catholic dogma. The consciousness of thorough scholastic training and superior theological insight, which had given him courage in 1518 in Augsburg to confront the papal legate, is also characteristic of the generation of theologians upon which he (and Melanchthon even more) drew.

The Lutheran Reformation grew from the soil of late medieval scholastic theology. Its relationship to its predecessor, therefore, has long been treated with great thoroughness, especially biographically, and especially since the strong attacks of Catholic investigators upon the originality of certain essential Lutheran ideas. A doctrinal study of the vast scholastic or half-scholastic commentaries on Biblical books in Luther's early period should make an important contribution in this regard. The main task will be to separate the evolving, gradually developing, new ideas from those which had been handed down.

But one can also proceed in the opposite way, i.e. by moving forward from late scholasticism instead of backward from Luther. Disregarding both the originality of Luther's ideas and their possible derivation from others, one could formulate the question thus: whether in the whole of late scholastic theology, but especially that of Germany before Luther, one may discover the germs—the beginnings of a development which points to the future. This is the formulation from which Carl Ullmann proceeded around the middle of the last century, when he wrote his much used and much abused book on the "Reformers before the Reformation." He found it striking that there was so much talk about pre-Reformation phenomena in other countries—England, Bohemia, France, and even Italy—but no serious search for corresponding beginnings in German territory. Yet Germany (including Switzerland and the Netherlands) was indisputably the heartland of the Reformation. Ullmann believed that he discovered such "reformatory" elements in German mysticism, and in the lay piety of the

Brethren of the Common Life and its close-knit circle of theologians, Johann von Wesel, Pupper von Goch, and Wessel Gansfort. (Luther, as is well known, obtained his very first knowledge of the writings of these theologians in the twenties.) Their immediate influence on his theological development interested Ullmann less than the fact that in the fifteenth century "reformatory" ideas were already in circulation in German territory and outside Wittenberg. Since then, of course, following the example of Ritschl,[1] the fundamental differences between this supposed "pre-reformatory" theology and genuine Wittenberg teaching have been disputed with such trenchancy that hardly anything seemed to remain of Ullmann's thesis. But his formulation of the problem is still by no means disposed of, as is recognized by more recent theologians. It seems to me to deserve more than merely ecclesio-historical interest.

Yet how difficult and almost impossible it is to grasp the concrete traits of national individuality within the framework of a medieval intellectual history which is only comprehensible as a general European history. How thick lies the covering of a foreign spirit, especially over German life! How much more than the nations of the European West and South does Germany struggle to break free from dull dependence on what is foreign and reach clarity about herself! Yet she achieves this most decisively—and this should be beyond confessional disputes—in the quarrel with Rome. From the decline of German imperial dignity in the struggle with the papal hierarchy, from Walther von der Vogelweide's nationalist songs of mourning and praise to the conciliar battles in Germany territory, to the German humanists, and finally to the German Reformation, this opposition appears in ever new forms and overshadows all other national antagonisms (toward the neighboring French, for example) in its importance for awakening a national self-consciousness.

But this denotes primarily only something negative, only an opposition. To determine the positive contribution which European intellectual history had already received *before* the Wittenberg Reformation from unquestionably original German sources is a very difficult and ticklish undertaking. Here one should discuss first of all (omitting the visual arts in the fifteenth century as a separate chapter) German mysticism, Meister Eckhart, and the Neoplatonists of the Dominican order in Germany. It is well known how extremely tricky it is to distinguish between scholastic tradition and independent thinking, and how difficult it is to answer the question whether there was any special *German* variety of Western mysticism with a characterizable peculiarity. An attempt has, indeed, just recently been made to derive the peculiarity of all German philosophy to a significant extent from the persistence into the modern era of mystical streams of thought from the Middle Ages.[2] Such a view, however, will have to follow with loving care the various beginnings of another view of the world —besides contemplative mysticism in the style of Eckhart—which, as early as the fifteenth century, seems to transcend mere negation, mere criticism of the Roman hierarchical structure, and affirm a positive new ideal of life. Whether this ideal points in the direction of later Lutheran theology and even scales the height of Lutheran thinking seems less important to us, who have no dogmatic interest to defend, than the problem of distinguishing as exactly as possible between the new and the traditional, and, within the new, between the positive and the merely critical and negative.

II

In order to find a sure answer to such questions, however, it will be necessary first to sketch the actual form of German scholastic theology in the fifteenth century.

Theology as a public study practiced in the manner of a guild was, as is well known, transplanted from Paris to German soil only at the end of the fourteenth century—later than anywhere else in Europe. This fact has had far-reaching consequences for the level of education and the mentality of German secular clergy, and for the esteem in which they are held by the public. Scholastic theological studies, indeed, had existed earlier, but they were limited mainly to the academic houses of the mendicant orders. Their literary contribution consisted for the most part in practical, edifying writings (many of them in the German language), rather than in scholarly tracts. These works are not without significance for understanding religious life in Germany in the fourteenth century, but they cannot compare with the great theological controversies of the time, and, understandably, they had no effect on the general development of theology. The latter is true also, for the most part, of the Platonism of the German Dominicans, mentioned above. The mystical movement in Germany evolved entirely within the area of preaching and pastoral care, i.e., as practical devotional teaching. It operated, at least in the beginning, not as a new theology but as a special kind of lay piety, which was originally of a highly aristocratic nature. Scholastic theology in Germany, together with the universities, arose not through organic development from primitive beginnings, but as artificially transplanted foreign growth.

The shape in which scholastic theology had the greatest impact within the German universities was an especially highly-developed late form, mature Ockhamism. Commonly associated with this form is the conception of a "self-dissolution of scholasticism"—by virtue of newly emerging intellectual ferments which prepared the way for the Reformation as both germs of decomposition and fertilizing sperm. This conception, though certainly not without a profound basis, has on the whole produced a great deal of confusion. Considered purely logically, it is doubtless correct that the one-sided emphasis on the volitional dimension of the religious, initiated by Duns Scotus and then pursued with far greater consequences by Ockham, was naturally fitted to undermine the artistically balanced harmony between faith and knowledge on which the unity of high scholastic systems— classically that of Thomas in particular—had rested. The artful fusing of these two historically quite different elements, the ancient concept of knowledge and Christian revelation, had, in the last analysis, con- stituted the purpose of all scholastic work. Their inner antagonism was recognized clearly for the first time when Ockham took seriously the achievement of Aristotelian science, denied that theology was scientific in the strict sense, and simultaneously revived the patristic "credo quia absurdum" in the form of a ruthlessly pursued supra- naturalism and ecclesiastical positivism.

In this tendency, in the theologian's mistrust of the ability of natural reason to judge revealed truths, the continuance of Ockhamist trains of thought in Luther is clearly recognizable. In place of a rationally conceivable order of salvation, there appears everywhere the uncomprehended arbitrariness of divine commands. But one should beware of overestimating the practical consequences of this theoreti- cally constructed antagonism in the Ockhamist system. Within the framework of medieval theology this did indeed loosen the unity of the metaphysical-theological picture of the world, but by no means destroyed it. The school traditions, long established through the great textbooks (with Peter Lombard and his commentators in the fore- front) and not least through the Aristotelian texts, the elucidation of which was the main part of all philosophical instruction, had an effect which cannot be overstated. The final goal inspiring medieval theology, even after Ockham, was at least to make dogma unassail- able—if it could not be demonstrable—to make it somehow as probable as was possible with the help of human *ratio*. The drive toward metaphysical-theological speculation, then, remained paramount even when Ockhamist epistemology, with its nominalist features, seemed to place in serious doubt the metaphysical validity of the general concepts formed by the intellect.

The importance of this nominalist critique of knowledge for the development of late medieval theology and philosophy has been very much overestimated. This has probably been strongest in the customary representations of the history of philosophy, which, misled by analogies from modern critical theories of knowledge, attempt to find in the old scholastic, Ockham, certain elements of a modern subjectivist concept of knowledge. In place of traditional Aristotelianism they find rudiments of a sensualist-empirical method of knowing, and even a skeptical view of the possibility of knowing anything outside of sensory experience. In fact nothing was further from Ockhamism than disbelief in the ability of the human intellect to grasp the true essence of things with the help of universal concepts. And this is true not only of the objects of sensory experience,[3] but also of metaphysical essences. I have, incidentally, documented this with regard to the philosophy of Marsilius of Inghen, the most important of the older German Ockhamists; it holds true in all the separate ramifications of the philosophical and theological system.[4]

But even if one wanted to grant the possibility that a liberation of human *ratio* from the spell of the scholastic tradition—the "modern critical sense of subjectivism"—*could* develop from Ockham's critical beginnings in the theory of knowledge (Seeberg), the fact remains that this advance in thought beyond scholasticism was simply not carried out. It may in fact have appeared for a moment that a philosophical-theological radicalism might develop in Paris from the soil of Ockhamist theorems. The high-flown epistemological subjectivism and the extreme separation of the idea of God from all *ratio*, which John of Mirecourt and Nicholas of Autrecourt dared to defend, would have meant, had it been carried through consistently, something like a "self-dissolution of scholasticism." But the ecclesiastical officials assailed it quickly with excommunication and inquisition. After that no Ockhamists abandoned the ground of strictest conformity to the church, which was at the same time the ground of the Aristotelian scholastic tradition. The philosophical harmlessness of their nominalist epistemology was defended vehemently by later Ockhamists themselves, with Jean Gerson at their head, against the attacks of inimical scholastic cliques.

Common in all late scholasticism is a clever opportunism, inclined to shun delicate oppositions and problems. This often comes to the fore in an especially crass form among the Ockhamists, since the role of natural reason in their tradition is particularly ambiguous. Indeed, the more the shrewd criticism of nearly all traditions, which Ockham himself pursued with increasing penetration throughout his life, was neglected by his later followers in favor of scholarly precision and thoroughness, the more the soul vanished from this erudition. For the soul of the scholastic method is controversy, disputation, just as the defense of dogma is its final goal. By seeking to avoid extreme positions as dangerous, one dulls the opposition. The controversy continues, but it is supported for the most part only by the tiresome customs of the school, seldom by the ardor of the original profound convictions. From unpublished sources of the history of the University of Heidelberg, I am able to show in detail [5] how scholastic disputations in the fifteenth century, particularly within the Faculty of Arts, had long since become empty rhetorical displays and had completely lost the character of conflicts between convictions.

Corresponding precisely with this development is the style of scholarly writing, especially along theological literary lines. At the end of the fourteenth century it still bears traits of the fully-developed Parisian tradition and shows clearly that frequently mentioned hypertrophy of logical subtleties, that typically late Gothic system of awkwardly embellished and complicated disputations and questions. It was a style comprehensible only through centuries of cultivation as a professional art and released its essentially formal charms most fully in French territory. This was true in *all* schools—Thomist as well as Ockhamist. But their oppositions were no longer retained in a pure form. I have already demonstrated this in a particular, but especially significant, example [6] and could today add numerous others.

The literary model of the fifteenth century, at least on German soil, was twofold. On the one hand there is the colorless compendium for school use, the principal theological position of which can hardly be recognized by external features (the number of such books from all camps is legion). On the other hand, there is the *collectorium*, the collection of flowers and sentences in which all possible opinions of all possible doctors are put together in a more or less neutral way. The most outstanding representatives—because they are theologically not completely colorless—are the German Dominican of the fourteenth century, Thomas of Strassburg, the favorite of all domesticated Ockhamists, Dionysius Rickel the Carthusian from the realist camp, and, in a certain sense, Gabriel Biel. The ensuing romantic-artificial revivification of the scholastic oppositions (*via antiqua* and *via moderna*) around the middle of the fifteenth century brought no really new life into the increasingly listless literary and scholastic activity. I have already demonstrated this in detail elsewhere [7] and need not repeat it here. Even the outward technique of organizing the questions seems to have lost its authority and charm. Anyone conversant with the scheme of these things will be astonished by the excessively simple and artless manner with which such a respected teacher as Johann von Wesel (to whom we will later return) was able to deliver his questions on Lombard in Erfurt around the middle of the century.[8] Yet there were many others like him. Present-day literature is dominated by completely exaggerated and distorted conceptions of the form of late medieval academic instruction.

This rapid leveling of problems and oppositions, however, is by no means limited to the philosophical or theological sphere. It is repeated in at least the same degree in the realm of ecclesio-political literature. Here, too, one must be wary of prematurely judging Ockhamism by Ockham. Certainly the conciliarists of the fifteenth century, the Germans in particular, move completely (as K. Wenck first showed) [9] along the lines of criticism laid down by Ockham, even when the name of the *venerabilis inceptor,* having fallen under the stigma of heresy, is never mentioned. But insofar as they belong to the academic guild, especially that of theology, they have carefully and thoroughly broken off the really dangerous points of this criticism.

This difference is immediately apparent when one compares the general tone. In spite of the scholastic cumbersomeness of Ockham and the strangely flickering twilight in which all things appear, no one can read his great *Dialogus* without being deeply moved by the incessant restlessness of a burning drive for truth attempting to break through the burdensome layers of historical tradition and authoritarian ties. One sees here a man pulling at his chains but unable to break them. By comparison, the reform tracts of Conrad of Gelnhausen, Henry of Langenstein, and even Jean Gerson read almost like Sunday devotionals. I intend soon to publish a more exact analysis;[10] here a few hints must suffice.

Ockham struggles to force the deposition of a hated tyrannical and "heretical" pope; Gelnhausen and Langenstein attempt to end the schism with the help of the council, and thereby make possible the restoration of the papacy to its old splendor and dignity. The summons of a general council without papal authorization seemed to them, as we know, an emergency measure, undesirable and indeed justifiable only in rare, exceptional cases. The thought of a continuing limitation of absolute papal power was far from their minds. Conrad found his consolation in the hope that the pope, who was to be elected by the council, could and would subsequently confirm the council's decisions and thereby remove its illegal character. There is no doubt that for these German theologians any compromise would have been welcome which made it possible to avoid summoning a general council without the pope. It is of the greatest importance symbolically as well as materially, and no mere coincidence, that Conrad, the Ockhamist, took the core of his theses, the doctrine of equity (ἐπιείκεια), not from the suggestions of Ockham but from the *Summa* of Thomas. While Ockham's *Dialogus* had at least closely brushed, if not actually overstepped, the boundary of revolution, his German followers took a wholly romantic, restorative tack. Their gaze was directed backward, not forward; their ideal was the reestablishment, not the transformation, the restoration, not the rebuilding, of the debased papal church.

I must forgo a demonstration that the whole of German scholastic theology and, in its train, the greater part of fifteenth century scholastic canon law are to be judged from exactly the same point of view. It is futile to attempt to deduce traces of revolutionary criticism pointing to the future from isolated statements on natural law and biblicism in Ockhamist school literature. The dogmatic tradition of the thirteenth century and the papal hierarchy—in spite of all the zealous criticism of the moral condition of the church—have never found more faithful and devoted defenders than the German scholastic theologians of the pre-reformatory epoch. Illustrations could easily be accumulated, ranging from the struggle of the Heidelbergers against the Pisan council (1409) to the uneasy reserve of the German universities in the face of the Basel radicals, and their willing submission to the newly emerging papal omnipotence. The sociological and economic backgrounds of this series of facts could also be demonstrated easily; meanwhile, the assertion suffices that there was no recognizable difference in these matters between the various theological schools, cliques, and parties. (In this connection it is more than just a curiosity that the only Heidelberg theologian who, in contrast to his colleagues, sometimes opposed Eugene IV at the Council of Basel was no Ockhamist but the founder and oldest representative in Heidelberg of Neo-Thomism, Johannes Wenck.) The conciliar movement, insofar as it championed class demands as such in its struggle with the papacy, was furthered by princes, secular clergy (especially those of the lower class) and practical churchmen of all kinds. German university theology had never established a real relationship to actual political questions.

One might almost believe that high church politics—the problem of a secular state and the changing relationship between church and state—never existed at all for these theologians. They may have disputed with all sorts of learned arguments whether in the case of a struggle between curia and council one is commanded to follow the pope or the synod. But this is purely academic, not meant seriously; the preeminence of the pope is established as self-evident from the beginning.[11] Or one may write a thick book [12] *de republica;* but it consists of no more than a collection of moral commonplaces from Augustine, Aristotle, and John of Salisbury among others, on the duties of the different classes; it is appropriate for the preacher in the pulpit. When Gregory Heimburg fought his great battle with the curia, not a single German professor came to his aid—this might be said to be self-evident. This renders comprehensible the cool, deliberating smile with which the only theologian of German descent who was at the same time a church politician of no mean stature, Gregory's highly gifted opponent Nicholas of Cusa, looked down on the isolated and insubstantial book-wisdom of these schoolmen. He himself had fully outgrown this atmosphere in Italy.[13] The lack of instinct with which Martin Luther faced actual political problems throughout his life is explained to a significant degree by his purely scholastic theological education. Compare him to Calvin, the trained jurist!

German theology, however, was not without its contributions to the conciliar movement. But they lay in another area. This is best recognized when we compare the zealous, indeed too zealous, political activity of the University of Paris. (In passing it should be remarked that the importance of the "Ockhamist" school traditions for the ecclesiastical politicians of Paris is also often overestimated; these traditions may be considered completely insignificant when compared with the strong influence of the actual political situation.) The antipapal and purely political radicalism, the origin of which Johannes Haller has so incisively depicted for us, unfolded in Paris around the turn of the fourteenth century.

At the same time Matthew of Krakow wrote his treatise, "On the Filth of the Papal Court," by far the most brilliant publicizing achievement of German scholastic theology. Its *political* content (if one disregards the depiction of mismanagement in Rome, which was not written by Matthew) does not go beyond what Langenstein and

Gelnhausen had already expressed; the author himself is apparently unaware of the political significance of the more radical-sounding phrases. But Matthew, in stating that the council was above all to serve the inward renewal of the church, directed the conciliar movement, even more strongly than had his predecessors, in a direction which would find response and participation by theologians in almost no country outside Germany. It was the most powerful penitential sermon on the corruption of the clergy which had been heard in a long time; and Matthew hoped for much from man's penitential sentiment—he had no suggestions on how the work of reform was to be implemented practically.

Precisely this, however, seems to me to be characteristic of the period which follows: the reform attempts of German theologians lie in the area of pastoral practice, not in that of high church politics. Within the boundaries thus delineated men strove with great fervor for reform, or, more correctly, for the restoration of the church according to the demands of the councils. German libraries harbor masses of sermon books and edifying writings of all kinds: confessional manuals ("Beichtspiegel"); instructions for a blessed death; indulgence and communion treatises; discussions of difficult questions which arise in the confessional (the priestly *forum internum*) and concern such matters as the binding power of vows and the collection of interest and usury; advice on the Jewish question; warnings against superstition and astrology; polemics against heresies of all kinds, and the like. I will report soon on a whole series of such writings within the framework of the history of the University of Heidelberg, which are characterized by complete theological and ecclesio-political colorlessness. Concerning the great church-political questions of the time there is almost nothing, at least in the material I have gathered.

The merit of this sermon and tract literature, however, for the moral and spiritual elevation of the clergy and the inward upbuilding of the church as a whole must not be undervalued, though it would be vain to seek therein new thoughts pointing to the future. Everywhere it is a matter of restoring the old, not of reform. All German authorities had been eagerly preoccupied with this since the close of the great councils. The oft-cited prohibition of German lay Bibles by Berthold of Henneberg, the great restoration politician, clearly marks the general direction of these efforts. The reasons given were that the German language was inadequate to grasp the meaning of Holy Scripture and, above all, that it was not fitting for the unlearned and, furthermore, for women to interpret this meaning. It is the typical attempt of an aristocracy threatened from below to assert with force its position of exclusive privilege. And just as the imperial reform movement led by Berthold very soon showed that the patriotism which inspired it was not strong enough to force the desire for power among the various classes into the service of the imperial design, so the conciliar movement in Germany failed largely because, from the beginning, it had not gone all out; the powerlessness of theological motivation was fatal. The practical churchmen who were to carry out the movement remained dependent for their ideas on the theological garrisons of fourteenth century polemical writings, which, in their most incisive formulations, had long been considered heretical. But the great mass of the laity inclined toward reform were handed over to the unbridled fantasies of obscure, demagogic preachers.

III

The fifteenth century, however, was filled with the unrest of a growing but theologically undirected lay movement, which increased on all sides and surged not only against the foundations of the ecclesiastical hierarchy, but against the firm structure of church dogma itself. Even outside Bohemia, and especially in southwest Germany, heretical movements of the most varied kinds were so strong at the beginning of the century that the best modern expert on them once stated that, if the church had not suppressed the danger with fire and sword at just the right time, there would have been acute danger of an uprising comparable to the Albigensian wars. There were also a great many revival and devotional movements within the church; for them the official church's apparatus of salvation, along with its scholastic foundation, became increasingly meaningless.

Was none of this heard in the lecture halls of the theological faculties? Was it discussed solely in the form of heresy cases? One would have to answer affirmatively were it not for the three reform theologians whom we are considering: Johann Wesel, Wessel Gansfort and Pupper von Goch. To be sure, probably only the first two were academic theologians, and for only a part of their lives. But the historically important aspect of their work is, nevertheless, the theological-scholastic foundation which they provided, for the first time in German territory, for the widespread opposition to ecclesiastical tradition. Furthermore, they developed theologically the basic premises of their own positive ideal of piety, which clearly and self-consciously opposed the traditional ideals of ecclesiastical piety. In comparison with the conservative, rather backward-looking, romantic and restorative tendencies of customary scholastic theology, they represent quite clearly a *revolutionary* element. How was this possible? Where is the seed of their opposition to be sought? What kind of incentives enabled them to break through the otherwise overpowering constraints of church custom and tenacious scholastic traditions? Were the motives predominantly practical or theoretical? Did the Ockhamist tradition, from which Johann von Wesel and Wessel Gansfort descended, in any sense play a role?

Unfortunately, the source material for answering such questions is extremely scanty: one can form only a rough picture of the intellectual atmosphere in which the theology of Wessel and Goch flourished. Even the reading of their work and that of Wesel is impeded by the loss of texts; much that is important has been lost, some of it probably destroyed early by the Inquisition. But, in addition, scholars heretofore have been only partially successful in distinguishing between the genuine and the spurious. Most studies have dealt with Goch and Wessel. About the first we even possess an outstanding new monograph by O. Clemen; [14] on Wessel there are a number of diligent, if not completely satisfactory and penetrating, specialized studies.[15] Most scanty, however, is our knowledge of Johann von Wesel. Here the penetrating criticism of O. Clemen [16] dissected the literary tradition to such an extent that the remains were extremely meager. I would not dare to express my opinion if I were not in the position, through a Stockholm manuscript of which a note by K. Burdach [17] made me aware, to evaluate a whole series of previously unknown passages. I intend to publish the most important of these soon in a specialized essay.[18]

What was previously known of Wesel consisted mainly in his long treatise on indulgences and a series of remarks extracted from him as a physically and intellectually broken man of eighty under fierce questioning by the inquisitor before the heresy tribunal. Finally, there were some pronouncements of denunciators concerning assertions in earlier sermons alleged to be too daring. But no one who knows the tendency of late medieval preachers to keep alive the flagging interest of their listeners through occasional bold statements will take these seriously. The most important parts of the newly disclosed source are: the complete draft of a correspondence with the Mainz preacher Johann of Kaiserslautern on the spiritual authority of the pope and the councils (previously we knew only a few sentences of this from the excerpts of Usingen in a Würzburg manuscript),[19] a copy of the familiar indulgence treatise, more complete than the reproduction furnished by Walch; a long essay on the immaculate conception of Mary which contains a complete doctrine of original sin; two confessional verdicts on the binding power of vows and a synodical sermon to the clergy of Worms. Other pieces, such as the treatise "De scientia et veritate astrorum" and some university lectures from the domain of the Faculty of Arts, are of lesser importance for our purpose.

Johann von Wesel began his career as schoolmaster in Erfurt and also worked for a while at the university in Basel, but after 1463 he was cathedral preacher in Worms and outside the academic sphere. During this time he began to run into trouble with ecclesiastical tradition; this finally cost him his office and brought him soon thereafter before the Inquisition. Thus it is pertinent to compare the writings of his early academic period with the later ones. For this purpose his main theological lectures, the Commentary on the *Sentences,* are available in two copies.[20] Unfortunately, in both copies the important fourth book in which, among other things, the indulgence question must have been treated, is missing.[21] What remains reveals a vagueness in theological controversy which makes the academic origin of this *magister* of the Ockhamist school almost unrecognizable. It emphatically confirms the conjecture I expressed earlier [22] that the authority of St. Thomas had almost become canonical in Erfurt (by repute strictly Ockhamist), as well as elsewhere around the middle of the fifteenth century, and that by that time the great party oppositions were almost forgotten.

Only on one topic can we see clearly how one of the later heresies of the Worms cathedral preacher could grow out of certain beginnings in the Ockhamist tradition. In the work on the *Sentences* Wesel still defines original sin quite in accordance with Duns Scotus and the Ockhamists (Ockham, of course, is named nowhere); he sees it as negative, a mere deficiency (*carentia iusticiae originalis*), but he does not deny it.[23] Later he identifies it as a "nothing" and in the end as much as denies it.[24] It is worthwhile to pursue the motives of his denial, because from this standpoint the position of our theologian in the history of dogma is immediately illuminated.

Wessel Gansfort and Goch, whose close intellectual affinity with Wesel will become clearer to us shortly, also made a purely negative definition from the Augustinian idea of original sin. With them the strongest factor was presumably the mystical motif of the incompatibility of a positive blot of sin in man with the idea of union with God; with the Ockhamists the effort to secure the idea of human freedom of will worked in the same direction. Johann von Wesel, in whose writings I am otherwise unable to find actual mystical strains, gave expression to a third, much more primitive motif (if I am correct), beyond the Ockhamist tradition and the presumed influence of Wessel. His is a naïve humanitarian effort, springing from certain considerations of *bon sens,* to alleviate the terrible severity of the old Augustinian doctrine of sin which transmits the damnation of all flesh even to the newborn. He polemicizes vigorously against Augustine in this connection: "If none of the doctors had ever discovered this word 'original sin,' Holy Scripture would still stand unaffected." The authority of the Bible is thus invoked against Augustine, and to the fifteenth century mind this amounted to an attack on church dogma itself. For us, however, it constitutes a warning not to classify our author and his intellectual companions under the popular category "Neo-Augustinian" without further investigation. In the end none of the theological reform and restoration movements of the late Middle Ages were able to avoid an appeal to the always stimulating Augustine. Yet Wesel had no intrinsic connection with the recently much discussed [25] theologians of the Augustinian order, whom he cites often in his work on the *Sentences* because of their frequently neutral middle position. As far as Pupper von Goch and Wessel are concerned, I find no reference to this group in any of their writings. If they were really "Augustinians" in any sense, they would signify a new beginning far more than a continuation of existing scholastic tradition.

Thus our theologian calls the Bible into play against Augustine, and this is the basic position from which he defends all further heretical theses. He defends the exclusive value of Holy Scripture, but especially of the Gospels (he cites them almost exclusively) and the Pauline Epistles, exactly according to their literal meaning which no one need distort. Human authorities, even the traditions of the ancient church, he rejects, if they contradict Scripture, even more harshly than do Goch and Wessel.[26] He dares even to dispute the "a patre filioque" of the Nicene Creed because (as Peter Lombard already knew) it is not strictly attested in the Bible.[27] Now *all* opposition inside and outside the church in the later Middle Ages was accustomed to appeal to Scripture against human ordinances; [28] the "Scripture principle" as a formal definition was by no means new. What was new was that a scholastic theologian of the fifteenth century dared to exegete the Bible in a way other than that prescribed by church custom;[29] even the Ockhamists—in spite of the founder of their school—had long since abandoned this. But what content did Wesel give to the *lex evangelica* which he found in the Bible? On this it all depends.

Most important is the renewal of that ancient distinction, already established by Augustine, between the *ecclesia universalis* as an external community of the church and the *vera ecclesia*, the invisible mystical unity whose head is Christ. This distinction had been used again and again to salve the ecclesiastical conscience when it was necessary to assault the secularized papal church. Ockham had taught it in this sense; on it Dietrich of Niem had based his great treatise, "De modis uniendi et reformandi ecclesiam," the source of numerous partially or completely heretical pamphlets. Then Wyclif and Huss had actually tried to set up a community of the predestined within the whole church in a strict Augustinian sense. It alone, the true, genuine *communio sanctorum*, was to possess infallibility; the visible church was to be subject to it.

The difficulty about this idea lay only in the question of how this invisible communion was to be made visible and effective in practice. Marsilius of Padua had pointed in a very naïve and direct way to the general council; Ockham, probing deeper but doubting as usual, finally clung to the indefinite idea of a general good sense which, with God's help, would and must prevail against pope and council. Since that time the belief in the infallibility of a general council had been shattered; the actual revolutionary result of this idea had long since appeared, quite horribly, in the Hussites' bloody battle of the *praedestinati* against the *reprobati*. Our reform theologians, taking up the old distinction again, avoided speaking of the predestined (in this, too, deviating from Augustine).[30] Wessel Gansfort chose the expression *communio sanctorum;* he apparently meant by this a community of love among genuine, revived Christians, who meet in the common struggle for the *imitatio Christi* without constituting an external authority over the consciences of believers; in the last analysis everything was left to the inner relationship of the individual to God. For this reason the external form of this community is also a matter of indifference; true Christians can lead a godly life even under perverse prelates. One is reminded of Luther when one sees how everything here depends on the inward disposition, and when one hears the continual demand that the theologians and not the lawyers should rule in the church.

The idea seems indeed to have completely lost its revolutionary impact, but this only appears to be the case. While the more peaceable Goch (he represents in our circle the theology of quiet devotion) contents himself with the idea of a Christian community of conviction, without wanting to reorganize the visible church in a practical way, Wessel keeps in mind the possibility that a reformation through action could become necessary. If the ecclesiastical authorities act against God's law, their subjects have not only the right but also the duty to oppose them in order not to share their damnation. "No one destroys the church more than a corrupt clergy. It is the duty of all Christians down to the last peasant to oppose those who corrupt the church." [31] Their relationship to their superiors, after all, rests only on an agreement of natural law; whoever breaks it deserves to be deposed. This sounds quite revolutionary and is even, in particular phrases, directly reminiscent of Dietrich of Niem. Wessel indeed knew that in a practical sense more evil than good can come of rebellion; he himself kept quiet and bemoaned the imprudence of Johann Wesel, who brought everything before the people from the pulpit. But the possibility of a revolutionary turn to his thought persisted nevertheless; Wessel was an honest and obstinate man, as portrayed by the letters of his acquaintances, and he, the *magister contradictionis*, did not shirk conflict, at least in his early years.[32]

On the whole, of course, with him as with Wesel, it is more a matter of theoretical than of practical criticism. In the forefront is the denial of the vicariate of Christ; they agree in this, using familiar arguments such as Gregory Heimburg had last repeated in Germany. Councils, as well as the pope, can and often do err. Peter must have been pleased at the shortcomings of Paul. Wessel regards it as blasphemy to bind the conscience of Christians in matters of faith simply to the mandates of ecclesiastical superiors. Only to the extent that they agree with God's Word are they to be followed; if the pope errs, he must allow himself to be set right by a simple layman or a woman. In a concluding part of the indulgence treatise, previously unknown, Wesel denied the binding force of the *canones* of decrees in matters of faith to the extent that they are not in accordance with Scripture. Since divine inspiration is not to be attributed to them, conscience is not bound to them. Neither pope nor council has the right to command anything under penalty of mortal sin.

Shocking as all this sounded in the mouths of German theologians, there was little that was basically new. Not one of these statements is missing in Marsilius of Padua and Ockham—in the former openly and logically developed from his premises, in the latter veiled by endless vacillation on various kinds of considerations. It is not necessary to assume a direct dependence; the ideas had been expressed so often that one need not go back to their originators. It is important only that now they enter theological literature from secular polemical literature and are newly developed out of the presuppositions of the latter. In other words, our reform theologians have laid themselves open to the influence of the antihierarchical *lay* movement against all academic tradition. This fact in itself urgently needs an explanation.

But they did not stop there. They also took over the second, much discussed vein of thinking, according to which the clergy's power of office should be restricted to purely spiritual tasks, to the mediation of divine salvation. This train of thought ultimately originated in Franciscan ideals of reform. Denial of the jurisdictional power of the priesthood, even in the sacrament of penance, and limitation of all church legislation to the *lex evangelica*, the command of love, were the most extreme consequences of these ideas; Wyclif and Huss had already progressed to this point. Johann von Wesel denies priestly jurisdiction in all forms, even sacramental; to him it is heathen and forbidden by Christ.[33] With Goch there is a distinction between divine law and church ordinance, again, to be sure, without revolutionary consequences; Wessel Gansfort and Wesel, on the other hand, expressly dispute the right of the papal church to burden believers with regulations which go beyond the commandments of love for God and neighbor as required by Christ.

From this point Wesel, in particular, proceeds to radical negations: the pope had illicitly made the advice of Christ on celibacy into a *regulation* for the clergy. Commandments to fast, consecration of the altar, anointing oil, holy water, church decoration, extension of the prohibition of marriage to distant degrees of relationship, the distinction between bishop and simple priest, and more, are mere human institutions [34]—they do not bind the conscience. Clearly these demands could lead only to a reform of the church, to a return to the conditions of the early church. They do not actually point outside the sphere of medieval conceptions. Only when the necessity of priestly mediation in salvation is fundamentally denied does the medieval concept of the church receive the fatal blow.

Such ideas had already been toyed with for a long time. The official church teaching on the sacrament of penance, as offered by Lombard,[35] obviously recognized that God himself forgives sins through the mediation of the priest. From this Marsilius of Padua had drawn the conclusion that the activity of the priest was not absolutely necessary; but he had not thought of destroying the Catholic concept of ministry on this account. Even Wycliffism did not go so far; nor did it recognize a universal priesthood of believers. Nevertheless, especially in Bohemia, this teaching devalued priestly absolution through a strong emphasis on the exclusive efficacy of God in the sacrament of penance. A penitent disposition, an earnest conversion of the heart is more important than the pronouncement of the forgiveness of sins through the priest. Johann von Wesel also moved in this direction. The priesthood is only a service, an administration of the mysteries of God; its power is not *potestas principalis*, only *ministerialis*. It is God who effects everything; He alone has the power of the keys. How can the priest presume to remit even the penalties for temporal sins if God himself does not remit them? The whole idea of indulgence is nothing more than a pious deception of the faithful. This, in a few words, is the content of Wesel's treatise on indulgence. He moves completely on the level along which Wyclif and Huss had moved before him, if not in exactly the same direction. This was astonishing for a German scholastic theologian, but these ideas are not, in the highest sense, original. The kernel of Catholic teaching, the belief in the miraculous infusion of grace in the sacrament of penance, he left untouched: it was self-evident. As long as there was no other way to attain salvation, however, the action of the priest remained practically indispensable, no matter how much one might disparage it as the work of a mere underling.

At this point the paths of our reform theologians part; only in comparison with Wesel do the accomplishments of the other two become truly visible. Time does not permit me to reproduce explicitly their finespun teaching on sin and grace, on penance and the forgiveness of sins. A few remarks must suffice to characterize their historical position.

The theology of Goch and Wessel moves in a completely different direction from that of Luther—in spite of the striking affinity of many isolated statements, which surprised no one more than Luther himself. The actual core of their thought is not the redemption of the will fallen into the bondage of sin, nor reconciliation with an angry God, but rather the completion of human striving for perfection through divine grace and the example of Christ which we attempt to approximate. The transfiguration of the human soul toward higher perfection is emphasized more strongly than the idea of absolution from guilt. The bent of their concept of God and salvation, more metaphysical than ethical, makes the origins of their theologies in medieval mysticism clearly recognizable. It has been correctly stressed that they lacked the "actual reformatory nerve" in the sense of Luther; [36] their ideal of life is more a mystical contempt of the world with its externalities than the actual moral conquest of the world—pious devotion instead of reformatory action.

On the other hand, they did not stem from the speculative mysticism of the German Dominicans, directed essentially toward inward devotion and contemplative submersion, but rather from the practical, active "new devotion" (*devotio moderna*) of the "Brethren of the Common Life" of the Netherlands.[37] This means, first, that the concept of sin had not faded to the same extent with them as with the mystics, and that they stood a good deal closer to the Pauline teaching on salvation and justification. It implies, furthermore, a preference for those aspects of religious tradition which had practical application for the active life over the purely speculative ones. An immediate consequence of this was a tendency toward sober, realistic simplification and reinterpretation of old and complicated dogmas in the light of natural reason; [38] humanistic influences have often been blamed for this trait, which at times touched closely on Enlightenment ways of thinking.

Important in our context is what distinguishes our reformers from traditional scholastic theology on the decisive questions of sin, grace, and justification. Briefly stated, it is the incomparably greater liveliness of religious feeling. God's omnipotence and glory stand at the center of their thought. The traditional conception of the cooperation of the human will with divine grace in the act of salvation is unbearable to them—this is clearly expressed by Goch. It is exclusively God's grace which frees and transfigures man. They (Goch especially) particularly emphasize the *sola gratia,* much more firmly than Thomas, indeed in some respects even more clearly than Augustine.[39] That "good works" can be accomplished only with God's help was a common ancient Catholic idea; but now "good works" are conceived not only as God's work in us but simply as "signs" of the new life which blossoms in communion with Christ. They have no merit at all, considered in themselves—only God's acceptance makes them appear valuable.

All these turns of thought could be brought into formal agreement with the usual scholastic teaching. They do not in any way signify a clear-cut transcendence of Catholic thinking in the manner of the Wittenberg Reformation. Ockhamism, too, was capable of tracing all merit finally to God's "acceptance." But one must close his ears in order not to hear the decisive shift of accent with which the old formulas here reveal a new intellectual life.[40] Anyone who has wandered for a long time in the desert of traditional scholastic theology breathes a sigh of relief when he steps on this soil; here fresh spring water bubbles from the depths. With what formality, inward indifference, and professionalism were the schools accustomed to separate, in a clean, logical way, the divine and human in the act of grace. How mechanically was all intellectual effort directed toward harmonizing the Augustinian and Aristotelian elements of tradition (if it may be permitted to sketch the opposition in such an abbreviated way)! The attempt ended in a colorless obliteration of all the original strict antinomies in the concept of God and in a confusion of all the important theological oppositions which sprang from these antinomies. Here, with Wessel and Goch, we sense again the warm, beating pulse of religious experience. This is not the impetuous passion, the heroic strength of will of the Wittenberg reformer who daringly destroyed the old, but it does possess a genuinely spontaneous liveliness, which quietly seeks new channels for the outpouring of religious thoughts without destroying the framework of the old forms.

This is especially true, also, for the concept of the priesthood and the church. Here too our reform theologians are at the point of freeing themselves from the Middle Ages (hesitatingly and only half-consciously, but in the end unmistakably). This, again, is done without expressly denying the old formulas: the "infusion of grace" in the sacrament, the authoritative mediating activity of the priest therein, and the miracle of the sacrifice of the mass through the hand of the minister are denied formally by them no more than by Huss and Wesel. They are repeatedly taken as unalterably fixed. But Wessel, as well as the others, is not satisfied with devaluing the activity of the priest, in a practical sense, as merely the work of an underling. To the first, traditional train of thought he adds a second, which, pursued logically, robs priestly activity of its actual meaning. In the first place, the penitent sinner must, even *before* absolution through the priest, attain the essential parts of the sacrament of penance—his inner conversion, union with God, and forgiveness of sins. Moreover, there is no basis for a special position of the priesthood which would set it apart in principle from the spiritual powers available to every individual Christian. The power of the keys belongs to every saint, no matter what class or sex. The universal priesthood of believers is *de facto* declared. Indeed in the final analysis there is no need whatever for any official power of binding and loosing, since God himself works all in all. And, like the priesthood, the sacraments are not indispensable. In the Lord's Supper the remembrance of Christ is so exclusively important that corporeal eating and drinking almost completely lose their importance. The true believer possesses the body and blood of Christ by the aid of the Holy Spirit even without wine and bread. True communion of love with Christ is always assured them, while the reception of the sacrament without such a disposition remains worthless.

We see here how the concept of the sacrament is spiritualized in such a way that the doctrine of the miracle of the host has almost completely lost its practical meaning. Perhaps it is no coincidence that the oldest collection of Wessel's writings, which appeared several times in 1522, once with a preface by Luther recommending it, did not contain the teaching on the Lord's Supper. Luther could have taken offense; in fact he had very definitely rejected it in the form put forward by Cornelius Hoen. On this point Wessel, although he formally held fast to the dogma of transubstantiation, actually detached himself further from the Middle Ages than did Luther himself.

The question arises whether all this was somehow already plotted in the development of late scholasticism. One is reminded, first, of familiar Ockhamist principles when one sees how our reform theologians destroy the original meaning and context of the teachings of the sacraments and the priesthood, without denying the holiness of the institutions as such; they are to remain simply the external, divinely willed order of spiritual life, the basis of which is essentially unknowable. Is that not merely a more radical usage of the Ockhamist denial of rational relationships, of the scientific intelligibility of positive divine ordinances? It appears thus only when regarded from afar. What Ockham disputed was the ability of reason to interpret God's intentions in his order of salvation. Wessel's attack went deeper; he denied the ultimate value of ecclesiastical institutions and their indispensability for the salvation of the human soul. Their incomprehensibility was not unsettling; this caused no great concern for the German scholastic theology of the fifteenth century. But whoever doubted their religious necessity—even with a thousand reservations—made an attempt on their life and on that of the church itself.

Looking backward, it becomes clear for the first time how our reform theologians found the courage to abandon the old, established conservative traditions of the schools and embrace all those ecclesio-political heresies which had been, so often and variously, refuted by the schools and condemned by the church. The spiritual foundation of their teaching—piety itself—had shifted to a deeper level, and the whole artificially ordained structure of late medieval tradition began to crumble under their feet.

IV

Let us summarize. The motives which we have come to recognize as impulses toward new ideas among our reform theologians are, throughout, those of practical piety and practical ecclesio-political experience—not those of scholastic, learned tradition. With them, as so often happens, life proved to be stronger than knowledge. In the case of Johann von Wesel, who was charged before the court of inquisition with epistolary and verbal communication with a Bohemian adventurer, one might suspect immediate Hussite influence. It does not seem probable to me. The ideas stemming from the lay movement, on which his opposition to the church rests, show no specifically Hussite or Wycliffite coloration anywhere in his work. He was, however, undoubtedly influenced by the writings of Wessel. There are many instances of literal agreement between the two. How he got hold of these works, which circulated in manuscript form within the author's narrow circle of friends, we do not know. But one sees clearly here how foreign thought stole little by little into the broad inheritance of traditional scholastic thinking. An investigation of the whole literary bequest would show this even more plainly. Only in this way is the fragmentary, unconnected manner in which Johann von Wesel developed his heretical ideas—as mere isolated theses—understandable. One finds in him, to a certain extent, the consequences of a new theological teaching without its premises—criticism of the tradition without a thoroughgoing change in his basic view of the world. He stands out for his courage in public avowal, for the bold aggressiveness which Wessel and Goch avoided. Not without emotion does one sense the depth of his spiritual struggle, in the short report of the minutes of the heresy case, and how the frantic pressure of well-meaning friends and advisors finally succeeded in moving the old man to a formal retraction and thereby saved him from death by fire.

Of disparately greater intellectual significance, indeed, was the effect of the appearance of the other two reformers, especially Wessel.[41] The decisive source of his thoughts has already been mentioned: the *Devotio moderna* of the Netherlands Brethren. He came out of their schools, and after years of academic wandering he ended his life in their circles on the Agnetenberg near Zwolle and in Groningen. But he was a highly educated and well-traveled man, who managed to take an ironic view, above the restrictedness of the Brethren, beyond the devotional gatherings of the inspired. The great ecclesio-political and religious polemical literature of the previous generation could not have been unfamiliar to him. He began his academic career as a champion of Cologne Neo-Thomism. As a learned disputant of repute and bold assurance, for whom the Heidelberg stage seemed too small, he dared to step into the hotbed of Paris as *magister contradictionis* and even disputed with papal lawyers in Rome concerning indulgences. Inwardly independent, free from external ambition, abundantly endowed with the obstinate willfulness and drive for autonomy of the Frisians, he ran through the scholastic university methods of the time one after another and learned to scorn them all. He renounced the professorial chair early, in order to spend his days studying and teaching among his intellectual comrades in proud but modest independence. In the end he considered himself nominally of the Ockhamist school. But how little this meant is shown, to cite one example, by his discussion of the writings of Jean Gerson, who was apparently highly regarded by the Brethren. In connection with the historical influence of Gerson, it is noteworthy that the writings of this leader of the Ockhamist school were held up to Wessel (and to Johann von Wesel) as evidence of correct church teaching.[42] Wessel handled him with great respect, but he reproached the opportunism which left Gerson standing halfway on the path to truth.

A question worth special investigation is whether there were *humanistic influences* at work in Wessel's theology. He was certainly in close contact with humanist literary stimuli at an early date—any Netherlander who attended a West European university, especially Paris, in the second half of the fifteenth century, could not possibly escape them. But he also lived for a time in Italy—in Rome, with short visits to Florence and Venice. To be sure, where he speaks of Italy, there is no word of association with humanist circles; only church matters are mentioned. He speaks of the Florentines with undisguised aversion and only occasionally remembers Antoninus Florentinus and his grave with respect.[43] Nevertheless, there are unmistakably clear traces of humanist-literary training in his writings. Most striking is the knowledge which he intentionally displays of certain elements of the Greek and Hebrew languages[44] and of the names of ancient authors, some of which were unfamiliar to scholasticism.[45] His literary style, which in general had by no means outgrown the medieval scholastic tradition, occasionally reveals an effort to approach an example he admired—Cicero's forensic speeches—through rhetorical pathos and artistic sentence structure.[46] Thus we find a very strange attempt in the second and third parts of the *Scala meditationis* to enrich the art of spiritual communication through an indiscriminate conjunction of the most varied rhetorical traditions—Christian and pagan, Biblical and ancient forensic, medieval scholastic and modern humanistic. The pleonasm of Old Testament Psalms, the rhetorical arts of Cicero and Theophrastus, the pettifoggery of Raymond Lull, the dialectics of Aristotle, samples of style from Plutarch, Demosthenes and other ancient authors—all these must serve, though somewhat mechanically, to supply *instrumenta abundae orationis* and to produce the longed-for "fullness" (*copia*) of speech and thought.[47]

Because of such external symptoms of humanistic training, Wessel's basic theological ideas have also been customarily associated with Italian humanism, especially with the religious ideas of the Florentine Platonists. This is clearly unfair. Not a single phrase in Wessel's work impels us to make this connection; on the contrary, much of it speaks loudly against Italian models. Whatever one might attribute to the Platonizing influences of the Florentines—the conception of the eternal idea as *verbum aeternum,* as uncreated love in God, for instance—can be explained in a far less forced way by the traditions of medieval Platonism, especially of traditional mysticism, than by the bland intellectual world of the Florentine Academy. As far as I can see, he shows no interest in the literary disputes between the Platonists and the Aristotelians. He is very far from approving the historically most important religious ideas of the Florentines—their "universal theism," their regard for great Hellenic thinkers, especially Plato and Socrates, as "divine teachers" and predecessors of Christ, and their interpretation of Christ as a teacher of Platonic wisdom and human example rather than as the incarnation of God and Savior. Instead, in passionate words at times almost reminiscent of Luther, he calls Aristotle a foolish, blasphemous pagan, worse than all heretics in that his view of God stands in contradiction to the Christian doctrine; [48] he expressly denies Plato as well as Aristotle the understanding of true Christian virtue, in spite of all their teachings on virtue.[49] All pre-Christian philosophy, including that of Pythagoras, Socrates, Plato, and Aristotle, he considers pagan, citing the condemnation of the apostles; he even calls it bestial and demonic insofar as it springs from mere human curiosity instead of genuine longing for God. It was this curiosity, he says, that sent those philosophers to Persia and Egypt "in order to make a name for themselves there and to expand their devilish curiosity by associating with demons."[50]

We need not go to the trouble of proving that a man who could write such statements was far removed from the rationalistic, secular-skeptical criticism of Bible and dogma of a man such as Laurentius Valla. All these ideas of the Italian humanists concerning religious matters belonged to a fundamentally pagan pre-Christian sphere of culture (in spite of its Christian cloak) which was by nature foreign to Nordic thought and sensibility. Not until Erasmus was it transplanted into the sphere of "Biblical humanism" in the Netherlands.[51] The tendency, however, to appeal to the ideal of a primitive Christian community of saints against the corruption of the contemporary church, and to the Bible and church fathers, especially Augustine and Jerome,[52] against the papal-ecclesiastical doctrinal decrees cannot be regarded as a special characteristic of the humanistic spirit. On the contrary, it is common to all late medieval opposition to the pope. A similar observation could be made regarding the predilection of Wessel's circle for Paul, from whom the Augustinian doctrine of grace had descended. It seems to me of the greatest importance in our considerations of humanism that we distinguish between what it borrowed from the critical thinking of other opposition efforts and what it added of its own. Furthermore, we need to separate those aspects of ecclesiastical opposition which sprang from the root of human *ratio* and those which were based on genuine religious motivations.[53]

If we stand by our assertion that Wessel Gansfort's criticism of the church and scholastic theology did not stem from learned scholastic or literary humanist influence but from another, deeper sphere of life,[54] we can evaluate more impartially his friendship with humanistically attuned spirits such as Rudolf Agricola and Reuchlin, his stylistic attempts at Ciceronian Latin, and his earnest effort to understand the Bible in the original languages.[55] These become signs of a broad, liberal education in the manner of the time. If I am correct in this, Wessel may serve as confirmation that the "humanism" which in Italy helped to bring about a new view of life and of the world remained in Germany purely a matter of education. It received whatever it needed for its view of the world from other, more fundamental, life tendencies. In the decisive crisis of German religious development, humanism did not actually make a creative contribution, but served only to assimilate and to mold.

V

The fact that Wessel's friends and admirers belonged, for the most part,[56] to the humanist circle is connected with the general influx, probably furthered by Wessel Gansfort, of humanistic educational interests into the cities, monasteries, and schools of the Netherlands. But humanist circles apparently soon became interested in Johann von Wesel also; his heresy trial, conducted with Heidelberg theologians as jurors, caused a great sensation. We are most probably indebted to this interest on the part of Upper Rhine humanists for the preservation of a portion of Wessel's writings, in spite of their official burning, and also for a detailed report of the trial, glossed by Wimpfeling with passionate attacks on the chroniclers of the church and the inquisitors. I will have more to say about this in another place. It suffices to remark that the humanists found in the trial a welcome sensational event, an excellent opportunity for their drive toward publicist activity. Wimpfeling in particular found opportunity for the sharp and somewhat rash invective which he liked.

But the effect of this reform theology reached significantly deeper and further. Penetrating studies of the problem are lacking, and in conclusion I will only hint at the direction in which the effect is presumably to be sought.

There is a widely read anonymous pamphlet, "De auctoritate, officio et potestate pastorum ecclesiasticorum," which used to be ascribed to Johann von Wesel.[57] It would not be difficult to show that it is full of Wessel's thoughts and obviously based on the theological presuppositions of his circle. But here the writer is no longer the silent, scholarly, reserved observer of the world; he has taken up the sword as an ardent champion of the truth. One seems again to hear Matthew of Krakow's resounding calls to repentance, his thundering complaints against the corrupt clergy. But this fighter's thrusts penetrate much deeper: the incisiveness of his theological argumentation goes to the roots of the hierarchical system, it does not merely lop off excrescences. The defiant battle-call of Johann von Wesel—"I scorn the pope, the church and councils, my love belongs to Christ; Christ's Word dwells among us superabundantly"—is sounded here even more intensely as the basic theme of the whole treatise. It is one of the strangest and most spirited pamphlets of the whole pre-Reformation epoch.[58] It has been established that the pamphlet, in Latin and in translation, must have been widely circulated during the era of the Reformation; it was prosecuted again and again by the Inquisition in all civilized European states. There is thus hardly a doubt that certain fundamental ideas of the quiet scholar on the Agnetenberg did move the world, if only in this presumably derivative form; in this way they helped to pave the way for the Lutheran Reformation.

But we have already noted that the path of our reform theologians does not lead immediately to Luther. Should they then have no continuing importance for intellectual history and be completely overshadowed by the greater Luther? We do not know very much about Wessel's circle of admirers, but we know enough to recognize that he exercised a highly significant influence both mediately and immediately on the religious attitude of German humanism.[59] Obviously we have here an important middle term, leading from the simple lay piety of the Netherlands Brethren to the educated religiosity of many German humanists. The significance of the *Devotio moderna* for the origin of German humanism as a whole has frequently been overestimated. We are familiar with the perhaps too often stated thesis: the efforts of the Brethren of the Common Life for education and schools gradually produced an original German humanism. It seems enough if we see in their religious disposition something like an original form of German piety. The theology of Wessel Gansfort is indeed essentially nothing other than the instructional form, the scientifically precise expression of this piety, stamped by the spirit of an independently and broadly trained man. Should not this also constitute the middle term for the theology of the greatest German humanist?

The connection of Erasmus with the *Devotio moderna* has just begun to be closely investigated. This worldling had from time to time passionately and ironically rejected the intellectual narrowness and the converting zeal of the Brethren; nevertheless it seems now to be an established fact that he, as a theologian, was in many ways their heir. What did he take from them through Wessel's mediation? Mestwerdt [60] has reported that the two are in close accord on the point of the (greatly moderated) doctrine of purgatory. Their agreement on the doctrine of the Eucharist appears—at first glance at least—no less close. This is particularly significant since the Erasmian view of the Eucharist had, according to W. Köhler,[61] an important influence on Zwingli; moreover the corresponding teaching of Wessel (as further developed by Hoen) was brought immediately to the Zurich and Strassburg reformers and is supposed to have made a strong impression on them.[62]

In both cases it is a matter of a spiritualizing reinterpretation of old, miraculous dogmas. Are these connecting threads to remain the only ones? One can consider the peculiar middle position of Erasmus between late medieval, reformatory, and modern enlightened religiosity. Is it not natural to explain his thought as a kind of mollification, amplification and, finally, moralizing dilution of two streams: the Modern Devotion, as formed by Thomas à Kempis and Wessel, and a Stoic-Neoplatonic, universal theism, which stems in the final analysis from Italy and was perhaps mediated to Erasmus through Colet? I can, in conclusion, only hint at this line of connection in the form of a question—no more than this. Yet it will be enough if our observations have conclusively established one thing: it will not do to include, in the manner customary since W. Maurenbrecher,[63] all possible reform efforts of the fifteenth century which run outside the line of development of later Protestantism under the collective concept "Catholic Reformation," and to have them lead finally into the Tridentine Council. From the very advanced position to which our reform theologians had ventured no easy path led back into the ecclesiastical heritage, as long as the purity of their basic ideas was retained. Conversely, no path led easily to them from the restoration efforts of scholasticism (including Dionysius Rickel, who is often classed with the *Devotio moderna*); yet a straight line led directly from the late scholastic *via antiqua* to Trent.

In other words, the revolutionary character of the reform theology of the Netherlands seems indisputable to me, although no actual will to overthrow is noticeable. (In a strict sense, by the way, this was also lacking in Luther.) Destructive gestures reveal themselves only in their German disciple Johann von Wesel. Because they kept quiet—they were doubly cautious after Wesel's catastrophe—the criticism was denied any far-reaching or visible significance. In addition a change in the historical situation came about shortly: the humanists who took up Wesel's reform ideas (Erasmus most crucially) were quickly ready to dilute them in a moralizing, paganizing direction. As a religious movement, however, the "new devotion" was soon surpassed on the right by the Wittenbergers. Thus, remarkably quickly, our reform theologians were in danger of being forgotten; as we know, Luther himself helped to save them. Yet it seems worth remembering that German life in the age of the Reformation was rich enough to allow a second, original form of German piety rebelling against Rome to bloom beside the Lutheran Reformation. This form derived less exclusively from the depths of original religious experience, was nourished more extensively by medieval mystical traditions, and at the same time was more openly accessible to sober rationality, practical *bon sens;* such a form could not have unfolded with any freedom until the end of the Middle Ages. From this standpoint, then, the intellectual content of humanistic secular education, from which Luther kept much more aloof, might eventually flow into theology. The representatives of this point of view would run the gamut from the *Devotio moderna,* through Wessel, theologically its most authentic architect, to the various humanistic views of reform. Zwingli, who drew equally from them and from Luther, would in a certain sense signify both their apex and their conquest. Yet they continued to be effective in many ways after Erasmus and Zwingli.

When one indulges in such thoughts one realizes with painful resignation how very much the political loss of the Netherlands and its rich culture has meant for the cultural history of Germany.

NOTES

1. *Die christliche Lehre von der Rechtfertigung und Versöhnung* (1870 [1]; 1889 [3]). Long before, the Reformed Catholic, J. Friedrich (*Joh. Wessel,* 1862), had attempted to show the bona fide Catholic character of Wessel's teaching.

2. Cf. H. Heimsoeth, *Die sechs grossen Themen der abendländischen Metaphysik und der Ausgang des Mittelalters* (1922).

3. As O. Scheel, *Luther,* I §15, 5 (3rd ed., 184ff.), showed with regard to Luther's teachers in Erfurt.

4. I am relying here and in the following on the results of my *Studien zur Spätscholastik,* I–II, which appeared in the *Sb. d. Heidelberger Akad.* in 1921 and 1922. Cf. also my summary account, "Aus dem geistigen Leben der Heidelberger Universität im Ausgang des Mittelalters," *Zs. f. Gesch. d. Oberrheins* N.F., Vol. 37.

5. I refer to the first volume of my history of the University of Heidelberg, most of which has been completed in manuscript form.

6. *Studien zur Spätscholastik,* I: *Marsilius von Inghen.* I yield to the criticism of O. Scheel (*Theol. Lit.-Ztg.* 1922, no. 11) that I have overestimated the influence of Augustinian-Thomistic themes on Marsilius' doctrine of grace in some important points. His use of the *gratia gratis data,* nevertheless, as well as his rejection of the *meritum de condigno,* does not seem to me to be simply a universal Ockhamist position (Marsilius himself stresses the differences); rather it is clearly influenced by Gregory of Rimini (*frater magister noster*). It is neither necessary nor possible to show further proof of this; the general result of a mixture of different traditions has not been disputed by Scheel. I see, by the way, that Denifle, *Luther und Luthertum* I, 529, makes a judgment similar to mine concerning Marsilius' doctrine of grace.

7. *Studien zur Spätscholastik,* II.

8. Berlin cod. theol. fol. 97 (=Val. Rose II, 1, 572).

9. *Historische Zs.* 76 (1896).

10. I refer again to my history of the University of Heidelberg.

11. Cod. Pal. lat. Vat. 608, f. 304–19 (Rad. de Bruxella).

12. Cod. Pal. lat. Heidelb. 729 ("Henricus de Hassia[?] de republica").

13. Cf. "Apologia doctae ignorantiae," *Opera* (1502), t.i.

14. *Johann Pupper von Goch* in *Leipz. Studien a. d. Gebiet der Geschichte* II, 3 (1897).

15. Theologically most valuable is the article of van Veen, *Realencyclopädie f. protestantische Theologie u. Kirche*, 3rd ed. (1908), 21 (hereafter *PRE*[3]). It contains also a listing of older (in part confessionally slanted) literature. The Groningen dissertation of M. van Rhijn (s'Gravenhage, 1917) treats thoroughly and creditably the questions of sources and literary history, but is less satisfying in the parts on intellectual history. Ödön Fizély (Göttingen diss., 1911) offers little more than a superficial report on Wessel's writings. Also without an independent scholarly contribution is the treatment of Wessel in J. Lindeboom, *Het bijbelsch humanisme in Nederland* (Leiden, 1913), pp. 39–56.

16. *Deutsche Zs. f. Geschichtswiss.* N.F. (Vierteljahrsheft) Jahrg. II, 142ff.; also, by the same author, *PRE*[3] 21, 127ff. (with complete bibliography). Cf. also N. Paulus in *Katholik* (1898) I, 44–57.

17. Concerning the national appropriation of the Bible and the beginnings of Germanic philology, see *Festschr. f. Mogk* (1924), p. 259, n. 1 (also appeared separately). It deals with Stockholm Cod. V. a. 2, fol. 283ff.

18. There I hope to be able to submit references for at least part of the following assertions. I am aware, however, that my sketch would need a more detailed exposition in order to offer more than provisional conjectures and suggestions.

19. U.-B. Cod. M. ch. o. 34, fol. 69–71, cited by Paulus, *Katholik* (1898) I, 55f.

20. Berlin Hs. theol. fol. 97 (=Val. Rose II, 1, No. 572) and Rome Cod. Vat. Pal. lat. 337 (=H. Stevenson and de Russi, *Codices Palatini Latini Bibliothecae Vaticanae* I [1886] 90).

21. Also in the Roman copy; the statement of Stevenson, *Codices Palatini*, is imprecise, as the administration of the Vatican library (Mons. Mercati) has kindly informed me. The designation of the Pal. lat. 336 as a writing of Wesel is unfounded and was taken over by Stevenson without verification from a catalogue of the 17th century.

22. *Studien zur Spätscholastik*, II, p. 46.

23. I. II, *dist.* 30 (Berlin Cod. fol. 119ff.)

24. In the treatise "De virginis Mariae conceptione"; cf. also the report of the trial, question 18.

25. Cf. A. V. Müller, *Lutherschriften*, esp. *Luthers theologische Quellen* (1912).

26. The opposing position of Clemen, *Goch*, p. 189, n. 4, turns out to be erroneous.

27. The correct teaching of the church is still found in the Commentary on the *Sentences* (l. 1, dist. 29, fol. 66[a]). J. v. Wesel himself invokes there the "anathema" of canon law upon those who deny it and he must, therefore, have been conscious of his heresy as such.

28. Cf. F. Kropatschek, *Das Schriftprinzip der luther. Kirche.*, I: *Die Vorgeschichte* (1904).

29. Noteworthy among other things is the thoroughly unusual form of his "potestacio" at the beginning of his indulgence treatise (C. W. F. Walch, ed., *Monimenta medii aevi*, I [Göttingen, 1757], 114f.: "nihil velle dicere . . . quod veritati fidei, que in scripturis sacris continetur, quovis modo sit contrarium"). Here, as in other places, there is no mention of ecclesiastical tradition. Likewise Wessel, *Opera* (1617), p. 830, par. 2; also *ibid.*, 759, par. 1. Goch expresses himself less radically (cf. Clemen, *Goch*, pp. 82, 86, 189). J. v. W. appeals (in the correspondence with Joh. von Kaiserslautern) to the quotations of Augustine in the *Decretum* I, dist. 9, which had first elucidated for him the exclusive importance of God's Word.

30. Cf. van Veen, *PRE*[3] 21, 140.

31. *Opera*, p. 769, par. 3.

32. *Opera*, pp. 864ff.

33. *Adversus indulgentias*, Walch, *Monim. medii aevi*, p. 42.

34. Goch goes still another step at this point. Apparently because of his sad experiences as monastic advisor, he declares every external constraint toward the observance of monastic vows to be contrary to the Gospel. Gansfort and Wesel, on the other hand, only warn the weak (in almost literal agreement) against entering rashly into vows which they might find intolerable.

35. l. IV, *dist.* 18.

36. Van Veen, *PRE*[3] 21, 140.

37. It would not be difficult to produce detailed evidence for this, but it must be left for another place.

38. In this context it could be significant that neither Wessel nor Goch strove for or attained academic theological degrees. They are not to be considered "lay theologians" (Friedrich), but neither were they actually guild theologians. As far as I can see, however, our information on this question is obscure and insufficient.

39. Compare with this O. Clemen's carefully weighed comparisons: *Goch*, pp. 221f., 249.

40. This is in no way contradicted by the fact that Goch (as Clemen demonstrates) takes over many phrases, even literally, from older literature. It is not the display of his own extensive learning which makes him interesting, but rather his new sense of what is essential to religion.

41. Concerning his relationship to Goch, cf. van Rhijn, Groningen diss. (1917), p. 72, and Clemen, *Goch, passim*.

42. Correspondence with Hoen, *Opera*, pp. 880ff. For J. v. Wesel, cf. his correspondence with Joh. v. Lautern.

43. Cf. the citations given in van Rhijn, p. 106, esp. *Opera*, p. 888.

44. What Hardenberg's "Vita" reports regarding the extent and, especially, the supposed base of these studies in Cologne, I must accept with even greater doubts than van Rhijn, pp. 64ff.

45. A list of these is in van Rhijn, appendix, p. XLIII.

46. This is most noticeable in the prefaces to the various "exempla" of the *Scala meditationis*, e.g. *Opera*, 365. Concerning Cicero's sentence structure, cf. *Opera*, pp. 42, 237, 245, 249ff., 325.

47. The *Scala meditationis*, which describes itself quite aptly as a *tractatus de cohibendis cogitationibus et de modo constituendarum meditationum*, belongs in general to the strangest works of the author. It appears to be the mature result of a long tradition of medieval mystical arts of "submersion" and devout

meditation on the "facts of salvation." To my knowledge it has never been studied in context. I would venture to point out in this connection that much attention has recently been devoted to the (hypothetical) dependence of Ignatius' *Book of Spiritual Exercises* on the devotional writings of German mystics (Ludolf of Saxony and Thomas à Kempis); I confess that the techniques of *cohibere cogitationes* presented here remind me vaguely of Ignatius. Incidentally, an important source for the *inventio dialectica* of R. Agricola might be found in the *Scala meditationis*.

48. *De Magnitudine passionis*, cap. 43, *Opera*, p. 548; *De Cervis incarnationis*, cap. 4, *Opera*, p. 420; cf. also *Opera*, pp. 722ff. (Criticism of Aristotle's teaching on the soul.)

49. *Opera*, p. 582 (*De Magnit. pass.*).

50. *Ibid.*, p. 785 (*De Sacramento poenitentiae*).

51. I consider the agonizing attempts of Mestwerdt (*Die Anfänge des Erasmus*, 1917) to construct an inner affinity between the *Devotio moderna* and the "stoic" disposition of Italian humanism unfruitful for intellectual history. They obscure the insight that it is a matter of two intellectual worlds of fundamentally different origin.

52. Here it must be stressed again that for Joh. von Wesel even the *patres*, esp. Augustine, enjoy no preferential authority.

53. Only thus can we steer clear of a hopeless confusion of intellectual-historical concepts which has long been threatening; cf. for instance (in addition to innumerable other examples) the already mentioned book of Lindeboom, which correctly recognizes the origin and significance of the lay movement in the Netherlands as an original form of late medieval piety. He sees its independence from the Reformation and the central position of Wessel in the movement; but in the depiction of its progress he does not distinguish with sufficient clarity between the humanistic and the religious elements. The height of conceptual mixtures (already obvious in the title) is the book by Albert Hyma, *The Christian Renaissance* (Michigan, 1924).

54. He expressly resisted such rejection of scholastic education as the humanists displayed: *Opera*, pp. 893 and 920, lines 11ff. from bottom of page. Cf. also his recommendation of the scholastic technique of questions: *Scala meditationis*, l. III, cap. 4, *Opera*, 256ff.

55. This effort, by the way, was not restricted to "humanistic" circles in the 15th century, nor did it need to spring from "humanistic" stimuli. This is shown most vividly in the report (almost moving in its simplicity) by Conrad Pellikan (*Chronicon*, ed. Riggenbach, Basel, 1877) concerning the beginnings of his Hebrew language studies.

56. Cf. van Rhijn, pp. 248ff. Melanchthon also, thanks to Reuchlin's intervention, was greatly interested in him all his life.

57. Walch, *Monim. medii aevi* II, 2, 117ff.; on older editions, cf. *ZKG* 19 (1898), 467ff.

58. Haussleiter, *ZKG* 19 (1898), 467ff.

59. Cf. van Rhijn, pp. 248ff.

60. *Erasmus*, p. 232.

61. *Zwingli und Luther* (1924), pp. 49ff.

62. Van Rhijn, pp. 257ff., and the bibliography listed there.

63. *Gesch. d. kathol. Reformation* I (1880). Cf. recently Clemen, *Goch*, p. 246.

2

BERND MOELLER

Piety in Germany Around 1500 *†

[TRANSLATED BY JOYCE IRWIN]

Bernd Moeller, Professor of Church History at the University of Göttingen, is best known for his study of the impact of the Reformation on the imperial cities: Reichstadt und Reformation *(1962), now in French and soon to appear in English translation. In addition to studies on Johannes Tauler (dissertation) and Johannes Zwick (Habilitationsschrift), Moeller has recently published* Geschichte des Christentums *(1965) and* Spätmittelalter *(1966), both bibliographically rich. The article on "Piety in Germany Around 1500" shows how, on the very eve of the Reformation, late medieval piety evinced loyal acceptance of the dogmatic authority of the Church. "The willingness, and indeed the desire to sanctify worldly life within the framework of*

---

* This is a partially revised version of a lecture, expanded with notes, which served as a basis for discussion at the colloquium for religious history in Lyon organized by the *Commission internationale d'histoire ecclésiastique comparée* and its French subcommittee on October 3, 1963, under the title "La vie religieuse dans les pays de langue germanique à la fin du xvᵉ siècle." The preliminary version was printed in the preparatory volume for this colloquium (Grenoble, 1963, pp. 35–48); a very abridged and not completely satisfactory rendering of the discussion following the lecture may be found in the concluding volume of the colloquium, *Cahiers d'histoire* 9/1 (Grenoble, 1964). I am indebted to this discussion, and above all to the contributions of G. Ritter, H. Heimpel, H. Bornkamm, O. Vasella, and M. Pacaut for many suggestions, both in agreement and in contradiction, which I have tried to utilize in part in the following article.

† *ARG* 56 (1965), 5–30.

the institutions created by the Church and with the help of the trea-
sures of grace she offered were hardly as generally widespread at any
other time in the Middle Ages and have never been more clearly
visible." The aberrations and subjectivism of renewed religious fervor
notwithstanding, Moeller finds the defining characteristics of late
medieval piety to be consistent "churchliness" and "traditionalism."
His conclusion is: "In my opinion, one could dare to call the late
fifteenth century in Germany one of the most churchly-minded and
devout periods of the Middle Ages." This leaves the reader with an
apparent puzzle: the Reformation broke out in a country where there
was not only intense religious fervor, but also deep respect for the
religious authority of the Church.

IT IS NOTEWORTHY, but not accidental, that the age before the
Reformation has consistently stimulated scholarship as has almost no
other period. Especially in the last generation, which was so intensely
oriented to problems of intellectual history, historical research in
Germany strove for a broad and comprehensive presentation of the
conditions and thoughts of this period. Confessional struggles regarding the legitimacy of the Reformation gave rise to such attempts, but
recent motivation, though still partially determined by the individual
involved, has been more general. Interest has focused on the "puzzling
complexity," [1] the richly colored and contrasting picture of the decades of the end of the Middle Ages and the beginning of the
modern era.

This situation explains the fact that our historical view of this age
is peculiarly dominated by the comprehensive approach. Exacting
specialized investigations have not satisfied the demand for the general view. At the same time, since the questions asked about this
period concerned its future development, its own contours were not
always recognized sharply enough. Finally, the methodological difficulties of attempting to grasp an era in its entirety and to stress its
inner life were not recognized or taken sufficiently into consideration.
For example, which phenomenon is to be regarded as "typical" and
deserving of emphasis: the normal and often banal observation or the
unfashionable but possibly weighty one, the loud and ordinary, or
the unostentatious one which may well look to the future?

In spite of misgivings, the present study aligns itself with previous
attempts [2] and is indebted to them in many respects. It is even di-

rected toward the realm of piety—that sphere of historical life which so easily escapes the grasp of the historian. As a whole it cannot claim to be more "correct" than older works or to overshadow them in pertinence and breadth of view. It merely attempts thoroughly to comprehend the era before the Reformation as an age in its own right and of its own kind. In this way it hopes to succeed in placing the accents more appropriately and hence to assess the significance of this period for the ecclesiastical revolution of the sixteenth century in a somewhat different light.

The one determining characteristic of the piety of this era which has not been thoroughly grasped before is its consistent churchliness. One cannot speak of a dissolution of the medieval world in connection with the external picture of religious life in Germany in the later fifteenth century. On the contrary, there has hardly been an age in the second millennium of Church history which offered less resistance to the dogmatic absolutism of the Catholic Church.

In what follows we will clarify and define this judgment, but in any case it is easy to show that the opposite conclusion is not tenable. For in these decades heresy—the general and fundamental revolt against the medieval Church—lost all vitality; indeed for all practical purposes it disappeared. To be sure, scattered groups of Waldensians apparently persisted in outlying mountain regions into the sixteenth century, but they went underground.[3] The last heresy trials against Waldensians or Hussites on German territory were held—with one exception [4]—before 1470.[5] After that time almost all those who came before the Inquisition were more or less harmless troublemakers,[6] blasphemers,[7] or pious zealots such as the members of the sect in Augsburg who created a stir in 1480 because they wanted to receive the Sacrament every day or several times a day.[8] But for the most part the history of heresy is now concerned with witch trials.[9] Nor was the disappearance of the heretics caused only by forcible suppression. There is symbolic significance in the resigned statement, in 1456, by the German Hussite Friedrich Reiser regarding himself and his friends: "their cause is as a fire going out." [10] The great heresy movement of the Middle Ages, which had troubled the German Church continuously since the twelfth century, came to an end in the late fifteenth century. All its energy and missionary spirit disappeared; heretical thoughts were no longer inflammatory.[11]

It cannot be said, however, that religious passion and fervor decreased in any way. The opposite is rather the case: there are many indications that the intensity of piety actually increased greatly in these decades. Perhaps the most impressive illustration is the detailed proof offered by Karl Eder that between 1450 and 1490 in Upper Austria, the region he investigated, the number of new endowments of Masses increased steadily, and faster than ever before. It remained at this peak until 1517, declined suddenly around 1518, and then almost completely stopped: the region became Protestant for a long period.[12] A list of medieval Silesian bequests to St. Anne compiled by Arnold Oskar Meyer, though full of gaps, points in the same direction.[13] Another study asserts that in one north German city, Hamburg, most of the 99 brotherhoods in existence at the beginning of the Reformation had arisen after 1450.[14] We should also add that no other period celebrated as many festivals [15] and processions.[16] But above all, from Alsace and Upper Austria to Holland and the Baltic, these decades were filled with a general resurgence of church construction.[17] The whole German-speaking world seems to present an essentially identical picture until the last, most vulnerable blossoming of late Gothic.[18]

One must not overlook, however, the fact that external factors partially explain these phenomena. The spread of the veneration of Anne was almost a fad and, of course, by no means limited to Germany.[19] Undoubtedly one significant ingredient in the enthusiasm for endowments in this era of early capitalism and the economic rise of the great trading companies was the need of the citizenry for a form of representation which could provide an outlet for the new wealth.[20] One bequest followed another and, significantly, the altars were often no longer named for the saints but for the donors.[21] Yet it is obvious that these superficial facts in no way really explain the phenomena. Corroboration from the records of the endowments is hardly necessary: one may hope for "attainment of eternal beatitude" [22] from an endowment, or for "all good things and salvation for both body and soul" [23] from a brotherhood. The church and religious realm of life was very closely entwined with the worldly. The willingness, and indeed the desire to sanctify worldly life within the framework of the institutions created by the Church and with the help of the treasures of grace she offered were hardly as generally widespread at any other time in the Middle Ages and have never been more clearly visible.[24]

In details, of course, the expressions of piety and churchliness in this period differ greatly. Two fundamental, but in many ways contradictory, tendencies or moods may first be recognized. On one hand, there is a trend toward massiveness, toward wild and, wherever possible, violent excitement, an inclination to simplify and vulgarize the holy; on the other is a tender individualism, a propensity for quiet inwardness and devout simplicity.

To be sure, the first tendency is not specific to our period but is characteristic of all of the late Middle Ages after the middle of the fourteenth century. It is explained by sociological shifts, the rise of towns and their bourgeoisie, as well as by shattering collective experiences such as the plagues. As never before, "the folk" in this age becomes not only a participant, but a molder of religious life within the Church.

Mass pilgrimages would catch fire like psychoses, from one day to the next, and just as suddenly they might collapse.[25] Often some marvelous occurrence was the cause, usually a miracle of the host.[26] In some cases, as at Sternberg in Mecklenburg in 1492, where a priest was burned to death because he had sold a consecrated host to a Jew,[27] the cause appears completely inappropriate and unreasonable. In others, as for instance in the strange children's pilgrimage to Mont St. Michel in Normandy in the year 1457, which consisted mainly of South Germans, no concrete cause is even discernible.[28] The era, however, produced not only mass religious achievements but also mass religious attacks, as, for instance, that brought about by the agitation of the Dominican inquisitor Heinrich Institoris. This systematic persecution of witches, the first in South Germany since the 1480's, at the outset, to be sure, met much resistance among officials and no general following among the people;[29] yet it belongs in the picture of these decades as much as do the innumerable local persecutions of the Jews in this era of rising capitalism.[30]

The supernatural world was still present, close to men at every moment. Agitation over the horrors and the periods of anxiety in this era—though in comparison not yet particularly strong—intensified the awareness of dependence on the heavenly powers and the desire for harmony with them. Miracles multiplied everywhere; they were found in every corner of the empire, and they were often based on blatant deception.[31] Occasionally such an undertaking ended in terrible scandal as did the Jetzer affair in Bern in 1509, in which four Dominicans were condemned and burned to death because they had— either maliciously or as innocent victims of an impostor—attempted to arrange a miracle of the Blessed Virgin directed against Franciscan mariology and they had failed.[32]

The veneration of saints reached its peak at about that time and also changed its outward form. The saints were brought steadily closer to personal everyday life. In sculpture they were no longer limited to a size practicable in gold, and were individualized and modernized in costume and facial expression.[33] They were met with familiarity and even intimacy in the cult, and especially in the intimate atmosphere of the brotherhood. This gave rise to touching and curious events such as the letter to St. Peter that the Brotherhood of Our Lady gave to a deceased member in 1456 so that, through the assurance of the brotherhood's good deeds, he might go freely through the gate of heaven.[34] Along the same line, the development of the patronage system was completed in this period: the responsibility of individual saints for particular groups of the population and particular emergencies was finally fixed, and the sphere of the saints was adjusted precisely to the arrangement of human society and human fate.[35] In addition, the practice of giving children the names of saints became common, so that the old Germanic given names all but disappeared.[36]

Behind all this was doubtless hidden an oppressive uncertainty about salvation together with the longing for it. By capturing the mediators between them and God, men attempted to force a guarantee of salvation. Death seems never to have been more realistically considered [37] than in this era,[38] and hardly ever so anxiously feared.[39] We know from these decades the struggles of many of the rich, gripping in their own way, to exhaust to the end the possibilities of pious accomplishments opened up for them by the late medieval Church. In this connection one thinks of the strange and vast collections of relics which originated particularly in the first years of the sixteenth century. The determining incentive for these collections was sometimes the wish to assure oneself of correspondingly immense periods of indulgence. In Halle Cardinal Albrecht of Brandenburg managed to accumulate 39,245,120 years,[40] or so he believed. In general, the extraordinary prosperity of the indulgence trade since Sixtus IV had become pope was certainly also motivated by the wishes and needs of believers and not merely, as earlier critics of the papacy believed, by the financial interests of the Church. Other legacies from these decades were no less grotesquely overdone and pursued no less vigorously than were the relic collections. Count Werner of Zimmern, for instance, had 1000 requiem masses read for him in 1483.[41] In 1569 Duke Adolf of Geldern, on the death of his wife, ordered the bells to be rung in all the churches of Arnheim for three days; moreover, offices for the dead were to be celebrated in all the churches and all priests were to read masses.[42]

These anxious, craning gestures, indicating spiritual destitution and the misery of existence, were of a greater extent and higher intensity than before that time. They contrast strangely but not accidentally with various expressions of the strong, even coarse worldliness displayed in these decades by the lower as well as the higher levels of society.[42a] But they presupposed the competence and capacity of the Church for the achievement of salvation just as naturally as they did the value and necessity of good works for the same purpose. It was also a medieval trait to rely on the quantity rather than the quality of these efforts. In addition, it was precisely the central mystery of the Church, the Mass and the Eucharist, from which, as in earlier times, strength and comfort were primarily to be expected. What increased at this time was mainly an awed, reverent recognition of the remoteness of the Sacrament, shown in the way the people crowded eagerly to see the consecrated host,[43] even though participation at communion did not increase[44] in spite of the Church's many efforts.[45]

Ardent and urgent forcefulness was not the only, probably not even the dominant characteristic of the piety of this era. In addition, in Germany, there was a second, essentially different current of piety.

The two broad streams of religious tradition, which flowed from the preceding period into the later fifteenth century, arose in the world of the monasteries. There were, on one hand, the offshoots of German Dominican mysticism of the fifteenth century and, on the other, the vigorous reform ideas which seized all the orders. The latter attained their most brilliant success in Germany in the first half of the fifteenth century and revitalized the Benedictine order in particular,[46] but by 1450 both traditions of piety had long since leapt the monastery walls. A large number of edifying ascetic treatises of many kinds had resulted from the renewal and deepening of religious life in the monasteries, but they were also distributed widely in lay circles, and undoubtedly stimulated sermons and pastoral care in the churches. Most important, however, was the rise of the *Devotio moderna* in the Netherlands at the end of the fourteenth century. The program of this spiritual movement sought to bridge the gap between secular and monastic life by realizing the ideals of monasticism in a modest social unit, not set apart and limited by rigid obligations, but at the same time free from the commotion of the world.[47] In the *Devotio moderna* the influences of mysticism converged with those of the reform movement.[48]

Superficial or exaggerated forcefulness was foreign to the piety of these monasteries and of the lay circles controlled by them. Yet here, too, it is impossible to doubt the drive toward churchliness; since the fourteenth century it had grown wherever possible. And the deep, anxious longing for salvation, which we have already noted, does not seem to have diminished. But precisely for this reason men turned away from all externality, all "wis-wis-wis-Gemompel." [49] The ecclesiastical means of grace were pushed aside, as in the heyday of mysticism, in favor of an inner relationship with Christ,[50] and theological speculation was approached with caution.[51]

By 1450 the impulses of mysticism and monastic reform, as well as those of the *Devotio moderna*, were crippled, their energy abated. The increase in observances and in reforming congregations was now to a great extent no longer a matter of enthusiasm but of intrigues and party struggles; [52] ideals had congealed into a certain formalism and literary activity had ceased.[53] And yet it was precisely in this condition of exhaustion, shallowness, and monotony that this piety moved history; precisely in this form it had a powerful impact.

The fifteenth century has been called "the inflation period of German mystic literature" [54]—a phrase which well characterizes the mystical-ascetic piety of the time. On one hand, it had gained exceptionally broad influence. This is most evident in the literary realm, where printing (the discovery of which was motivated to a certain extent by the newly-aroused need for books) made possible the spread of intellectual matter and enormously increased the enthusiasm for reading and education.[55] An abundance of religious writings of all kinds became generally accessible, from prayer books and books of comfort [56] to sermon manuals [57] and missals,[58] from scholastic summas [59] to dances of death.[60] We have no exact compilation of the spiritual publications which appeared in Germany in the age of incunabula; [61] but it is obvious that they comprise by far the greatest portion of the gigantic book production [62] in the first decades of printing.[63]

If one looks more closely at the spiritual literature, however, it becomes evident that, to an astonishing degree, it is lacking in originality and frequently also in depth. When it is not simply a reproduction of older works, it consists, at best, of more or less skillfully prepared compilations or revisions of those works.[64] Even fifteenth century writings conform slavishly, as a rule, to older prototypes;[65] and the independence of famed ecclesiastics and writers of the time such as the Dominican Johann Nider (d. 1438) and the Strassburg cathedral preacher Johann Geiler of Kaysersberg (1445–1510) consists mainly in simplifying, making innocuous, and popularizing the systems and thoughts they had appropriated.[66]

A general and fundamental characteristic of this age is the paucity of great men.[67] For the literary realm, at least, this is not to be traced simply to intellectual impotence; rather, the astonishing traditionalism that we observe was intentional. Men actually avoided originality and serious thought. The famous Viennese preacher, Nicholas of Dinkelsbühl, a theologian of the first half of the century, had formally boasted of this: "Nihil locuturus sum de proprio ingenio . . . , sed omnia, que locuturus sum, sunt omnipotentis dei dona et sanctorum doctorum katholicorum virorum doctrinae; solum enim laborem habui in colligendo." [68] Geiler remarked: "They are more praiseworthy who understand simply, in a common superficial way, what virtues are." [69] And the scarcely less famous Dominican, Johannes Meyer of Basel, turned against mysticism, telling his readers that there was less use for visions than for virtues.[70] Here an affinity to the *Devotio moderna* —admittedly in somewhat crude form—is noticeable, as is the influence of Gerson, who could be called the church father of the German spiritual writers of the fifteenth century. Men were afraid to touch the principles of existence and of thought. No works such as the profound and turbulent *Ackermann aus Böhmen* appeared in the second half of the fifteenth century; the consuming desire for knowledge and the vast theological passion of one such as Nicholas of Cusa stood alone in this period. Heresies, conciliarism, and the reforming zeal of the conciliar era [71] had largely disappeared; so had the daring aspects of mysticism and piety; [72] heretical works or even those criticizing the Church were as unusual in the printed matter of the fifteenth century as were original treatises from the golden age of German mysticism.

Even in the early days of printing the demand regulated the supply.[73] The books people wanted to read were the books printed. The trend toward simplicity, the adherence to the traditional order, and the flight from extremes were not forced on the age from outside; the tendency was a fundamental and general characteristic of piety in the Germany of the time. Mysticism became a spiritual and religious force precisely in this popularized, inoffensive, diluted form.

The printing of the Bible had very great importance in the period of incunabula; in no other country did as many Bibles appear in the vernacular as in Germany.[74] But the complete editions of the Bible, totaling twenty-two by 1522, were not the most successful, but rather the more practical partial printings. By the time of the Reformation at least 62 complete or partial editions of the Psalter and 131 *plenaria* (Gospel and Epistle readings for Sundays) had appeared in print.[75]

There is plenty of evidence that the new reading matter had a deepening effect. Occasionally, Bible reading may have been pursued as ascetic exercise; there is, for instance, the testimony: "In 1476, I, Madalena Krefftin, read this book from cover to cover between mid-Lent and Holy Saturday to the glory of the Holy Trinity." [76] But there is also much evidence that Biblical history and Christ, above all the suffering Christ, won increased importance in relation to that of the saints. We are familiar with the deeply moving and realistic crucifixes and depictions of the man of sorrows produced by German late Gothic,[77] as well as with the representations of the Passion which engaged the great German painters—Cranach, Grünewald, Dürer, and Tilman Riemenschneider—at the turn of the sixteenth century.[78] In this case, too, the relationship of supply and demand should be observed; the zeal for establishing foundations in this period is intrinsically connected with the blossoming of the arts. The new devotion to Christ was even occasionally capable of purifying and enriching traditional forms of piety. This is seen in the Christocentric direction taken by representation of the dance of death in some parts of North Germany in the second half of the fifteenth century. In the Berlin Dance of Death of 1484 Death is no longer the leader and focal point; the Crucified, not Death, has the last word: "Come all of you with me to the dance of death!" [79] It was a few years after the turn of the century, however, that the Isenheim altar was produced.

Bound up with the fervor to appropriate simple, innocuous, trustworthy ideas, there was thus much depth of feeling and inward sympathy. Veneration of Mary also brought forth moving and sincere expressions.[80] And in the history of religious drama [81] and of music,[82] as well as in the visual arts,[83] there is a major turning-point in the later fifteenth century—a change from the dominance of the symbolic and ornamental to that of the individual. Viewed broadly, it is by no means indifference, formalism,[84] or even worldliness which is the dominant trait of the piety of this age,[85] but rather—the formulation Lucien Fèbvre used with regard to France is also appropriate for Germany—"un immense appétit du divin." [86] The readers of the books of comfort—of the paradise of the soul and the art of dying—and the donors of the Passion representations as well as those who gazed upon them longed no less for salvation and were no less fearful of death than were the enraptured pilgrims. They too were gripped by the thought that humility and resignation—the virtues recommended to them—could open the way to their beatitude.

If the picture we have painted is correct in its basic features, we have on the whole—granting all the differences in detail which can only be hinted at in a study such as this—a connected and in certain respects a completed picture. The religious excitement, in many cases amounting to mental disturbance, the "mobilitas seu mutabilitas animarum et inconstantia mentis nunc in hominibus" which an Erfurt theologian identified in 1466,[87] was seeking an answer, seeking repose in the ancient and holy, and gained peace within the structure of the Church. In my opinion, one could dare to call the late fifteenth century in Germany one of the most churchly-minded and devout periods of the Middle Ages.

To be sure, men did not primarily seek the Church as such but rather the salvation which it possessed. In their intense and largely, it appears, subjectivistic concern for salvation, men grasped the forms of religious life and the possibilities for devout exercise which the Church offered with a new and independent zeal, and to a certain extent they gave those forms new content. This activity went beyond an exaggerated and overzealous manner; indeed the feeling of responsibility for the Church on the part of the laity increased markedly (it had been a lively impulse for a long time, particularly in the cities).[88] Rulers and aldermen, for example, but also individual citizens, energetically undertook the reform of the monasteries. And the practice, begun at the turn of the fifteenth century, of founding benefices for preaching in order to guarantee regular and engaging preaching (as is evidenced by the frequent requirement of an academic degree for preachers) had in many regions, especially Southwest Germany, procured a preacher for nearly every town by the end of the century.[89]

This measure, and others like it, occasionally had an unmistakable self-serving character. The general churchly devotion of the later fifteenth century did not mean unconditional and uncritical recognition of the claims of superiority and leadership on the part of ecclesiastical officials.[90] Admittedly, viewed broadly and compared with the preceding century of reforms, there was thoroughgoing criticism of the Church only in isolated cases and in relatively modest form. Utterances of this kind have, in my opinion, often been overrated as far as both their substance and their historical importance are concerned.

There are, for example, the so-called *Gravamina* of the German nation,[91] which are directed against particular, mainly financial, grievances. There are some more penetrating pamphlets which articulate the demand for church reform, such as the so-called *Reformatio Sigismundi* [92] which appeared in connection with the Council of Basel in 1439 and was quite widely circulated in the later fifteenth century. Another example is the wild pamphlet of the so-called Upper Rhine revolutionary,[93] which, however, remained almost unknown.

The most important critics of the Church within the territory of the German Empire in the fifteenth century were three theologians who were more or less closely connected with the *Devotio moderna:* the two Hollanders, Johann Pupper von Goch (d. 1475) and Wessel Gansfort (d. 1489), and the Rhinelander Johann Ruchrath von Oberwesel (d. after 1479).[94] German school theology of the fifteenth century, which had otherwise been characterized by "complete theological and ecclesio-political colorlessness" (Ritter) [95] and had run only along traditional scholastic tracks, heard the sounds of reform and saw an independent religious element for the first time through these men. To be sure, transmittal of their reforming zeal remained fairly limited and weak. Even when they determinedly stressed the Scripture principle and turned it to some extent *against* previous exegesis, when they raised various objections to the institutions of the Church—indulgences, the merit of monastic vows and the like—and even when they defended a concept of the Church which exalted the invisible communion of the righteous, as did the Ockhamist-trained Gansfort, they reached only a few, and still fewer were interested enough to be carried along.

Only among the humanists did they find an echo.[96] In these circles, small indeed at first, a general change in outlook and in piety occurred for the first, in fact for the only, time in the fifteenth century.[97] With some humanists, Celtis for instance, one senses a deeper, more fundamental alienation, the rise of a mood related to and partly influenced by the Italian Renaissance, consisting of a new optimism in man's point of view. Here, too, one must beware of the danger of false evaluation. Though the German humanists were supposed to have played such an important role in the breakthrough of the Reformation,[98] there is little conscious turning away from the old churchliness around 1500. In 1485 Rudolf Agricola had himself buried in his cowl; [99] quite a number of humanists enlisted in the service of popular religion as poets and writers, and some, such as the Basel preacher Surgant, as well as Reuchlin and Erasmus later on, tried to establish the new ideals precisely in order to deepen the Church's influence.[100] Moreover, the later historical effect of humanism, and the tendency of its representatives to appear to have greater force than they actually possessed, easily mislead the historian into overevaluation. The humanists are not representative of piety in Germany in the late fifteenth century.

Nevertheless, the criticism of the Church in humanism and popular literature and the struggle for an extension of lay influence in the Church are, with their implied reproach, elements of color which belong in our picture, if one carefully observes the limits of their extent and significance. Along with a certain subjectivism in devotion, a veiled emancipation which allows a man to choose his own means of salvation, disappointment was expressed that the clergy corresponded so little to the demands and expectations of the faithful. The criticisms raised concerning lack of education and immorality among priests and monks, and the attempt to combat these abuses within the framework of one's own possibilities, were, so to speak, acts of self-defense. They, too, presupposed that one was seeking salvation and was certain to find it with the help of the Church.

To what extent were this disillusionment and criticism and the attempt to help oneself justified? We will attempt to summarize the state of research with respect to the much-discussed and much-disputed problem of the moral and intellectual condition of the hierarchy on the eve of the Reformation.

With regard to education,[101] it has been proven that at least in South Germany a third to a half of all clerics had attended a university and had belonged to the faculty of arts.[102] The percentage of learned pastors in North Germany was undoubtedly lower,[103] and in any case one must keep in mind the fact that very few of these men had studied theology.[104] Only with the Reformation was the principle established that the study of theology should be a prerequisite for a spiritual vocation and that a pastor should be a learned theologian. Even the examinations required of prospective clerics in the dioceses set extremely modest requirements.[105]

In the area of morality, the situation around 1500 was also not completely catastrophic. Precise and reliable figures obviously cannot be obtained, but the best contemporary expert on these problems, Oskar Vasella, recently, and certainly with justification, painted a thoroughly gloomy picture of the conditions in Switzerland.[106] Undoubtedly the number of clerics who lived in concubinage was extraordinarily high. Relationships similar to marriage,[106a] however, already prevailed in many ways, and the beginnings of legalization and therewith some recognition of the morality of these unions could be observed.[107]

Finally, as far as the pastoral activity of the clergy is concerned, this was limited for the majority, the altarists, to the reading of Mass. In the many parishes which were provided only with a vicar for the nonresident incumbent,[108] pastoral leadership of the congregation and preaching were often completely neglected. We also have evidence that even in the case of responsible pastors with a sense of duty, activity was largely restricted to a completely formalistic attendance to the Sacraments and the saints.[109] To be sure, there was much preaching by mendicant friars, preachers, and even pastors; considering the level of these sermons, the judgment may be justified that in this area there was too much rather than too little. As far as we can discern from extant outlines and transcripts,[110] which naturally contain passages held in especially high esteem, this level corresponded to the mood of the time and was often astonishingly, and sometimes unbelievably, low.[111]

Abuses among the late medieval clergy and how they offended the piety of 1500 present a complex state of affairs. One of the conditions leading to these abuses was the extraordinary increase in the number of clerics and their consequent deprivation and frequently also impoverishment.[112] Yet piety itself was the cause of this situation, because of its zeal in founding benefices and masses. In pre-Reformation Worms some 10 percent of the population were secular and regular clergy;[113] the situation had reached a point where the Church had to react,[114] but there was no profound impulse[115] in theology or spiritual life to guide men out of the maze into which the historical development of the Church had led. No suitable and appropriate answer could be given to the longings and explosive passions of the men who submitted to the leadership of the Church. The significance attained in this period by the indulgence sermon[116]—so sub-Christian in its materialism and so misunderstood in its essence—is the most distinctive symptom of this negative state of affairs.

It seems, therefore, that the general revitalization and enrichment of devotion in the later fifteenth century found no echo worth mentioning among the clergy.[117] Indeed, there are signs that the condition of the clergy merely deteriorated even more up to the threshold of the Reformation.[118] The clergy's leadership role, well established since the early Middle Ages, was indeed still claimed in Germany around 1500, and still recognized almost everywhere; but the clergy were in fact hardly capable of assuming the part. Most of them were bound to the feudal age in conceiving of their office as a benefice, but at the same time they were accustomed to being set apart from the laity on the basis of their sacramental function and the *opus operatum*. Now, for the first time in the Middle Ages, high and differentiated intellectual and spiritual demands were placed on them, and their power slipped through their fingers. Their deterioration in rank must have seemed all the more unbearable as the status of the laity rose— particularly in Germany, which at the beginning of the sixteenth century, for the first time in history, was the focal point of intellectual and religious life in Europe north of the Alps.

Undoubtedly, what we have been discussing belongs to the "prerequisites"—if not also to the "causes" [119]—of the Reformation, but here we can only hint at the problem on which this touches. Nicholas Glassberger, the Frankish Franciscan chronicler of the later fifteenth century, at one point complained about the wretched condition of the French Church of his time; in contrast he calls attention to the flourishing situation in Germany, where services are festive and the people devout and faithful to the Church.[120] He may have been correct: Germany in the later Middle Ages was "an especially medieval country" (Heimpel),[121] and clearly remained so right up to the threshold of the Reformation. Luther's victory in Germany, his ability to carry men along with him, are easily misunderstood if one does not recognize that one of the prerequisites for his success was the extreme intensification of medieval churchly devotion.[122] It is no accident, and must be borne in mind, that the Reformation emerged in Germany, a sluggish, medieval country where authority was still respected, rather than, for example, in France.

NOTES

1. J. Lortz, *Die Reformation in Deutschland* I (1949 [3]), 96.
2. Among the general presentations in which our theme is treated from varying points of view, the following seem particularly valuable, in addition to the largely dated work of G. v. Below, *Die Ursachen der Reformation* (1917): W. Andreas, *Deutschland vor der Reformation* (1959 [6]); J. Lortz, *Die Reformation in Deutschland,* I (1949 [3]), with the important in-depth supplement in the essay "Zur Problematik der kirchlichen Missstände im Spät-Mittelalter," *Trierer Theol. Zs.* 58 (1949), 1–26, 212–227, 257–279, 347–357; R. R. Post, *Kerkelijke verhoudingen in Nederland voor de Reformatie* (Utrecht and Antwerp, 1954). Cf. also Post, *Kerkgeschiedenis van Nederland in de middeleeuwen,* above all vol. 2 (1957), 268ff. Also instructive are G. Schnürer, *Kirche und Kultur im Mittelalter,* 3 (1929), 206ff., the survey of O. Clemen, *Die*

Volksfrömmigkeit des ausgehenden Mittelalters, in *Stud. z. relig. Volkskunde* 3 (1937), and the important, though in their own way one-sided, books of R. Stadelmann, *Vom Geist des ausgehenden Mittelalters,* in *Dt. Vierteljahrsschr. f. Literaturwiss. u. Geistesgesch.,* Buchreihe 15 (1929), and W. E. Peuckert, *Die grosse Wende* (1948). Less satisfying, on the other hand, is the literature report of P. Wunderlich, *Die Beurteilung der Vorreformation in der deutschen Geschichtsschreibung seit Ranke,* in *Erlanger Abh. zur mittleren und neueren Gesch.* 5 (1930), as well as the lecture series of K. Eder, *Deutsche Geisteswende zwischen Mittelalter und Neuzeit* (1937). My general interpretation has been most determined by the essay of H. Heimpel, "Das Wesen des deutschen Spätmittelalters," *Archiv f. Kulturgesch.* 35 (1953), 29–51=*Der Mensch in seiner Gegenwart* (1957²), pp. 109–135.

3. H. Haupt, *Die religiösen Sekten in Franken vor der Reformation* (1882), pp. 48ff.; H. C. Lea, *Gesch. d. Inquisition im Mittelalter,* 2 (1909), 473f.

4. There were persecutions of Waldensians in the Brandenburg Marches from 1478 to 1483, followed by their migration to Moravia: W. Wattenbach, *Über die Inquisition gegen die Waldenser in Pommern und der Mark Brandenburg,* in *Abh. der Königl. Akad. d. Wiss. zu Berlin* (1886) Philos.-Hist. Klasse 3, pp. 87ff.; G. Brunner, *Ketzer und Inquisition in der Mark Brandenburg im ausgehenden Mittelalter* (Diss. Berlin, 1904), pp. 26ff.

5. Trials were held in 1458 against Hussites in Strassburg: H. Köpstein, "über den deutschen Hussiten Friedrich Reiser," *Zs. f. Gesch.wiss.* 7 (1959), 1068–1082 (the importance of this man is greatly overestimated in this work; he is made to resemble a Communist Party official in a capitalistic country); cf. Köpstein's previous study in *Aus 100 Jahren deutsch-tschechoslowakischer Geschichte* (1958), pp. 22ff. In the same year there were trials in the Brandenburg Marches against Waldensians influenced by Taborites: Wattenbach (note 4), pp. 71ff.; Brunner (note 4), pp. 18ff.; in 1461 against Waldensians in the bishopric of Eichstätt: Haupt (note 3), p. 47; in 1462 against Taboritic Waldensians in Saxony and Thüringia: H. Boehmer, "Die Waldenser von Zwickau," *Neues Archiv f. sächsische Gesch. und Altertumskunde* 36 (1915), 1–38; in 1467 against the apocalyptic sect of the "Wirsbergers," who were probably connected with the Hussites: G. Ritter, *ZKG* 43 (1924), 158f.; O. Schiff, "Die Wirsberger," *Hist. Vierteljahrsschr.* 26 (1931), 776–786; R. Kestenberg-Gladstein: "The 'Third Reich,' " *Journ. of the Warburg and Courtauld Institutes* 18 (1955), 245–295 (the writer overestimates the importance of these groups: heresies are not "characteristic of this epoch in general"). Other individual heretics are discussed in J. Döllinger, *Beiträge zur Sektengesch. d. Mittelalters* 2 (1890), 626ff.; G. Ritter (note 5), pp. 150–158 (a spiritualist who says "Ecclesia tota inferior est dampnata et haeretica"); K. Schornbaum, *Zs. f. bayerische Kirchengesch.* 8 (1933), 203f.

6. For example, Hans Böhm, the "Pfeifer von Niklashausen," executed in 1476, and the movement which flocked around him, singing against priests, and which collapsed rapidly after the death of its leader: Haupt (note 3), pp. 57ff.; Peuckert (note 2), pp. 263ff.; G. Franz, *Der deutsche Bauernkrieg* (1956⁴), pp. 45ff. It seems clear that the revolutionary character of this movement, which traced itself back to an appearance of the Virgin, was stamped on it through the reaction of church officials. Concerning executions of Flagellants in Quedlinburg and Halberstadt in 1461 and 1481, see most recently G. Zschäbitz, *Zur mitteldeutschen Wiedertäuferbewegung nach dem grossen Bauernkrieg,* in *Leip-*

ziger Übersetzungen und Abh. zum Mittelalter I (1958), 123 (Bibliography).

7. For example, Post, *Kerkgesch.* (note 2), 2, 338ff.

8. A. M. Koeniger, *Ein Inquisitionsprozess in Sachen der täglichen Kommunion* (1923); A. Schröder, "Die tägliche Laienkommunion in spätmittelalterlicher Auffassung," *Archiv f. d. Gesch. d. Hochstifts Augsburg* 6 (1929), 609–629. The church officials no doubt perceived Hussitism behind this: P. Browe, *Die häufige Kommunion im Mittelalter* (1938), pp. 32ff.

9. Enumeration in H. C. Lea–A. C. Howland, *Materials Toward a History of Witchcraft,* I (New York-London, 1957 [2]), 237, 241, 251, 253.

10. A. Jung, *Timotheus* 2 (Strassburg, 1822), 256. Reiser intertwined Waldensian and Hussite themes, as was shown after Köpstein particularly by V. Vinay, "Friedrich Reiser e la diaspora valdese di lingua tedesca nel XV secolo," *Boll. della Soc. di Studi Valdesi* 109 (1961), 35–36.

11. This important fact, in my opinion, has not been sufficiently noticed. This holds true even for the recent instructive investigation of the matter: C. P. Clasen, "Medieval Heresies in the Reformation," *Church History* 32 (1963), 392–414. It infers, as do numerous older works, a historical continuity from the affinity of Reformation sects with medieval sects in matters of theology and church discipline. Even if the covert survival and influence of medieval sects cannot simply be denied, the conclusion as a whole is not compelling. It does not take into consideration the fact that the breadth of variation in sectarian themes within the realm of Christianity is relatively limited.

12. K. Eder, *Das Land ob der Enns vor der Glaubensspaltung* in *Studien z. Ref.gesch. Oberösterreichs* I (1933), 105ff., 421ff. Similarly, for Styria, K. Amon, *Die Steiermark vor der Glaubensspaltung* I, in *Gesch. d. Diözese Seckau* 3/1 (1960), 85f. Comparable, though less comprehensive and precise, figures for the Netherlands are found in Post, *Kerk. verh.* (note 2), p. 402. Similar results are reached for the parish of St. Gangolf in Trier by A. Schüller, "Messe und Kommunion in einer stadttrierischen Pfarrei vor und nach der Reformation," *Trierisches Archiv* 21 (1913), 65–98. Endowments for the Carthusian monastery at Marienkron in Pomerania, on the other hand, balanced each other for the first and second halves of the fifteenth century (totaling 2570 headings between 1406 and 1528): ed. H. Lemcke, *Liber beneficiorum des Karthäuserklosters Marienkron bei Rügenwalde,* in *Quellen zur pommerschen Geschichte* 5 (1919–22). The register of benefices found in Lüneburg seems to give the same result: G. Matthaei, *Die Vikariestiftungen der Lüneburger Stadtkirchen im Mittelalter und im Zeitalter der Reformation* (1928), pp. 151ff.

13. A. O. Meyer, *Studien zur Vorgesch. d. Reformation aus schlesischen Quellen,* in *Hist. Bibliothek* 14 (1903), 42ff. General work: B. Kleinschmidt, *Die Heilige Anna,* in *Forsch. z. Volkskunde* 1–3 (1930), 138.

14. G. Brandes, "Die geistlichen Brüderschaften in Hamburg während d. Mittelalters," *Zs. d. Vereins f. hamburg. Gesch.* 34 (1934), 75–176; 35 (1936), 57–98; 36 (1937), 65–110. According to Th. Kolde, *Friedrich d. W. und die Anfänge der Reformation* (1881), pp. 15 and 74f., the councillor of Electoral Saxony, Pfeffinger, who died in 1519, was a member simultaneously of no less than 35 brotherhoods, to which he bequeathed legacies at his death.

15. For example, Amon (note 12), pp. 211ff.

16. In 1475 there were, for example, 22 in Bruges alone: Post: *Kerk. verh.* (note 2), p. 398. In Breisach in 1502 they were even held weekly in honor of the town's patron saint: W. Müller, "Der Wandel des kirchlichen Lebens vom

Mittelalter in die Neuzeit, erörtert am Beispiel Breisach," *Freiburger Diözesan-Archiv* 82–83 (1962–63), 227–247, esp. 231.

17. Cf. the following, in part with enumeration of the edifices: A. Barthelmé, *La réforme dominicaine au XVe siècle en Alsace,* in *Coll. d'études sur l'histoire . . . de l'Alsace* 7 (Strasbourg, 1931), p. 151; Eder: *Land ob der Enns,* pp. 123ff.; Post, *Kerkgesch.* (note 2), 2, 266f.; E. Schnitzler, *Das geistige und religiöse Leben Rostocks am Ausgang des Mittelalters,* in *Hist. Studien* 360 (1940), 63.

18. The following comprehensive monographs on local history are still important: E. v. Lehe, *Die kirchlichen Verhältnissè in den Marschländern Hadeln und Wursten vor der Reformation,* in *Jb. der Männer vom Morgenstern* 24 (1928–30), 136–215; G. Rücklin, *Religiöses Volksleben des ausgehenden Mittelalters in den Reichsstädten Hall und Heilbronn,* in *Hist. Studien* 226 (1933); W. Jannasch, *Reformationsgeschichte Lübecks—1515–1530* (1958), pp. 7–79.

19. P. V. Charland, *Madame sainte Anne et son culte au moyen âge* 1–3 (Quebec, 1911–1921); Kleinschmidt (see note 13 above).

20. The standard monograph on Augsburg is J. Strieder, *Zur Genesis des modernen Kapitalismus* (1935 [2]). H. Bechtel, *Wirtschaftsstil des deutschen Spätmittelalters* (1930), only partially succeeded in integrating economic events into intellectual history.

21. H. Witte, *Archiv f. Kulturgesch.* 29 (1939), 276.

22. From the Württemberg endowment for preaching: J. Rauscher, *Württembergische Jb. f. Statistik u. Landeskunde* 2 (1908), 156.

23. Rücklin (note 18), p. 134.

24. The struggle for spiritual command and assurance on the part of the merchant class is shown clearly in the essay of A. Schulte, "Die grosse Ravensburger Handelsgesellschaft und die Pflege der kirchlichen Kunst in ihrer Gesellschaftskapelle," *Archiv f. Kulturgesch.* 26 (1936), 73–88. Abundant corresponding material is offered in N. Lieb, *Die Fugger und die Kunst* 1 (1952). E. Maschke has announced a comprehensive investigation of the piety of medieval merchants. In the meantime, see his essay, "Das Berufsbewusstsein des mittelalterlichen Fernkaufmanns," *Miscellanea Mediaevalia* 3 (1964), 306–335, esp. 323ff.

25. G. Schreiber, "Wallfahrt und Volkstum," *Forschungen z. Volkskunde* 16/17 (1934); L. A. Veit, *Volksfrommes Brauchtum und Kirche im deutschen Mittelalter* (1936), pp. 54ff.; J. Staber, *Volksfrömmigkeit und Wallfahrtswesen des Spätmittelalters im Bistum Freising* (1955).

26. P. Browe, *Die eucharistischen Verwandlungswunder im Mittelalter* (1938), *passim.*

27. Schnitzler (note 17), p. 56. Bauerreiss (see below, note 77), p. 62, is apparently incorrect.

28. In this regard see Veit (note 25), p. 54, and the literature he names p. 221, n. 76.

29. In addition to Lea-Howland (note 9), see particularly the specialized investigation by F. Byloff, "Hexenglaube und Hexenverfolgung in den österreichischen Alpenländern," *Quellen zur deutschen Volkskunde* 6 (1934), 30ff. Further literature in *Lex. f. Theol. u. Kirche,* 5 (1960 [2]), col. 319.

30. Cf. R. Straus, *Die Judengemeinde Regensburg im ausgehenden Mittelalter,* 1–2 (1932/60). General work: S. Dubnow, *Weltgesch. d. jüdischen Volkes* 5 (1927), 322ff.

31. For example, F. Roth, "Die geistliche Betrügerin Anna Laminit von Augsburg," *ZKG* 43 (1924), 355–417.

32. See the most recent treatment of this topic, K. Guggisberg, *Bernische Kirchengesch.* (1958), pp. 38ff., and the literature listed on p. 742.

33. J. Braun, *Tracht und Attribute der Heiligen in der deutschen Kunst* (1934), *passim;* W. Messerer, "Verkündigungsdarstellungen des 15. u. 16. Jh. als Zeugnisse des Frömmigkeitswandels," *Archiv f. Liturgiewiss.* 5/2 (1958), 362–369.

34. Post, *Kerkgesch.* (note 2), 2, 246, n. 1.

35. The Augsburg patron saint Ulrich even appears as a partner with the Fuggers in 1515. But as Lieb (note 24), p. 131, remarks, this practice was introduced from Italy, where it had already been current in the High Middle Ages.

36. A. Bach, *Die deutschen Personennamen* 2 (1953 2), 22ff., is a survey of the topic. Still important as explanation is J. Trier, *Der hl. Jodocus,* in *Germanist. Abh.* 56 (1924), 138ff. The specialized study of J. Scheidl, "Der Kampf zwischen deutschen und christlichen Vornamen im ausgehenden Mittelalter, nach altbaierischen Quellen für das Dachauer Land dargestellt," *Zs. f. Namensforschg.* 16 (1940), 193–214, on the other hand, is valuable only as a collection of material.

37. Consider, for instance, the gravestones dating from these decades in Marburg (Lahn), Lorch in Upper Austria, and elsewhere, which show the corpse of the deceased eaten away by worms.

38. Some general observations are found in W. Rehm, "Der Todesgedanke in der deutschen Dichtung vom Mittelalter bis zur Romantik," *Dt. Vierteljahrsschr. f. Literaturwiss u. Geistesgesch.* Buchreihe 14 (1928), 73ff.

39. Cf. below, note 60.

40. N. Paulus, *Gesch. d. Ablasses im Mittelalter* 3 (1923), 292. Ph. M. Halm and R. Berliner, *Das Hallesche Heiltum* (1931). But smaller territories such as the city of Heilbronn also tried with special zeal to increase their relic collections: Rücklin (note 18), pp. 118f. Regarding the monastery of St. Peter in Erfurt see O. Scheel, *Martin Luther* 1 (1921 3), 130.

41. H. Tüchle, *Kirchengesch. Schwabens* 2 (1954), p. 385.

42. Post, *Kerkgesch.* (note 2), 2, 293. Similar examples: Eder, *Land ob der Enns,* p. 259; Schnitzler (note 17), p. 59; R. Wackernagel, *Gesch. d. Stadt Basel* 2/2 (1916), 869f.

42a. This is sometimes closely connected with religious accomplishments and institutions themselves. Thus in 1504 in Lüneburg there was a feast of the brotherhood of the Calends which lasted three days; 124 persons took part, and devoured approximately 20 casks of beer: *Die Altertümer der Stadt Lüneburg* 5 (1862), 2.

43. Compare the annoyed commentaries and the strange penalties inflicted on those who, in attending Mass, congregated in the choir of the churches "in order to see the unveiled Sacrament," cited from the decades around 1500 in H. B. Meyer, "Die Elevation im deutschen Mittelalter und bei Luther," *Zs. f. kath. Theol.* 85 (1963), 162–217, esp. 194.

44. Communion once a year was customary: *vid.* Schüller (note 12) as well as Post, *Kerk. verh.* (note 2), p. 407.

45. Along with the brotherhoods of the Holy Sacrament and similar institutions, which aimed at more frequent communion, there were also counter-move-

ments; these were sometimes motivated spiritually by the after-effects of the view represented by German mysticism and the *Devotio moderna* regarding the superiority of spiritual nourishment over corporeal (see below, note 50) and sometimes by resistance to the Hussites, which demanded frequent communion (see above, note 8; furthermore, in addition to Browe's book cited there, see Post, *Kerk. verh.* [note 2], pp. 405ff., and S. Tromp, "S. congregatio concilii de communione frequenti," *Divinitas* 1 [1957], 550–557; 4 [1960], 61–80).

46. Lortz, "Zur Problematik" (note 2), pp. 212ff., shows impressively how manifold and complex the motivations and manifestations of monastic reform were in the fifteenth century.

47. "Non sumus religiosi, sed in seculo religiose vivere nitimur et volumus," say the brothers in Hildesheim: E. Barnikol, *Studien z. Gesch. d. Brüder vom gemeinsamen Leben,* in *ZThK,* Ergänz. H. 27 (1917), 109.

48. The best introduction to the thought world of the *Devotio moderna* is still the summary of P. Mestwerdt, *Die Anfänge des Erasmus—Humanismus und Devotio moderna,* in *Stud. z. Kultur u. Gesch. d. Reform.* 2 (1917), 78ff. Next most important are the works of R. R. Post, "Studiën over de Broeders van het Gemene Leven," *Nederlands Historiebladen* 1 (1938), 304–335; 2 (1939), 136–162; and *De Moderne Devotie* (Amsterdam, 1950 [2]). Post showed that the spread of the *Devotio moderna,* and its immediate influence, were more limited than was previously thought. The standard study of its extension into Germany is B. Windeck, *Die Anfänge der Brüder vom gemeinsamen Leben in Deutschland* (Diss. Bonn, 1951). Concerning a certain emanation to France, see G. G. Coulton, *Five Centuries of Religion,* 4 (Cambridge, 1950), 365ff.

49. S. Axters, *Geschiedenis van de vroomheid in de Nederlanden* 3 (1956), 76. [Translator's note: The phrase represents the muttering sound made by those who say their prayers audibly without directing their thoughts to God.]

50. Thomas à Kempis, *Imit. Christi* (ed. M. J. Pohl, *Opera Omnia* Vol. 2, 1904, pp. 22ff.).–Cf. Axters (note 49). W. Brüggeboes, *Die Fraterherren . . . im Lüchtenhofe zu Hildesheim* (Diss. Münster, 1939), pp. 87ff.

51. This aversion was occasionally extended in the *Devotio moderna* even to Thomas Aquinas. Cf. Godest van Toarn in C. van der Wansem, "Het ontstaan en de geschiedenis der Broederschap van het Gemene Leven tot 1400," *Rec. de Travaux d'hist. et de philol. de Louvain* 4/12 (1958), 104f.

52. Characteristic are G. M. Lohr, *Die Teutonia im 15. Jh.* (1924), *passim;* R. Molitor, *Aus der Rechtsgeschichte benediktinischer Verbände,* 2 (1932), 1ff.; G. Spahr, "Die Reform im Kloster St. Gallen 1442–1457," *Schriften d. Vereins f. Gesch. d. Bodensees* 76 (1958), 1–62.

53. For the Brethren of the Common Life, see Windeck (note 48), pp. 63ff. Strange formalizations of monastic piety are depicted in F. Rapp, "La prière dans les monastères de Dominicaines observantes en Alsace au XVe siècle," in *La Mystique Rhénane* (Paris, 1963), pp. 207–218.

54. G. Pickering, *Bulletin of the John Rylands Library* 22 (1938), 458.

55. This reciprocal relationship was worked out impressively by C. Wehmer in his instructive survey, "Inkunabelkunde," *Zentralbl. f. Bibliothekswesen* 57 (1940), 214–232, even though he perhaps emphasizes the character of Gutenberg's undertaking too strongly as a "discovery."

56. F. Falk, *Die deutschen Sterbebüchlein von der ältesten Zeit des Buchdruckes bis zum Jahre 1520* (1890); H. Bohatta, *Bibliographie der Livres d'Heures, Officia, Hortuli Animae . . . des XV. u. XVI. Jh.* (1924 [2]); A. Auer,

Johannes von Dambach und die Trostbücher vom 11. bis zum 16. Jh., in *Bei-träge z. Gesch. d. Philos. und Theol. d. Mittelalters* 27/1, 2 (1928), 367ff. Concerning the spirituality and piety expressed in this genre of literature, see especially H. Appel, *Anfechtung und Trost im Spätmittelalter und bei Luther,* in *Schr. d. Vereins f. Ref. gesch.* 165 (1938); F. X. Haimerl, *Mittelalterliche Frömmigkeit im Spiegel der Gebetbuchliteratur Süddeutschlands,* in *Münchener Theol. Stud.* 1/4 (1952), 34ff.; R. Rudolf, *Ars Moriendi,* in *Forsch. z. Volks-kunde* 39 (1957).

57. See below, note 100.

58. For the present see H. Bohatta, *Liturgische Bibliographie des XV. Jh.* (1911; reprint, 1961).

59. There is no comprehensive bibliography or investigation concerning the early printed editions of theological works.

60. P. S. Kozaky, *Gesch. d. Totentänze* 1–2 (Budapest, 1935–1944); H. Rosenfeld, *Der mittelalterliche Totentanz,* in *Beiheft z. Archiv f. Kulturgesch.* 3 (1954) has a good bibliography.

61. Cf. for the time being F. Falk, *Die Druckkunst im Dienste der Kirche* (1879). Also informative is the *Bibliotheca Catholica Neerlandica impressa 1500–1727* (The Hague, 1954), which lists no less than 784 printed editions of ecclesio-theological writings for the Netherlands alone in the years 1500–1520, very close to the period we are considering.

62. According to Wehmer (note 55) 40,000 works appeared between 1450 and 1500, 43 percent of which were in the territory of the German Empire.

63. To be sure, literature concerning early book production (see most re-cently, with its rich bibliography, L. Fèbvre–H. J. Martin, *L'apparition du livre* [Paris, 1958]), tends to overlook the basically conservative character of early printing output by focusing on curious or isolated phenomena pointing to the future. An exception is Wehmer's essay; see note 55.

64. Cf., in addition to the literature named, A. Spamer, *Über die Zersetzung und Vererbung in den deutschen Mystikertexten* (Diss. Giessen, 1910); F. P. Schmidt, *Beiträge z. thüringischen Kirchengesch.* 4 (1939), 155–176; finally the essays of W. Stammler and W. Schmidt in the collection of K. Ruh, *Alt-deutsche und altniederländische Mystik* (1964), pp. 386ff., 437ff., with their rich bibliographical data.

65. This is true for example—in spite of the exposition of J. Kalverkamp, *Die Vollkommenheitslehre des Franziskaners Heinrich Herp* (Diss. Freiburg i. Br., 1940)—of the "Spieghel der Volcomenheit," ed. L. Verschueren, 1, 2 (Ant-werp, 1931), by the most daring mystic of the time, the Dutchman Hendrik Herp. Also informative is J. Werlin, "Mystikerzitate aus einer Nürnberger Predigthandschrift," *Archiv f. Kulturgesch.* 43 (1961), 140–159.

66. Cf. G. Gieraths, "Johann Nider und die 'deutsche Mystik' des 14. Jahr-hunderts," *Divus Thomas* 30 (1952), 321–346; also his "Johann Tauler und die Frömmigkeitshaltung des 15. Jahrhunderts," in *Joh.-Tauler-Gedenkschrift* (1961), pp. 422–434; A. Vonlanthen, "Geilers Seelenparadies im Verhältnis zur Vorlage," *Archiv. f. elsäss. Kirchengesch.* 6 (1931), 229–324; F. Breitenstein, "Die Quellen der Geiler von Kaysersberg zugeschreibenen Emeis," *Archiv f. elsäss. Kirchengesch.* 13 (1938), 149–202.

67. The statement of K. Eder, *Dt. Geisteswende* (note 2), p. 181, "It would be difficult to name an age which produced such a great number of outstanding men as the period 1450–1530," cannot be supported in this form.

68. Quoted by F. Schäffauer, *Theol. Quartalschrift* 115 (1934), 539f.

69. Quoted by Vonlanthen (note 66), p. 285, n. 1.

70. Quoted by W. Muschg, *Die Mystik in der Schweiz 1200–1500* (1935), p. 350. This book is valuable for understanding the whole process described here.

71. A. Stoecklin, "Das Ende der mittelalterlichen Konzilsbewegung," *Zs. f. schweiz. Kirchengesch.* 37 (1943), 8–30; H. Jedin, *Gesch. d. Konzils von Trient* 1 (1949), 24ff.

72. Cf. in this regard the exposition of Stadelmann concerning "Die literarische Endstufe der Mystik" (note 2), pp. 98ff., impaired though it may be by its one-sided presupposition of the "morbidity" of our period.

73. Of course, the reference of Wehmer (note 55), p. 227, to the numerous bankruptcies of early printing houses must be taken into account.

74. The oldest German Bible, which appeared in print in 1466, *Gesamtkatalog der Wiegendrucke* 4 (1930), no. 4295ff., has been critically edited by W. Kurrelmeyer in ten volumes of the *Bibliothek des Litterarischen Vereins in Stuttgart*, 1904–1915. In interpreting this phenomenon, one should note the suggestion of H. Volz, *Bibel und Bibeldruck in Deutschland im 15. und 16. Jahrhundert* (1960), that the frequency of Bible printings in particular decades before the Reformation was subject to considerable fluctuation.

75. H. Rost, *Die Bibel im Mittelalter* (1939), pp. 363ff. The list is incomplete.

76. Quoted by F. K. Ingelfinger, *Die religiös-kirchlichen Verhältnisse im heutigen Württemberg am Vorabend der Reformation* (Diss. Tübingen, 1939), p. 141.

77. R. Bauerreiss, *Pie Jesu—Das Schmerzensmann-Bild und sein Einfluss auf die mittelalterliche Frömmigkeit* (1931), *passim;* G. Wagner, *Volksfromme Kreuzverehrung in Westfalen,* in *Schriften der volkskundlichen Kommission des Landschaftsverbandes Westfalen-Lippe* 11 (1960), 77ff.

78. G. Dehio, *Geschichte der deutschen Kunst* 2 (1930[4]), 182: "The visual arts tell us, better than theological and literary sources can, that the Christ of the people in the century preceding the Reformation was not the Christ of glory but the Christ in misery."

79. Rosenfeld (note 60), pp. 212ff.

80. Concerning the Marian lament of the monk Reborch of Bordesholm, cf. the judgment of W. Stammler, "Die mittelniederdeutsche geistliche Literatur," *Neue Jb. für das klass. Altertum* 23 (1920), 114–135, esp. 134. Regarding the devotional exercise of the "Marientiden," which began to spring up at the end of the 15th century in the cities of northwestern Germany, see Jannasch (note 18), pp. 43ff., 356f. and the bibliography mentioned there.

81. H. H. Borcherdt, *Das europäische Theater im Mittelalter und in der Renaissance* (1935), pp. 147ff.

82. *New Oxford History of Music,* 3 (London, 1960), 239ff. Also W. Wiora, "Der religiöse Grundzug im neuen Stil und Weg Josquins des Prez," *Musikforschung* 6 (1953), 23–37.

83. Especially informative is the essay by Messerer; see above, note 33.

84. There are, nevertheless, some significant, even fantastic examples of this, such as the calculation of Jesus' drops of blood in order to adjust the number of Our Father prayers accordingly: Post, *Kerk. verb.* (note 2), pp. 459f., as well as Rapp (note 53).

85. The study of E. Döring-Hirsch, *Tod und Jenseits im Spätmittelalter,* in

Stud. z. Gesch. der Wirtschafts- und Geisteskultur 2 (1927), though it does not go into much detail, concludes otherwise, as does the book of Bechtel.

86. L. Fèbvre, *Revue historique* 161 (1929), 39.

87. "The Augustinian Johannes Dorsten," in Kestenberg-Gladstein (note 5), p. 259.

88. Cf. A. Schultze, "Stadtgemeinde und Kirche im Mittelalter," in *Festgabe R. Sohm* (1914), pp. 103–142; B. Moeller, *Reichsstadt und Reformation,* in *Schriften d. Vereins f. Reformationsgesch.* 180 (1962), 10ff.

89. See J. Rauscher, "Die Prädikaturen in Württemberg vor der Reformation," *Württembergische Jb. für Statistik und Landeskunde* 2 (1908), 152–211; E. Lengwiler, *Die vorreformatorischen Praedikaturen der deutschen Schweiz* (Diss. Fribourg, 1955). Concerning the encroachments of laymen into preaching, see Amon (note 12), p. 276.

90. A general work on this subject is A. Störmann, *Die städtischen Gravamina gegen den Klerus am Ausgange des Mittelalters und in der Reformationszeit* (1916).

91. A standard work on this topic is B. Gebhardt, *Die Gravamina der Deutschen Nation gegen den römischen Hof* (1895 [2]). Concerning the beginnings see W. Michel, *Das Wiener Konkordat vom Jahr 1448 und die nachfolgenden Gravamina des Primarklerus der Mainzer Kirchenprovinz* (Diss. Heidelberg, 1929). See also H. Cellarius, *Die Reichsstadt Frankfurt und die Gravamina der Deutschen Nation,* in *Schriften d. Vereins f. Reformationsgesch.* 163 (1938).

92. Ed. H. Koller, *Monumenta Germ. Hist., Staatsschriften* 6 (1964). This work has lately been interpreted as strikingly medieval and conservative, particularly by L. Graf zu Dohna, *Reformatio Sigismundi,* in *Veröff. des Max-Planck-Instituts für Gesch.* 4 (1960). Characteristic of the overevaluation of this reform work in scholarly research is the completely misleading remark of M. Straube in *Die frühbürgerliche Revolution in Deutschland* (1961), p. 111: the fact that there were five printed editions of this work between 1476 and 1520 proves "that the demands of the *Reformatio Sigismundi* actually corresponded to the views of the widest [!] circles of the population in Germany and that they were current throughout many years." Compare with this note 61 above.

93. Partial edition by H. Haupt, *Westdeutsche Zs. f. Gesch. und Kunst Ergänzungsheft* 8 (1893). The most recent, though very unsatisfactory, study of this is O. Eckstein, *Die Reformschrift des sog. Oberrheinischen Revolutionärs* (Diss. Leipzig, 1939). The southwest German peasant uprisings of the early 16th century, which were perhaps ignited or strengthened by this pamphlet, were also distinguished by striking traits of medieval churchly devotion; thus, for example, Joss Fritz, after the failure of the Lehen uprising in 1513, went to Einsiedeln, dressed as a pilgrim, in order to consecrate the league's flag to the Mother of God. Franz (note 6), p. 74.

94. The best treatment of their thought is G. Ritter, "Romantische und revolutionäre Elemente in der deutschen Theologie am Vorabend der Reformation," *Dt. Vierteljahrsschr. f. Literaturwiss. u. Geistesgesch.* 5 (1927), 342–380 [=Chap. 1 in this book.—ED.]. For Wessel Gansfort, see also Stadelmann (note 2), *passim.* Concerning the reform writings of the Erfurt Carthusian Johannes Hagen, who was much more restrained in his criticism, cf. the monograph of J. Klapper, 2 vols. (1960–1961).

95. Ritter (note 94), p. 355.

96. Cf. for example N. Paulus, "Wimpfeling als Verfasser eines Berichts über den Prozess gegen Johann von Wesel," *Zs. f. die Gesch. des Oberrheins* NF 42 (1929), 296–300.

97. On German humanism of the 15th century, see above all G. Ritter, "Die geschichtliche Bedeutung des dt. Humanismus," *Hist. Zs.* 127 (1923), 393–453; P. Joachimsen, "Loci communes," *Luther-Jb.* 8 (1926), 27–97; O. Herding, "Probleme des frühen Humanismus in Deutschland," *Archiv f. Kulturgesch.* 38 (1956), 344–389, as well as the valuable, penetrating, and comprehensive presentation of L. W. Spitz, *The Religious Renaissance of the German Humanists* (Cambridge, Mass., 1963) and my review of it in *ZKG* 76 (1965). Also R. Newald, *Probleme und Gestalten des deutschen Humanismus* (1963), *passim*.

98. B. Moeller, "Die deutschen Humanisten und die Anfänge der Reformation," *ZKG* 70 (1959), 46–61.

99. H. E. J. M. van der Velden, *Rodolphus Agricola* (Diss. Leiden, 1911), p. 254.

100. D. Roth, *Die mittelalterliche Predigttheorie und das Manuale Curatorum des Johann Ulrich Surgant* (Diss. Basel, 1956), pp. 176ff.; D. Meinhardt, *Predigt, Recht und Liturgie* (Diss. Göttingen, 1957). Less profitable is F. Schmidt-Clausing, "Johann Ulrich Surgant," *Zwingliana* 11/5 (1961), 287–320. Cf. also the opinion of Dehio on architecture (note 78), p. 155: "What is traditionally called Renaissance is a changed cloak, under which late Gothic lived on undisturbed."

101. On the following, see above all O. Vasella, *Untersuchungen über die Bildungsverhältnisse im Bistum Chur,* in 62. *Jahresbericht der Hist.-Antiquarischen Gesellschaft von Graubünden* (1932); Vasella, "über das Problem der Klerusbildung im 16. Jahrhundert," *Mitt. des Instituts für österr. Geschichtsforschung* 58 (1950), 441–456; Vasella, "Reform und Reformation in der Schweiz," *Katholisches Leben und Kämpfen im Zeitalter der Glaubensspaltung* 16 (1958); P. Staerkle, *Beiträge zur spätmittelalterlichen Bildungsgesch. St. Gallens* (1939); A. Braun, *Der Klerus des Bistums Konstanz im Ausgang des Mittelalters,* in *Vorreform. Forschungen* 14 (1938); F. W. Oediger, "Über die Bildung der Geistlichen im späten Mittelalter," *Studien u. Texte z. Geistesgesch. d. Mittelalters* 2 (1953); Post, *Kerk. verh.* (note 2), pp. 50ff. Less fruitful on this and the following subject is J. Vincke, *Der Klerus des Bistums Osnabrück im späten Mittelalter,* in *Vorreform. Forschungen* 11 (1928).

103. Ibid. According to Post, *Kerk. verh.* (note 2), p. 53, some 20 percent
102. Oediger (note 101), p. 66.
of the candidates for ordination in Holland between 1505 and 1518 possessed an academic degree, mostly the *Magister Artium*.

104. In the diocese of Chur there was in the whole later Middle Ages only one *Dr. theol.* among the parish clergy: Vasella, *Untersuchungen* (note 101), p. 99.

105. Oediger (note 101), pp. 80ff.

106. Vasella, "Reform und Reformation," further bibliography there (note 101). Important also is the older work of this author, "über das Konkubinat des Klerus im Spätmittelalter," *Mélanges Ch. Gilliard* (Lausanne, 1944), pp. 269–283.

106a. The curious piece of information in the *Historia de Europa* of Enea Silvio Piccolomini, *Opera Omnia* (Basel, 1571), p. 429, that in Friesland celibates were tolerated "non facile," in order that the marriage bed should not be defiled, does not need to be taken literally.

107. Cf. Rücklin (note 18), pp. 56f., as well as the systematic presentation of F. Flaskamp, *Jb. der Gesellschaft f. niedersächs. Kirchengesch.* 58 (1960), 128ff. Also the proof by Vasella, "Über das Konkubinat" (note 106), pp. 275ff., that a whole chain of generations of priests lived in concubinage, points in this direction. But one must not go too far. Marriages of priests remained punishable, and their progeny were deprived of their rights.

108. On the Lower Rhine these constituted almost half of all parishes around 1500: F. W. Oediger, "Niederrheinische Pfarrkirchen um 1500," *Annalen des hist. Vereins für den Niederrhein* 135 (1939), 1–40, esp. 32. The evidence is similar in parts of the Netherlands: Post, *Kerk. verh.* (note 2), p. 44. Exact information for the diocese of Lüttich, though for our time period somewhat meager, is found in J. Absil, "L'absentéisme du clergé paroissial au diocèse de Liège au XVe siècle et dans la première moitié du XVIe siècle," *Rev. d'histoire ecclésiastique* 57 (1962), 5–44.

109. Cf. F. Falk, *Die pfarramtlichen Aufzeichnungen des Florentius Diel zu St. Christoph in Mainz (1491–1518)* (1904). Also J. B. Götz, *Das Pfarrbuch des Stephan May in Hiltpoltstein vom Jahre 1511* (1928), esp. pp. 87ff.

110. There are numerous publications and sketches of sermons of the fifteenth century. Among recent ones are the following: F. Schäffauer, *Theol. Quartalschr.* 115 (1934), 516–547; A. Murith, *Jean et Conrad Grütsch de Bâle* (Diss. Fribourg, 1940), pp. 60ff.; F. Landmann, *Archiv f. elsäss. Kirchengesch.* NS 2 (1947–48), 205–234; NS 3 (1949/50), 71–98; P. Renner, *Archiv f. Kulturgesch.* 41 (1959), 201–217; Amon (note 12), pp. 261ff.; Werlin (note 65).

111. The example of the Augsburg preacher who, in his funeral sermon for Cardinal Peter of Schaumberg in 1469, quoted the *Corpus Juris* no fewer than 60 times, each time with the reference (A. Schröder, *Archiv f. d. Gesch. d. Hochstifts Augsburg* 6 [1929], 704) is, of course, extreme.

112. In Mainz documents there appears in 1506 a curacy which apparently was in no way connected to any steady income and whose occupant "propter paupertatem aufugit": *Zs. d. Vereins f. thüring. Gesch.* NF 2 (1882), 58.

113. H. Eberhardt, *Die Diözese Worms am Ende des 15. Jh.* (1919), pp. 51f.

114. Marxist historians see the connections in the reverse. Cf. for example M. Steinmetz in *Die frühbürgerliche Revolution,* p. 43, n. 73: Religious excitement before the Reformation was consciously stirred up by the Church "in order to bind the masses to the Church, to redirect social unrest in a way which would be safe and reliable for the continuance of the feudal social order."

115. L. Meier, "Wilsnack als Spiegel deutscher Vorreformation," *Zs. f. Religions- u. Geistesgesch.* 3 (1951), 53–69, concerning the impotence of the theologians in regard to the pilgrimage to the holy blood of Wilsnack is informative in this regard.

116. The work of Paulus (note 40) is fundamental. The best specialized study is E. Laslowski, *Beiträge zur Gesch. d. spätmittelalterlichen Ablasswesens nach schlesischen Quellen* (1929). I am unable to see that the problem of the misunderstanding of the indulgence sermon is "niet van al te grote betekenis," Post, *Kerk. verh.* (note 2), p. 482.

117. Only a few signs point in another direction. One may think of Surgant (see above, note 100) or of the "Epistola de miseria curatorum seu plebanorum" of 1489, which A. Werminghoff published in *ARG* 13 (1916), 200–227; or of

the pastoral effort underlying the writings investigated by F. Falk, *Die deutschen Mess-Auslegungen von der Mitte des 15. Jh. bis zum Jahre 1525* (1889).

118. This, at any rate, seems to be the result of the otherwise methodically and substantively rather unsatisfactory investigation of J. Löhr, *Methodisch-kritische Beiträge zur Gesch. der Sittlichkeit des Klerus besonders der Erzdiözese Köln am Ausgang des Mittelalters*, in *Reformationsgesch. Studien und Texte* 17 (1910).

119. Cf. H. Heimpel, *Archiv f. Kulturgesch.* 35 (1953), 50.

120. *Analecta Franciscana* 2 (Quaracchi 1887), 439f. Cf. the similar judgment of an Italian in comparing devotion at worship services in Germany with that in his homeland: G. Vale, *Itinerario di Paolo Santonino*, in *Studi e Testi* 103 (Città del Vaticano, 1943), 195f. Agrippa of Nettesheim writes before the appearance of Luther: "Insignes sunt litteratura Itali, navigatione Hispanes, civilitate Galli, religione et mechanicis artificiis Germani," quoted by Stadelmann (note 2), p. 10.

121. Heimpel (note 2), p. 38.

122. In contrast with this is the recent statement of E. W. Zeeden in *Die Entstehung der Konfessionen* (1965), p. 7, that "around the year 1500 no one [denied] the necessity of a thoroughgoing reform" and "precisely for this reason Luther met with overwhelming response."

3

FRANTISEK GRAUS

The Crisis of the Middle Ages and the Hussites *

[TRANSLATED BY JAMES J. HEANEY]

For many years František Graus was Professor of Medieval History at the Charles University in Prague and a member of the Czechoslovakian Academy of the Sciences. In the fall of 1970 he accepted a chair in the Justus Liebig University in Giessen. Graus has written extensively on the social and economic history of the late Middle Ages. In addition to studies of the hagiography of the Merovingian period, his best known work is a two-volume study of Bohemia in pre-Hussite times (Prague, 1949, 1957).

More recently, Graus, keenly aware of contemporary crises in European society, has turned his attention, philosophically as well as in a historical sense, to the problem of "crisis" in the late Middle Ages. "The Crisis of the Middle Ages and the Hussites" is his most recent work, first presented in a lecture before the Czechoslovakian Academy of the Sciences in September, 1969. This study was preceded by an extensive and often critical investigation of the vast body of secondary literature on "crisis" in the pre-Reformation period. Its purpose is to analyze anew the phenomenon of historical crisis, espe-

* This article is translated from a French translation of a paper presented by Professor Graus to the Czechoslovakian Academy of the Sciences in Prague in September, 1969. Because of recent developments in Czechoslovakia it was not possible to obtain the original. Professor Graus kindly made the French version available for translation and inclusion in this volume.

*cially as manifested in the Hussite movement of the late fourteenth
and early fifteenth centuries.*

*In Graus's view the historical phenomenon of crisis is not ade-
quately dealt with by the sociological approaches, recently so popular,
which assign a secondary role to religious and quasi-religious factors.
The very root of historical crisis is a people's perception of a grave
threat to their most basic values and symbols of security. Social division and tension, economic difficulties and the loss of faith in institutions are not the root of the matter. Rather they aggravate the sense
of menace and force the creation of new values and symbols, even
radically new ones, which can restore the lost sense of security and
meaning.*

*For Graus, the Hussite movement is the most telling example of
genuine crisis in the late Middle Ages. In Bohemia the old religious
forms and rites, which for so long had given solace to so many, were
suddenly simply ineffectual. This cannot, in Graus's estimation, be
satisfactorily explained in terms of social and economic grievances—a
judgment already implied when one considers the immediate answer
to the crisis which set the people on the march: the dogmatic tenets
of John Huss. Huss, who was no more a social reformer than he was
an original theologian, set forth religious concepts which became, intellectually and institutionally, a rallying-point for the people. The
Hussite movement was, however, ineffectual in the long run; the
return to the simpler doctrines and social structures of an ideal past
was not a long-term answer to the crisis suffered by medieval man.
A truly effective resolution of the crisis awaited bold new directions.
It was, for Graus, forthcoming only with the more radical solutions
of sixteenth century humanism and the Protestant Reformation.*

E VERY AGE has its own way of seeing the past, its own precise and
different point of view. One would think it unnecessary nowadays to
insist that there are no eternally valid commentaries on the past,
"accurate" in the most ideal sense, which both accurately sum up
historical events and make all future commentaries superfluous. In
point of fact, however, it is well known that this has so far not
occurred, and that whether by accident or intention, knowingly or not,
we still find that a great deal of the contemporary infiltrates our images
of other periods. It seems almost ridiculous to repeat this, except
that so often when we look into this age or that we discover that

historians affirm this principle in theory, but decidedly deny it in practice because of the exigencies of a particular case. All the more reason, then, for me to seek exactitude at the very beginning of an endeavor in which I will consciously make use of a *contemporary* mode of interpretation to handle the close of the Middle Ages, with particular reference to the Hussite movement and the events connected with it.

Obviously we cannot permit ourselves to read our own opinions into the past, to bring it up to date, as it were, by smuggling into it today's ideas. Despite this, however, it remains true that *every* epoch is so variegated and heterogeneous that historians in each succeeding period must find in it—often for the first time—aspects which contradict previous research simply because of the differences in purpose discernible in each undertaking. Precisely on this account I wish to make it clear that I am going to pay a great deal more attention to the traits of "crisis" in the late Middle Ages than to its more obvious traditional and conservative features, in the hope that aspects of the period will be brought to light which have hitherto escaped attention.

Probably the most significant thing about current historiography is the downfall of the old evolutionist interpretation of the past. We no longer view the past as a necessarily and conveniently linked chain of epochs. Instead we have begun to consider periods of development, if not as mere collections of fortuitous occurrences, outrages, and absurdities, then at least as a series of unfinished events, sudden and unlooked-for eruptions, with some necessary consequences and some completely chance happenings. In short, history is to be seen as a tangled skein of phenomena and events. Because we sense that things are changing all around us with no discernible direction toward a better and happier world, we see a certain crisis in those values which had seemed to guarantee our efforts and desires in earlier times. We discover afresh that abiding irrationality which the Middle Ages schematized in strata of Good and Evil, and which still seems to us senseless, absurd, or simply incomprehensible. Without a doubt, it is because of the decline of our own certainties and most cherished notions that we read the equally important events of the past carefully enough to discover "periods of crisis" of different kinds, and eventually to have the past reveal to us the unending panorama of crises through which mankind has had to pass. We lose faith in the ineluctable course of evolution, in the ability of men to survive periods in history wherein "progress" no longer plays the primary role, though it may later do so thanks to "the cunning of history." It is at such times that we seem to rediscover the concept of destiny and its traces in history.

If we consider the fourteenth and fifteenth centuries, which are more often labeled the "late Middle Ages" or simply "the end of the Middle Ages," from such a point of view, we will find it very difficult to see this period as the "decline of the Middle Ages" (or, to go even further, its "autumn"), or to look down on it from the vantage point of today, which has put an end to the supposed "obscurantism of the Middle Ages." Rather we must strive to grasp this period as directly as possible, and in such a way that we discover therein what is most familiar to us from our own day.

Apparently, "signs of crisis" can be read with equal validity into every separate age and segment of the populace. Nevertheless, it is also fair to characterize "crisis" as a ground-swell facet of experience which is truly manifest both in the thought of a great many persons and in the feeling of the whole period. As such its effects can be seemingly ambiguous, since crisis gives rise to a general feeling of uncertainty as well as to the most strained attempts to grasp security of any kind or some abstract certitude. Not every period has these "signs." Where they do exist, they merit consideration as motivating forces only when they have brought about some plainly novel and reasonably lengthy movement.

The first hurdle in trying to apply any of this to the fourteenth and fifteenth centuries is the continuing influence of the traditional point of view, or, more accurately these days, points of view about the Middle Ages. Of course, when one thought of the Middle Ages as a period of darkness in which ignorance and a grim Church held soul and body relentlessly captive, it was easy to regard the end of that age in a more favorable light. It was, one could say, a period in which the first traces of the dawn of the new age were showing, harbingers of the light of progress. The demise of this way of looking at things has produced a counter-tendency to idealize the Middle Ages as the tranquil harbor from which mankind has perilously ventured onto the stormy modern seas. This view, of course, is no more true and dependable than the former one; it simply idealizes it a bit differently. Deriding the Middle Ages as a period of general obscurity is another way of glorifying our own day, of singing the praises of the "European Spirit." On the other hand, glorifying so-called medieval quietism is merely a way of suggesting that immobility and tranquillity are the solutions to contemporary unrest, and attempting to document this claim by reference to a false image of the Middle Ages.

Let us, however, leave aside for the moment such general considerations about the evolution of the medieval world and try to focus more clearly upon those two centuries which are generally referred to as the close of the period. When we call them an era of transition, we usually do so in a twofold manner: it was an age in which the old was coming apart and disappearing, or an age in which the foundations of later times were being laid. Both these characterizations are accurate and well substantiated, even though it *is* true that *any* epoch could be described as one of transition in which the old was disappearing and giving rise to the new. Furthermore, we must keep in mind that the events in question constitute a movement and change which is unique in character, and in which particular individuals gave substance in their own lives and troubles to these relatively abstract ideas. It is from this standpoint that the Middle Ages really does seem to be a period of social crisis, from which people tried to extricate themselves by every possible means. I think, therefore, that at this point I should explain more carefully what I mean by the word "crisis," seeing that it is the leitmotif of the period, as indicated by the title of this article.

The sense of "crisis" which I wish to communicate here has nothing to do with "decadence," "cessation of growth," "stagnation," or any analogous connotation which may attach to the word outside the sphere of historical terminology. Any such connotation would obviously be false because it tends inevitably to superimpose a "transitory" character on the period. It is only right to object to such a tendency: while the fourteenth and fifteenth centuries did see the decline of certain forms of life and society, they also provided the opportunity for the birth of newer and more viable forms, many of which were to have a decisive formative influence. We can, therefore, say of these centuries something which always remains true in history: at any given time in the past something was coming to birth and something else was dying; which process was the more intense in any one age, considering the fact that history is always different, is purely a debater's point. This is especially true of the so-called late Middle Ages. However, I think we really must take a little more space to understand the term "crisis," if it is to have any real content.

Clearly we can use the word differently in different sorts of discussions, depending upon whether the data with which we are working

are more or less precise. That, for instance, is the method of those
historians who have introduced and tried to give concrete meaning to
general expressions such as "monetary crisis" and "agrarian crisis," or
who have tried to use it in more specific cases such as "political crisis,"
"crisis of the Papacy," and so on. Using such notions on a small scale
is not objectionable; extending their use until they become overall
descriptions for the entire period is. Even vaguer meanings attach to
expressions such as "crisis of the aristocracy," "crisis of structure," or
"crisis of feudalism," and it becomes obvious that they are practically
useless for any sort of real historical endeavor. This is not so much
because historians have not thought about these terms before using
them; rather it seems that most of them have gone to great pains,
occasionally to an embarrassing extent, to employ the word precisely
and to document as clearly as possible all the events which are connected with and cause the "crisis." Such a desire for exactitude is the
real source of the problem simply because such a use of terms presupposes, without justification, a connection between the interpretive
scheme and the facts, with the whole business disguised as an elucidating commentary. We must still keep in mind, however, that any
attempt to interpret what evidently *is* a real crisis is going to shape
our commentary in a certain way.[2]

Actually, I neither wish to give, nor do I believe myself capable of
giving, a precise definition of the word "crisis." Furthermore, I consider such definitions to be of no value at all to the social sciences.
Most frequently they serve merely to sidetrack us, and can be about as
useful as the old sophistic and scholastic debates about how many
trees justify the use of the term "forest," or how many grains of sand
one must have for a "cupful."

All I can do here, then, is to give a description of social crisis as a
resumé of what I understand by the word. In such a description I wish
to include any and all phenomena which result in the breaking up of
a way of life in a society. Most important among them is the general
feeling that values which have hitherto been held in high esteem as
unquestioned "basics" seem to be either menaced or perhaps already
in the process of disintegration and disappearance. Such values are, of
course, seen in an entirely different light by contemporaries and by
later observers, who feel and appreciate them in a quite different way.
(For instance, everything usually associated with "religion" had a meaning for men in the fourteenth and fifteenth centuries entirely different
from its meaning for men in the twentieth century.) What is really

important is that *the people of those times* held these values to be vital and nevertheless menaced. What importance such values would have for their descendants is quite another question.

Naturally, not everyone in a society will feel that certain values are being challenged, and the feeling that they are penetrates only gradually, with very different effects upon different groups. When it does happen, the manner of penetration is always unique because of the nature of the values themselves, the available means of communication, and what values the society in question holds most dear. The "rhythm" of life in every society has a certain momentum and adaptability, which takes generations in stride as well as changes in living conditions (here taken in the broadest possible sense). This makes it possible for the rhythm to adjust its pace accordingly. However, if the values in question *really are* the basics of the society, and the whole social system is crumbling, those who live in it feel as if life itself— as it was up to their time—is passing out of existence.

Those most aware of the loss or menace to values are usually the intellectuals. For most other people there is a vague feeling of unhappiness, that things aren't really going as they should, an awareness, or simply a feeling of uncertainty. What is common to all parts of the population, however, is that when the moment of crisis reaches its peak no one alive can remain a spectator or preserve his neutrality. Each and every one must take a stand; verbal declarations of neutrality are impossible. When a crisis situation reaches its climax, when it has, as it were, "ripened," the reaction to it always divides with due formality into two camps, depending greatly on how such things are seen in that epoch. (In such cases we should take great care to divorce the *manifestations* of controversy from their *substance*. To later ages it always seems that the controversies which caused such violent clashes between contemporaries were not substantial. The reason for this is that men of a later age find the opinions of *both* disputing parties distasteful, and are thus at a decided disadvantage in trying to feel the crisis as deeply as did contemporaries.[3])

Such "crises" do not, of course, occur in a vacuum, and they need not be regarded as the result of some mysterious contagion. Quite the opposite: historical research can generally identify the factors leading to the crisis. But, for those who must live through it, there is the overall feeling that *everything* is in decline, and hence an effort must be made to restore the *whole*. In a given case, those factors which bring the crisis to fruition can be of many kinds (some of which will be discussed later). For a larger grasp of the matter, however, and really to see its significance, analysis is of value only insofar as those involved have felt themselves affected by such forces.

The feeling of crisis varies directly with the degree to which people feel their values menaced, and with the extent and importance of such values. Such a feeling can peak in complete despair and anarchy, manifested in the spheres of religion, politics,, or the social structure. As the groups affected by these feelings become more numerous, the effects of crisis on the heart of a society become greater. And if the crisis appears to give direction and ideological emphasis to some one group, it can give rise to a revolutionary movement or produce a revolution.

It is because of this that the differences between the geographical and social segments of the population are so clear in periods of crisis. These differences are more pronounced in a revolutionary period than in a supposedly "normal" one, since they are, in the former, clearly evidenced by opposing actions and attitudes. Of course, the notion of "crisis" does not *necessarily* entail an actual revolution, or any clear and definite goal or "explosion" which *must* occur.

Usually in such crisis situations, the return to the old and trusted values seems to people to be a rather simple matter. Because such values have proved themselves in the past, they easily give the impression that they are "good," would "work" in any period, and that the sole error was their abandonment. Despite this, however, there is still the feeling among the people that it is necessary "to do something" about things, a feeling which usually results in a frenzied search for a symbol around which they can unite. Historically, such symbols are indeed different and take different forms, but they do have one common problem: they merely focus on a certain issue without providing any real solution to it.

I should like to make it clear here, in order to avoid misunderstanding when I link the Hussites with the crisis in society in the late Middle Ages, that I do not think that the Hussite movement resulted from any historical necessity, nor did the form in which it occurred. In my opinion, the real connection between the Hussites and the "crisis" is that the feeling of loss and of menace to values, linked with the instability of the situation, made it absolutely necessary for all those involved, in the most diverse parts of Europe, to make *some* decision. This decision took different forms, depending on each country and its conditions. It could lead as easily to efforts to restore the old system of values as to efforts to create a new one. Popular feelings of being threatened and the consequent decision to do something about it gave the Hussite movement a special impetus, a grass-roots foundation which lent importance to its actions. It was the intensity and shock of earlier feelings of insecurity which gave the movement its power. Only taken in this sense, not in a causal sequence, can it be said that the Hussite movement is directly connected with the larger crisis of the late Middle Ages.

But before proceeding further let us take a brief general look at the spectrum of events which indicate a crisis in the late Middle Ages. (It should be understood that the length of this article allows only limited reference to a group of events with which one would suppose historians generally to be familiar.) If we now ask ourselves what it meant for the people in the fourteenth and fifteenth centuries to feel a "crisis" of society, we must first note that values, particularly the feeling of security, have quite different structures in different historical periods. Not only is there no overall system of such values, but they change constantly as do the connections between them. Thus, the way in which a crisis of values was perceived by a man in the Middle Ages differs completely from what we would understand it to be.

Compared to the modern European, the medieval man was *always* menaced, and that embraces areas which we today would no longer include in our understanding of crisis. Famine, crop failure and armed conflict were almost daily dangers in the Middle Ages, and, given the low productivity of medieval farming and the continual disruption, these dangers were all too real during most of the period. The average age of the people was fairly low, the infant mortality rate very high. Men had to face these difficulties continually in daily life, and in general were not afraid of them. The Lord gives, and the Lord takes away—in this particular sense, we could call the Middle Ages more fatalistic than later ones. Catastrophes had to be of extraordinary magnitude before anyone thought of them as truly menacing or outside the normal course of miseries which, by God's decision, oppressed the men of this earth. If a famine grew intense, or an epidemic became the Black Death depopulating whole villages and families, men did feel a sense of catastrophe, the scourge of God or divine chastisement. Never, however, was this the same as crisis, abandonment or loss of security. Their reactions to such distressing situations were strong, vibrant, even exalted in some ways, but always *within* the confines of their given social structure. The terror which such events aroused in them found an outlet in the usual sacrificial lambs of society—the Jews, whom they accused of having poisoned the wells. Or they took to prayer and pious processions to appease the wrath of God.

Of a somewhat different character were the processions of the flagellants, who exceeded the "limits" of contemporary society. Seeking to find a direct way to allay the wrath of God, without recourse to Church or clergy, they naturally found themselves in conflict with both Church and nobility.

The pillage and burning commonly resulting from military combat were nothing extraordinary for the Middle Ages. This was simply the way war was waged. Both enemies and friends lived by pillaging neighboring villages. But to those villagers who were reduced to total misery (as was the case in Bohemia), it was scant consolation to know that the military units which had just passed through were not the enemy but the soldiers of their own country. Combat had to attain an extraordinary intensity, as it did in France around the middle of the fourteenth century, before anyone considered it unusual, or before the peasants combined forces to save themselves or even thought such an unusual form of redress to be justified.

True crises, however, which affect the entire society, do not often arise solely from direct or immediate causes. Neither are they a reaction against a single event. Instead, they are usually directed against a whole chain of causes manifest in clearly defined moods, changes, problems, and the loss of certainty in the most varied domains. Furthermore, the question here covers not one but many sectors of life. The crises ripen, and in attaining their full effect become an overall tendency, a general impression, springing from experiences of life and from the most various dispositions and situations.

I would claim that the Middle Ages did not know the relative economic stability with which we moderns are familiar. This statement is surely justified, but needs some qualification in that the Middle Ages did indeed know periods of development and prosperity just as it knew periods of famine and depression. If a famine resulted from crop failure, bad times or military incursions, it was a misfortune which those with a stiff upper lip could handle, simply because the causes were obvious. It was different, however, if the peasant had a good harvest, and then suddenly found he could not sell it for a high enough price to meet his debts, or if the value of money continued to decrease, or if his lord decided that he could buy much less than in past years. Causes such as these were not at all clear, and so people began to think about them and to look for the guilty parties. It is noteworthy how impassioned and expressive the voices of men in the latter half of the fourteenth and first half of the fifteenth century became when they were seeking answers to these questions. Some *paranoid style*

conspiracy hunting

accused sovereigns and their financial directors of devaluing the money and thereby causing a general scarcity. Others suspected plots on the part of usurers who bought up goods, particularly wheat, to sell at higher prices in times of famine, just as they suspected merchants of getting together to rig prices on merchandise. A third group were up in arms against companies, accusing them of being enormous traps, endeavoring to fix prices and enrich themselves at the expense of others. There were as many guilty parties as one could wish, but no one knew anything precisely. Mutual suspicion grew, and the value of money continued to decline, deeply affecting the majority of the population, nobility as well as peasants.

In addition, a political and social crisis began to manifest itself. Obviously, we cannot in this regard judge the state of things in the late Middle Ages accurately, accustomed as we are to an ordered and functioning public administration. Even the periods of greatest "stability" in the Middle Ages were by our standards rife with anarchy, but it must be remembered that such a state of affairs was then considered to be clear, natural and perfectly in order. Attention was given only to deviation from the usual, which was interpreted as a menace to the organization of the kingdom. In this connection, we must remember the political impetus of a large number of cities throughout Europe, which turned against their sovereigns. Usually this resulted in alliances among the cities, the captivity or deposition of the king, or simply open resistance to him. Resistance to the king, inasmuch as it had fixed and precise forms and kept to certain rules, was then considered perfectly legal (some modern historians would even like to see therein the foundation of the juridical basis of medieval society). Revolt could occur if certain limits were passed, if what was considered the "basis of society" was challenged. Quite typically, then, the old question of the legality of assassinating tyrants came to the fore at the beginning of the fifteenth century.

"The basis of society" is a rather indefinite notion, and hardly clear to those who do not live in the society in question. For those who do, however, such a "basis" is so evident that it needs no more concrete definition. Such persons react almost allergically if the values of a society which has a set social structure and clear caste boundaries are challenged.

Compared to society in the nineteenth century, medieval society from the thirteenth century onward was fixed, though far from immobile. On the contrary, the fact that the limits of caste were fairly well

1) economic crisis
2) political crisis
3) social crisis

set, together with a marked slowdown in social evolution, gave rise to a certain amount of social unrest, of gradually growing animosity. This most frequently took overt form in social tension, but sometimes grew into the hatred which erupted in the peasant disturbances and urban uprisings of the late Middle Ages.

Social and economic change did not, however, affect all segments of society in the same way. Perhaps the most menaced of all in regard to their social status were the lower aristocracy, and they were forced to take account of it simply because it posed a daily and immediate challenge. A small part of this group managed to rise a little from a social and caste standpoint, primarily by means of service to the king. The majority, however, found the whole basis of their existence threatened. Their possessions were appropriated by more powerful lords or by cities, and sometimes even rich peasants represented a threat. Their sons no longer had much opportunity to make something of themselves, and the lower aristocracy itself became an object of mockery. All over Europe poets and writers made fun of the little aristocrat who had to do his own plowing with his little cattle, while still priding himself on his nobility. It was not by chance that this aristocracy formed the basis of the military companies which played such an important role in the history of Europe at the time.[4]

On the other hand, cities were now becoming powerful economic and military forces throughout the various countries of Europe, as well as the heart of its social structure. (Especially noteworthy in this regard is Flanders, which was in some ways the equal of the Empire. Also quite special and different was the situation of Italian cities, but that is another matter.) Politically, however, the cities remained of somewhat less importance. They retained their original social structure, which was quite different from the rest of society. Movement in society (remembering that such movement is absolutely impossible to compare with that of, say, the nineteenth century) was, relatively speaking, one of the most important issues in the medieval city. Cities were most often the scene of riots and disturbances, which everywhere seemed to be indications of social struggle. City life was dominated by tension between different groups in the population, by mutual suspicion and insecurity which often grew into open hatred. If one were to say that the stature of authority decreased in lay society in the fourteenth and fifteenth centuries, or that there was doubt about the justice and necessity of the existing organization of society, then it is in the cities, the greatest centers of population, primed to revolt and often in the process of revolt, that we find the unique developments which played an important part in the wars and disturbances of the late Middle Ages.

Of equal importance in some areas, however, we find another force at work, a force which had only begun to make itself felt in the Middle Ages, but would find full scope in modern times: national feeling. Antagonism toward and distrust of foreigners, expressed sometimes as simple distaste, are old phenomena. Even before the fourteenth century defensive reactions occurred, and in some areas, by the close of the Middle Ages, these corresponded reasonably well to what we call nationalism. One need only think of the Anglo-Saxon reaction to the Norman conquest or the Provençal reaction to the crusades of northern France. Such movements, however, had relatively minor effects, and were not the source of any later national movements. The national movements of the late Middle Ages are rather different. Equally diverse, unequal in their force, expressions, and capabilities, they can scarcely be likened to contemporary national movements, but they still constitute the source of the ground swell which would continue down to modern times. It is enough to remember the cultural developments in Italy or the vitality of the movements in France and Bohemia in the fifteenth century.

These factors were, of course, never equal in effect in every country in Europe, nor in every segment of society; in some they had hardly any effect. But something had indeed happened to the Church, and the reverberations were felt throughout all of Catholic Europe, though with different power and intensity. But *no part* of Europe escaped the shock of the so-called Papal Schism in 1378.

In order fully to understand this event, it is necessary once more to recall the differences between the consciousness of medieval man and that of man in the twentieth century. There is a profound difference, which the notion of "religion" almost conceals rather than clarifies. Medieval man was continually threatened by the cares of this world, by famine, disease, and war, but he was also threatened in the realm of ideas by demons, the devil himself, and snares of every kind. His temporal life was menaced by bodily ills and his eternal life by the powers of darkness, whether in the shape of the devil familiar to Catholic theology, or in one of the forms surviving from pagan times so prevalent among the country folk. The sacraments of the Church constituted a bulwark and a guarantee against such evils. This was no abstract Church symbolized by clergy in union with the Pope. Such a Church was often the target of criticism even more virulent than some expressed in modern times. The Church did not constitute a secure refuge on the basis of its faith and doctrine, but because of the security guaranteed by its sacraments. Everyone had need of the latter, even an obstinate usurer, a highwayman or a criminal fearful of dying without the last rites, who therefore hesitated to cut himself off from the Church.

Everyone, including men today, recognizes the need for security in some form. Feelings of insecurity arise when a threat impinges upon several different spheres of life, or upon the center of one's emotional life. But in the Middle Ages the center of life consisted of the sacraments of the Church, the sign of the Cross with its power to chase demons away. The sacraments, the cult of the saints, and many other rites were transformed in the minds of the people into magical means of protection. Preachers tried unceasingly to alter this notion, which they considered an "abuse," but they had little success in changing the popular conception of the Church. Popular baroque piety, in this regard, is quite different from that of the medieval period.

Obviously, the intellectuals for whom theology was of primary, although not always exclusive, interest, held a different view. In the intellectual centers of Europe at the close of the Middle Ages a gradual emancipation had already begun. It did not take the form of a denial of the Church (this particular phenomenon found its traditional expression only among heretics, who generally in the Middle Ages were even more isolated from things than were the Jews, and often even more persecuted). Instead, from the twelfth century onward, other systems of values began to arise outside the Church (beginning with the introduction of Aristotelianism), setting forth the values of antiquity—ever old and ever new—to which men could direct some of their needs for security and sustenance.

However, this was a help only to the "eminent" intellectuals. For the majority of the people, the Church itself continued to be the powerful administrator of the sacraments and the ultimate guide; it could guarantee a death safe from an infernal host of demons, or, at least, it could fend off the probability of eternal damnation. If faith, as the need for security, is so well established, scarcely any attack in this area will be seen as particularly fatal or even as having extensive consequences. I certainly do not believe it accidental that large numbers of people were greatly alarmed to hear that the sacraments were being misused or perhaps worthless, that the Church was corrupt, that it was not the true Church of Christ, or that the sacraments were vitiated.

The Schism was the external manifestation of internal stress, and shook the Church to its foundations. All the Catholic countries were touched by the Schism as well as by its practical consequences, but not all of them reacted in the same way. The situation was influenced by a number of things—the degree to which eminent intellectuals dedicated themselves to the Church and a great many other factors— all of which united in a single great current capable of giving varied impetus, intensity, points of view and policies to the most diverse movements.

The fourteenth and fifteenth centuries saw many movements which, using rather loose terminology, we could call riots, rebellions, uprisings, or revolutionary movements. We cannot enumerate every type of movement involved, nor is it necessary, since a great deal of attention has lately been paid to them and they are fairly well known. Therefore I should like to confine myself to a short sketch of the basic types.

One type was the urban mutiny, in which the inhabitants of a city gave substance to their economic or political demands within the city by the use of force. Another was the revolt of the country people, brought on by suffering and misery considerably above their usual level of tolerance. More often, however, and clearly distinguishable from the purely urban or rural cases (e.g. the French Jacquerie or Wat Tyler's uprising), these two types of revolutionary movement mingled somewhat confusedly, the better to serve the interests and progress of both sides. I am not ready to discuss in full a "typology" of late medieval uprisings; that would require a separate article. I merely wish to call attention to the fact that, while rancor and social discontent gave rise to different effects, these effects united to prove that they all sprang from discontent and irritation.

The Hussite movement belonged to quite another type, which will be discussed in the latter part of this essay. Of a somewhat similar nature, though with individual differences, are those events in France which we associate with the name of Joan of Arc. The distinguishing feature of these movements is that they exhibit what we moderns would call "ideological" characteristics. Both were directed not only toward providing a remedy for a given situation, i.e. a short-term solution, but also at indicating guidelines specifically tailored for the particular epoch. Obviously the two movements are very different. One need only recall the stern letter Joan wrote against the Hussites to realize what an abyss this French fighter for the rights of legitimate royalty believed to exist between herself and the mutinous Czech heretics. Actually, the two movements are not the same; they only exhibit certain analogies. One cannot ignore the fact that a certain "national movement" was taking shape in each of them (more so in Bohemia than in France), in which not only partial and immediate solutions were at stake, but also general policies.

Because of this aspect, these two movements were as different from the riots and revolts preceding them as were the later developments which we normally associate with the beginning of the modern era. As for the earlier revolts, they were generally isolated events, which never achieved any clear concept of their purpose, and usually remained local. The uprising of 1381 is an example. Cases of this sort achieved neither the creation of a unifying symbol nor even the distillation of any special doctrine. There is, however, one other parallel with the Hussites which is a bit more complex: the movement of "heretics" in southern France in the first half of the thirteenth century, which spread resistance far beyond the local level, and involved a definite doctrine. I should like, however, to leave the discussion of this for another occasion.

The reform movements of the fourteenth century, the late Middle Ages, are distinguished by the fact that they usually had clearly defined limits within a given country, and did not expand to embrace the whole Christian world. Much later they were to give birth to a new era, at least in the spiritual domain. Nevertheless, the effects of the two great earlier national movements (the Hussites being the more important) were particularly striking because they were of a *new* type. This novelty lay not only in their ability to encompass an entire country, but also in the fact that they had achieved an adequate organizational form. Above all, they did not pass into oblivion without having shown their true colors for a considerable length of time, which had not previously been the case. It is for this reason that I consider the Hussites to represent the first phase of the medieval crisis, serving as both a transition and a catalyst throughout the length and breadth of the Empire.

Because of its well-knit character, extent, and the amount of attention it provoked, the Hussite movement was subjected to analysis even by its contemporaries. They were well aware of the necessity to explain its origins. Indeed, the commentaries and explanations with which historians continue to describe this period were, with appropriate differences, actually formulated at the time. For those partial to the Protestant Reformation, the Hussite movement was substantially the product of Biblicism or a new revelation of divine truth. Insofar as the people were acquainted with sacred Scripture, they could see that the Church had moved far from the ideals and prescriptions of Christ, and they demanded reform in both the head of the Church and its members. It was enough for enthusiastic preachers to sow the word of God; the seed would then take root of itself, since the seed was good, and the truth of God could not be stifled.

Catholic pamphleteers had a somewhat different feeling about the origins of the Hussite movement (though one particular group of theologians maintained their own special point of view). As set forth in the teaching of the Church fathers, Satan had threatened the Church from the beginning, and had chosen to oppose it with the most powerful of weapons, the very seed of schism—heresy. Thus the Church will always be menaced by heresy (a necessary evil, but one which must be ceaselessly opposed), by deviations from the true faith fathered by the devil himself. The most recent spawn of the devil were Wyclif and Huss, his disciple. Seen in this way, the Hussite movement was not a renaissance at all, but a dangerous contagion which must be snuffed out. Furthermore, at this time a certain connection between medieval religious and national motifs had begun to appear. The Catholics suspected every Czech of being a heretic, no matter how passionately Czech Catholics defended themselves against such a suspicion. For the majority of Hussites, the Czechs had become the chosen people, successor to the chosen people of the Old Testament, Israel, heralds and protectors of truth, warriors of God.

Modern historiography accepted this notion quite literally for a long time, with differences only in accent. Some investigators concentrated on the religious aspects of the problem, others on the national, and the interpretation naturally varied according to the religious and national allegiance of the historian. Still, some form of the old scheme managed to shine through, and even to dominate the historiography of the period until today. The Hussite movement was taken to be both a national and a religious phenomenon, and this was undoubtedly true.

But this is not the heart of the matter. The real problem for the modern observer is the fact that a religious reform movement, a theological doctrine, could bring about such a tremendous and explosive effect in Bohemia. Contemporaries, of course, did not see this as a problem at all. Catholics thought it the work of a band of heretics, or, going even further, of the Prince of Darkness himself. The Hussites, on the other hand, thought of it as the victory of truth, the word of God and evangelical teaching. We cannot know, of course, the ultimate reasons for the occurrence of this movement at this time and in Bohemia. An observer with confessional commitments can adopt the confessional answer, and that is why modern historiography has chosen to replace the confessional point of view with the more general category of the "religious." In the eyes of modern historians, the people of the Middle Ages were truly "believers," and "religious questions" were of immeasurable importance. They were able to become excited about them and to decide them in a manner no longer comprehensible to us. This is not really an answer, however; such a general formula, even in modified form, is valid neither for Bohemia nor for the fifteenth century in general.

On the contrary, it is precisely here that the puzzle comes home to us. The medieval sources of information in Bohemia, and indeed in all of Catholic Europe, agree that the rural population, the very heart of the future Hussite movement, was, by our standards, more or less *indifferent* to religion. True, it was a believing population—there were no "atheists"—but their faith was a bizarre mixture of common and Catholic notions with venerable "superstitions," and most of their interest was centered on rites guaranteeing some sort of protection. Ideas, dogma, and doctrine, with very few and very diverse exceptions, were quite out of their realm. The preachers' handbooks, the official protocols, sermons, and formal histories present a remarkably unified picture: the lay people, particularly those of the countryside, were not at all interested in dogmatic theses, and were acquainted only with the most fundamental "truths" of the faith. Furthermore, the majority demonstrated very little interest or concern for most ecclesiastical regulations. Then, suddenly, these same masses were gripped by substantive dogmatic questions, and abandoned those rites which, despite the work of their preachers, had been the real heart of their religion.

From this point of view the Hussite movement was not a unique event, though it did have unusual extent and importance. Similar situations, in which the people were apathetic until they suddenly burst into frenzied activity, can be found from time to time in other periods. Examples could be cited from the era of the people's crusades, which began in areas where dogma had previously been of little concern, and suddenly spread like wildfire. There is the first crusade, the children's crusade, and the shepherds' movement, in which shepherds who had previously been content to tend their flocks suddenly organized a crusade to the Holy Land to liberate their king (St. Louis), held prisoner by the Saracens. Incidents such as this, in

previous centuries manifested only on the periphery of society,[5] became in the Hussite movement a central and all-important phenomenon.

This is the heart of the problem: why, suddenly, did a movement
like this become a national movement in Bohemia? And why did
Huss and his doctrine enjoy a renown greater than that of Wyclif,
his precursor and source, who was definitely more original and more
important in many ways?

Historians who approach this question by considering the nature of
the particular society have tried to meet the problem head-on. We
may characterize their version as sociological. Without denying the
importance of the national movement involved, these historians have
tried to determine exactly why reform doctrine had such a strong
impact on Bohemia in the fifteenth century. If they do not wish to
settle for an explanation adducing "the exalted and ardent Czech
soul," they are forced to turn to the economic, social, and political
situation in the country at the beginning of the fifteenth century,
when all sorts of small factors *could* have given substance and
strength to the Hussite movement. Eventually they find themselves
forced to consider all these material aspects of the movement, none
of which can properly be called a passionate "outburst" or "explosion."

In the flurry of excitement provoked by the new sociological analysis, and in reaction against traditional explanations, accounts such
as these were often given a lofty status, and the influence of the
so-called religious causes assigned a secondary role. Gradually, however, it has become clear that analysis of social factors cannot give a
true, independent, and adequate explanation of the Hussite phenomenon. Undoubtedly, a large number of such ordinary facts made the
movement potentially a national one. Furthermore, it was no accident
that people chanted in the streets of Prague, as early as the time of
Master John, that the *Germans* were going to march on Bethlehem.
Here the self-consciousness of the national reform movement is manifest. No matter how carefully we examine all these factors, however,
it is clear that none of them can be the *primum movens*.

It is just as necessary, therefore, to search for causes in the spiritual
life of the period in question as it is to examine everyday events in
its society. Furthermore, we must endeavor to understand how the
people of the time construed their situation, what motivated them to
oppose the two greatest authorities of the world, the Pope and the king
of Rome. It seems to me that one possible route to an answer to this
question is the definition we have already given of crisis in the

Middle Ages—that collection of events and causes creating a situation which demanded a solution and forced the people to act.

Undoubtedly the factors we have discussed in relation to medieval economics did have a strong and deleterious influence in Bohemia, especially since the economic structure was such that change affected it tremendously. The so-called agrarian crisis, i.e. the stagnation of prices for wheat, had an enormous effect on Czech agriculture, directed as it was toward the cultivation of grain crops. No city connected with Prague, the greatest city of central Europe, had an organized production of manufactured goods even at the end of the Middle Ages, nor, indeed, were there any others situated on the important commercial routes. The stagnant Czech balance of trade, compensated for occasionally by the exportation of native silver, gradually began to crush the rural population, the local aristocracy, and the poor of the cities. It is no wonder that there were so many anguished cries and moving laments about the cost of living, the depreciation and debasement of money, although the financial situation in Prague remained stable and prosperous. Despite the wealth of the Czech mines, the king, the archbishop, and the aristocracy were forced to use the most primitive means of acquiring silver during these troubled times; often they had to pledge property and revenues of all sorts to obtain precious metals. The situation in Prague grew worse because of the dangers of travel, which often tended to paralyze commerce, and the city was menaced by the impoverishment of great segments of the population, a situation not at all improved by the so-called eternal revenues accruing to Church institutions.

None of the foregoing, however, would justify the claim that these facts alone had created a "revolutionary situation" which forced the poor into an uprising against the more powerful elements of society. (Actually, no one has ever said this; it is merely a polemical tool.) The telltale signs of "crisis" in the economic and social spheres are only to be seen over long stretches of time; they do not suffice as direct and immediate explanations of events. Instead, such signs explain how a particular difficulty in economic and social areas can have a genuinely intense effect and can make the people far more sensitive to change than they would otherwise be. Conditions which under different circumstances would not be noticed can, in the course of extraordinary events, cause an excitement, an increment of rancor, hatred and animosity that may suddenly and furiously explode.

The other most important result of the Hussite movement was its great impact on the rural population and the lower aristocracy, a segment of the population fairly important on the military scene in Bohemia, although not, until this time, on the political. It is well known, and I have already mentioned it, what sorts of tension this situation created throughout all Europe during this period. In Bohemia, a small and enclosed country, this particular tension erupted in an especially fierce manner at a time when the military potential could not be focused and utilized (as it was in England). Even so, some of the lower aristocracy were able to better themselves socially and politically, although the position of the majority of this group obviously worsened.

The lower aristocracy, however, were not alone in facing a crisis; the power structure in the kingdom was also having a prolonged crisis. As was usually the case in the medieval world, the balance of power in society was basically determined by the relationship between the king and the aristocracy (though later there would be in some cases a third force, the cities). The equilibrium thus established was frail, at the mercy of many forces and changes in circumstances. After the thirteenth century, rulers in the most developed regions of Europe began to gather up those threads of power which had persisted during the reigns of weak kings, and even during periods when there had been practically no rule. In Bohemia we perhaps find such efforts on the part of Přemysl Otokar II, although he failed in the end because of resistance by a higher aristocracy unwilling to renounce any of its privileges. In the beginning of the fourteenth century, the higher aristocracy almost completely dominated the scene, but Charles IV forced them to retrench a bit. His reign, nevertheless, because of its internal structure, was a re-creation of the old type of rule. Charles set up no actual administrative offices (in Bohemia there was not even a financial office, which in the west was often the beginning of a small administration), no institutions which governed the country and gave assurance of some sort of continuity. The king himself reigned, an authentic sovereign, and thus the Czech pattern of governmental organization was determined by the fact that its most stable element, that with the greatest duration and tradition, became those regional institutions which expressly promoted aristocratic rights.

In a kingdom so organized, if the sovereign is either incapable or uninterested in the exercise of power, disorders of unusual magnitude are bound to occur. Václav IV (Wenceslaus IV) ceded his power for all practical purposes to his council; in the council, as was the custom at most royal courts, the lower aristocracy, the educated clergy, and the bourgeoisie assumed power—the nucleus of a future bureaucracy. This manner of governing—reasonable where the institutions to which power was entrusted were stable—could lead to nothing but disorder in a situation like that in Bohemia. Charles IV was able to reduce the power of the higher aristocracy slightly and for a short time. But he was completely unable to break its supremacy, or to stabilize royal authority in any form other than the person of the sovereign.

During the reign of Václav (Wenceslaus), disorders erupted which had long been brewing in the intrigues and interference in the affairs of the kingdom by Václav's brothers and his parents. It is well known that these disorders culminated, after the stage was set by small clashes throughout the country, in the captivity of Václav (in 1394 and in 1402). These two periods of captivity indicated the weakness of the royal power, but they also demonstrated that the aristocracy itself was not in full control. For in both instances Václav was able to re-assume power, albeit without actually governing except for some sporadic interference in particular affairs. The late Middle Ages had no knowledge of the kind of organized power or administrative apparatus familiar to us. At the time in question, however, anarchy in Bohemia reached a level high even for the Middle Ages, and sur-passed only by conditions in the same period in France.[6]

The king did not rule in Bohemia; his council wished to, but lacked the power. The sphere of influence of the higher aristocracy continued to spread, as did the power of the cities; moreover, the lower aristocracy and the people of the countryside, the largest part of the population, began to reassume importance. To these people the country seemed to be without rule, and they began to doubt the authority of king and crown. The tendency to renounce the king altogether in Bohemia clearly indicates just how acute the crisis of royal authority had become; indeed by the end of the fourteenth century it was almost impossible to govern in the ancient manner. The new governmental organization was too tentative and uncertain to gain real administrative control, and the structure of power in the whole country was threatened. This crisis of "temporal power," however, was slight in comparison with the situation of the Church, the primary spiritual authority. Contemporary conceptions of temporal power and ecclesiastical power were entirely different. The curial theory of the two swords managed occasionally to conceal the fact that the Middle Ages was quite capable of justifying and measuring power of both kinds.

I have already drawn attention to the central position of the Church in the life of medieval men, and it is quite clear that both the faith and the piety of these men were markedly different from those of men in ecclesiastical orders in the baroque age. (The later period is often projected backward toward the Middle Ages. But this is not to deny that the so-called Reformation and Counter-Reformation were important turning-points in popular piety.) The Middle Ages was primarily concerned with the guarantee of security the Church offered to believers, and only secondarily with doctrine. Even in the fourteenth century the Church remained the exclusive administrator of the sacraments, the body to which one could have recourse in the moment of supreme danger, when face to face with death. The sign of the cross dispelled demons, and the power of the devil stopped abruptly at the doors of holy places. This belief was so general, and indeed so dominant, that all resistance to the Church was heresy—once men had become at all ideologically conscious. Resistance could never take the form of paganism, atheism, or Judaism, though one could at times make choices leading to parallel phenomena. No resistance of any kind whatever could retain substantially the same premises as Catholicism; it was of necessity heterodox.

If the security guaranteed by the sacraments was the dominant idea in the minds of the common people, a security often of a purely magical sort, the doctrine of the Church was the matter of greatest concern to Bohemian theologians. Therefore we might say that the reform tendencies of the Church were not clearly based on either human or economic and social principles. To be sure these concerns were strongly manifested from time to time in the tracts or the preaching of some reformers, not so vibrantly in those of others. Never, however, were such ideas at the heart of their doctrines or their efforts. Unshaken and certain, the Church of Christ always appeared at the core of their doctrines, simply because the reformers still regarded it as the true foundation and center of everything.

The reform movement was thus based on the Augustinian tradition, the "unsubdued heritage" of medieval theology [7] in which, in contrast to the policy of the contemporary Church, no decision could be made as to being the church of the militant or the church of the elect. The problems of the Church necessarily came to the fore in the fourteenth century, including its difficulties in regard to temporal power and the reform movement. These were the problems of the Czech reformation as well, and if it is true that Huss displayed more social consciousness than his predecessor Wyclif, his main effort was still not to reform his society, but to reform his Church. Social ideas and compassion for the poor were secondary in his program, and this particular segment of society did not occupy the center of his thought. The center was, as it had been for Wyclif, the Church. In this sphere the battle was joined, rather than in that of social doctrine, morality (which was employed as a critique of clerical behavior), or nationalist thinking.

The crisis of the Church necessarily had powerful and even deadly effects in the spiritual realm, because Czech culture at that time had neither created other values and assurances outside the so-called religious sphere, nor begun to search for them. Even the earliest efforts of the new movement were blatantly religious, despite its somewhat humanistic underpinnings. This is clear if we compare the movement in Czechoslovakia with the contemporary situation in Italy and in France. Czech intellectual life still centered on religion, and the most intellectual segment of the population, the clerics who were the predecessors of modern intellectuals, had not discovered those values which their contemporaries in more developed regions had found in the arts or in the rediscovered ancient sciences. Czech intellectual life continued its monolithic way, and the shattering of its foundations was bound to produce violent effects.

The whole Czech Church was also a bit behind the times in comparison with others, and not only in the realm of ideas. It did not become involved in ecclesiastical upheaval, with all its financial, personal, and cultural consequences, until the time of Charles IV, but at that point the process of change agitated the entire Czech Church. The result was that large numbers of clergy and laity became involved in the question of the traffic in indulgences and the problem of simony. In the ecclesiastical centers of Europe this latter practice had been the target of satire for centuries, but remained a phenomenon easier to write about than to remedy. Bohemia, however, had not been conditioned to these practices; their arrival on the scene seems to have been relatively swift and sudden. All these things fit together. Security was nowhere to be found, or, at least, those certainties which man needed in order to live. The currents of discontent, fear, apprehension and excitement began to unite, and the temperature—one might even say the fever—at the heart of society rose to the point of explosion, an explosion of apparently unjustified proportions. The Hussite movement did not result from the death of its leader John Huss, the hero of its first stage. The real sign of the rebellion (although the people of Prague did not at first recognize it) came when the aldermen of the new city were thrown out of the windows of the town hall in 1419. It was a planned action, perhaps, but still anonymous, senseless, useless and only distantly connected with the reform movement. One basic facet of the revolutionary movement took shape at this time as an expression of security and certainty: the demand for the chalice. It fitted perfectly the pattern of what a new symbol should be. It guaranteed full security: only the Hussites, considered communally, were the real members of the Church. But the weakness of this approach was evident from the beginning: the symbol also contained latent sources of conflict. In some cases it even became apparent that it was quite meaningless.

The crisis of the late Middle Ages was clear and well developed in Bohemia, and as a result the Hussite movement spread over the whole country. It became, at least initially, a national movement. Its organizers came from the ranks of the priests, both those impoverished by contemporary developments and those with good livings. Most of them were good propagandists, since they were well disposed toward the new doctrine. Their activity was fruitful largely because social tensions and hatreds, economic difficulties, loss of faith, and the current organization of both society and Church transformed a sense of being menaced into a call to action. Those who spread the Hussite message were themselves the product of the crisis, and they carried on their work in the midst of a society in crisis.

The Hussite movement swept the country like a grass fire, but it soon became apparent that it really had no solution to offer and would have no results. The doctrine of the reformers, as I have already mentioned, was centered on the Church in its original form, and served only to glorify the popular notion that the old times were the best. The real popular movement had a certain chiliastic nature, resurrecting the concept of an original (mythical) state of pure humanity. From the standpoint of ideology the ideas of the new society were not clear, and perhaps could not possibly become so. The whole movement, therefore, ended in a fruitless heroic outburst. Then it began to decay internally, held together only by the symbol it had created, unfortunately as formal a thing as other symbols, and by the necessity for solidarity against its enemies. With the neutralization of these enemies the imposed unity of the movement came to an end.

Thus the Hussite movement could not be the source of later developments, and the Reformation had no direct connection with it. It is true that the Hussites instilled fear into the Church, and set in motion the search for heretics. It did force the Church to some extent to deal with "heretics" on an official basis for the first time, and thereby to admit them, at least formally, to a certain standing. But this was not much of an advance. The Hussite movement was not the only possible response to the contemporary situation. It was in no sense the final result of the whole crisis. Later developments were to show that the basic approach of the Hussites, concentrating on the traditional doctrine of the Church and on renewal of the conservative organization of society by returning to idealized ancient forms, could not answer the thorny problems raised by the crisis. On the contrary, those efforts which were to open new paths for doctrine and society abandoned the ancients' point of view and sought a new basis on which to build. But we cannot blame the Hussites for this; the possibilities open to reformers in the sixteenth century were not open to them. Only later was the new solution to take shape.

On the intellectual scene, there was so-called humanism, building its system of values on man and nature, while in the religious realm the center of gravity moved from the Church to the concept of faith. "The religious life" of the laity became just as individualized in Catholicism, but the Protestants were no more able to resolve the problems of ecclesiastical and social organization. It is not my place to take account of these developments, but I should mention that they were the means by which the intellectual crisis of the late Middle Ages was overcome and a new system built upon its ruins. Socially, the sixteenth century saw the formation of new kinds of states, able to handle the problems that had toppled medieval sovereigns. The new style of society, however, did not achieve its definitive form at that time, but in later epochs.

If, as I see it, the actual crisis of late medieval society ends here—manifested as it was in the loss of traditional values and certainties in the social and cultural realms as well as in the search for new ones—only the new formation of value-systems in the sixteenth century allowed the Hussite movement to be recognized as a turning-point of the greatest importance. This was not only because of its strength, clarity, and duration, but also because it really did bring the medieval period to a close, and demonstrated that the new problems were not to be solved by old methods. The attempt to form a new society on a primitive Christian model, to set the Church back by several centuries, could hardly meet with success. The new era demanded a new solution. Thus, perhaps, the most profound result of the movement was the reaction of Petr Chelčicky, who saw with his own eyes the downfall of everything he had worked for, yet remained deeply convinced of the necessity of reforming the Church outside the sphere of Catholicism. Like the Union of Brethren (the *Unitas fratrum*) which followed in his footsteps, he had only an individual answer, and one different from that of the official [and more moderate Hussite sect of the] Calixtines, whose ideas were already passé in the sixteenth century. One cannot, unfortunately, find until then any better individual response than Chelčicky's.

It seems to me that one cannot get a true picture of the Hussite movement unless it is closely bound to the crisis we have been discussing. It did not resolve that crisis, but because of its clearly defined character and the intense emotions it generated, the movement gives us perhaps the most suggestive picture of the depth and extent of the crisis of the so-called late Middle Ages.

NOTES

1. This paper was also a report given at the colloquium organized by the Historical Institute of the Czechoslovakian Academy of the Sciences at Smolenice from September 2–6, 1969. The colloquium was devoted to the problems of the epoch just previous to that of the Hussite movement, and to the place which the movement occupies in European history. I have omitted references; the general scope of the paper makes specific documentation implausible, largely because it could not be realistically useful in a paper of this length. I am, however, publishing in German (as a "supplementum" in the new journal *Mediaevalia Bohemica* [=Vol. 1 (1969)—ED.]) a catalog of literature on the topic up to the present time, and of opinions concerning this so-called crisis of the Middle Ages. There one can easily find verification for the points of view ascribed to different historians, as well as the more specialized literature dealing with different aspects of the crisis.

2. I have given up old attempts to explain the crisis of the late Middle Ages as a "crisis of feudalism," and to consider the changeover to monetary forms of rent as a decisive and definitive cause. The patterns which led me to make this decision can be found in more detail in the article mentioned in n. 1.

3. Karel Havlíček Borovsky, in truly classic fashion, puts this ahistorical, noncomprehending attitude into an epigram: "Why did the Hussite troubles occur? They really wanted to know whether the divine body should be eaten with or without sauce."

4. Wherever I speak of "Europe" in this article, I am thinking specifically of the Catholic part of it, leaving out for the moment eastern and southern Italy. For many reasons the Italian situation in the Middle Ages was unique, and the criteria applicable to other countries apply there in only a *very* conditional way. Further, what is in question here, if we are to make use of this notion at all, is a set of very general limitations. In reality regions differ greatly among themselves, and in diverse countries even distant resemblances are not in the least like the cultural unity of modern times. There *are* some general characteristics of the Middle Ages, however, and to handle them I should like to make use of the incorrect term "European" in an effort to avoid getting bogged down and involved in useless repetition.

5. I am obviously dealing here with something that is worth considering not

only in regard to the Middle Ages. Similar mass movements have also occurred in recent times. I have tried to set forth some general ideas about the connection of these events in an article entitled "La Crise actuelle de notre conscience historique," *Československý časopis historický* 16 (1968), 485–504.

6. The French kingdom, unlike Bohemia, not only created continuously functioning institutions, but also raised the kingdom itself to a sort of semisacralized state of which the Renaissance was later to make use. (One need only think of the importance of the royal anointing and crowning of Charles VII at Rheims in 1429.)

7. We could trace the continuation of this controversy even into modern times, most clearly in Jansenism.

PART TWO

MEDIEVAL
SCHOLASTICISM
AND THE
REFORMATION

4

PAUL VIGNAUX

On Luther and Ockham [*]

[TRANSLATED BY JANET COLEMAN]

Paul Vignaux, director of studies at the Ecole des Hautes Etudes in Paris, is well known in the English-speaking world through his challenging Philosophy in the Middle Ages: An Introduction *(first published in translation in 1959). He has made important contributions to late medieval philosophy and theology with his studies of* Justification et prédestination au XIVe siècle *(1934);* Luther commentateur des Sentences *(1935); and* Nominalisme au XIVe siècle *(1948). In this highly compact article "On Luther and Ockham," a test of intellectual agility for layman and professional alike, Vignaux analyzes the context and content of two propositions taken from Luther's* Disputation Against Scholastic Theology *of September 4, 1517. This disputation forms the immediate theological background of the famous 95 theses (c. October 31, 1517). The propositions discussed by Vignaux are directed against William of Ockham in particular and late medieval nominalism in general; the nominalist theologians, Pierre d'Ailly and Gabriel Biel, are also singled out for criticism by Luther. The issue is one which lies at the heart of nominalist theology: the possibility of man's obtaining divine acceptance without divine grace, of receiving divine favor simply on the basis of his natural moral ability and God's freedom to accept him for doing his best. Luther's*

* *Franziskanische Studien* 32 (Dietrich Coelde-Verlag, Münster/Westf., 1950), 21–30.

Agapistic God. By positing God's grace Luther got himself out of problems.

Ockham an true humanist Luther seemed to believe. That Agapistic man took away from the glory of

critical propositions are a sharp response to this teaching and the assumptions on which it rests. "God cannot accept a man who does not have His justifying grace. Against Ockham" (Proposition 57); "It is a subtle evil to argue that an act is both enjoyable [an end in itself] and useful [a means to another end]. Against Ockham, the Cardinal [Pierre d'Ailly], and Gabriel [Biel]" (Proposition 94). Luther had already argued in his 1516 comments on Biel's Sentences commentary (or Collectorium), that man could not merit divine favor by doing his moral best. In the arguments of this earlier work Vignaux sees important clues to Luther's rejection of Biel's teacher, Ockham, in the Disputation Against Scholastic Theology. Vignaux suggests that the basic theological differences between Luther and Ockham (and late medieval nominalism) stem, in the last analysis, from very different assessments of human nature: "One might say that man, as Luther conceived him, posed a problem for justifying grace quite different from that posed by man as Ockhamism saw him."

Since the beginning of the century, when Denifle suddenly stated the problem of the relation between Luther and Ockham and developed his interpretation of it, research on this issue has progressed not only with great reserve in regard to the ideas of its initiator, but also with more general considerations than detailed analyses. Therefore, we should like simply to find a means of determining, at least as a first approximation, the meaning of two propositions in the *Disputatio Contra Scholasticam Theologiam* of 4 September, 1517: theses 57 and 94. These theses are presented as opposed to the teachings of William of Ockham, who alone is cited by name in the marginal comment on thesis 57, but who appears along with Pierre d'Ailly and Gabriel Biel in the marginal comment on thesis 94.[1]

Karl Holl considers proposition 57 *contra Ockham* remarkable: "God cannot accept a man who does not have His justifying grace" *(Non potest Deus acceptare hominem sine gratia Dei iustificante).* Holl writes: "While Luther expressly indicated that he was alluding to Ockham in this thesis, he was still unable to prevent Denifle and others from maintaining that his doctrine of justification was Ockhamist."[2] The issue is important. Can we not discover a precise reason for Luther's inclusion of proposition 57 in the *Disputatio,* and at this particular point in the succession of theses, assuming there was some logic to it?

This proposition against Ockham is preceded by two theses *contra Gabrielem*. We need not be reminded of the importance of the commentary on the *Sentences* in which Gabriel Biel deliberately follows Ockham, the *Venerabilis Inceptor*.[3] This was the *Collectorium*, in which Luther, in 1515–1516, made marginal notes in the edition available in his monastery's library.[4] The relation of the *Disputatio* to Biel's commentary, to one question, one passage annotated by the "Augustine of Wittenberg," is evident in propositions 5–19 of the *Disputatio*. After the four initial theses, which maintain the authority of St. Augustine against a *dictum commune*—common to Biel, Duns Scotus and St. Bonaventure—and show that, in truth, *homo arbor mala factus,* these fifteen propositions are appropriately written as marginal comment on Book III of Biel's *Collectorium*, distinction XXVII, the first (and only) question, article 3, *dubium secundum.* The question bears on the idea of the virtue of charity—that disposition or *habitus,* which inclines the will toward the perfect observation of the commandment of love. Biel first develops some preliminary remarks, which analyze the act of loving in general and of loving God in particular. (Luther will refer to these in his *Randbemerkungen*.) Then Biel formulates and establishes his theses on the *habitus* and the commandment of love. Finally come the objections, notably the *dubium secundum,* which has the form and importance of an added question: "Whether the human will of the *viator* can, from its own nature, love God above all things and therefore fulfill the precept of love?" *(Utrum voluntas humana viatoris possit Deum ex suis naturalibus diligere super omnia et ita implere praeceptum dilectionis?)* It is a question of determining whether a natural love of the deity is possible, and whether such a love would fulfill the commandment to love God.[5]

Biel's response, *secundum opinionem Scoti, Occam,* rests on five propositions. Thesis 5 of Luther's *Disputatio* refers to the preliminary refutation of opposing arguments. The next fourteen theses are developed along with Biel's first proposition and the proofs he brings to bear: "The human will of the *viator,* from its own nature, can love God above all things" *(Viatoris voluntas humana ex suis naturalibus potest diligere Deum super omnia).*

But a natural love of God, expressed in this way, seems nothing but a "fiction" to Luther: *terminus fictus sicut chimaera* (thesis 18). For Biel, on the other hand, it constitutes a real possibility, implied in the very existence of a spiritual nature, a free will. We would, indeed, see its pure realization if a certain order of grace had not already been established by divine choice. In fact, Biel's subsequent propositions are viewed *de potentia Dei ordinata* (proposition II) and *stante lege* (proposition V)—according to God's historically ordained power and promulgated law. This is all in his hypothesis of a set order, a determined legislation of the way to salvation. His propositions, therefore, are not based on the simple presupposition of unlimited creative power, on what can be done through God's absolute power: *quod fieri posset per Dei absolutem potentiam* (proposition III).

When we come to Biel's fifth and final proposition, which appears to reverse the first by declaring man's natural incapacity to fulfill the commandment of divine love—"no man through his purely natural capacities can fulfill the precept of loving God above all things" *(nullus homo per pura naturalia potest implere praeceptum de dilectione Dei super omnia)*—we can regard the initial proposition as only a preliminary conclusion, abstract in itself, but still an abstraction based on the very nature of a created spirit and on an analysis of the concrete order and the complex arrangement of free will, grace, and [extraordinary] graces. This analysis reminds us how for Ockham, Biel's "chosen Doctor," the dialectic *de potentia Dei absoluta* has not only a religious significance, but also a critical function—discerning and probing the depths of objects under investigation.[6] As Ockham's disciple, Biel constructs his doctrine according to theological logic—*theologicus logicus*—a method which Luther came to think "monstrous" (thesis 45).

Having rejected *contra Scotum, Gabrielem,* the concept of man's natural love for God defined as "to will that God be God" *(velle Deum esse Deum)*, Luther allows only the love of friendship to relate to grace: "An act of friendship [toward God] comes not by nature but from prevenient grace" *(Actus amicitiae non est naturae sed gratiae praevenientis: Contra Gabrielem)* (thesis 20). In nature, with regard to God, there is only a concupiscent love, which, in every activity, is evil (theses 21 and 22). It is sufficient merely to consider this evil in order to reject, along with the idea of natural charity, the concept of hope as the regulatory virtue of concupiscent love, as proposed by Biel in the *Collectorium* (theses 23, 24, 25). This teaching had already been set forth by Biel in the preceding distinction (III *Sent.* d. XXVI), which was devoted to the virtue of hope. It is taken up again here, with particular regard to its origin, in the course of a preliminary analysis of love which is annotated by Luther.[7]

Once this false concept of Christian hope is out of the way, Luther returns in the *Disputatio* to the act of natural friendship toward God, which is set forth in Biel's proposition as a "preparation," or, since it is not a question of temporal priority, even as a "disposition" for the infused gift of grace, which is identified with charity. Theses 26-28 again are marginal commentary on the *dubium secundum:* "Second proposition . . . It is proved, because, according to the ordained law, he who does what is in him . . ." *(Probatur: quia secundum legem ordinatem cuilibet facienti quod in se est. . .).* The idea of "preparation for grace" evokes for Luther the idea of predestination, which he calls "the highest preparation and singular disposition for grace" *(Optima ad gratiam praeparatio et unica dispositio)* (theses 29-32). After another criticism of the *facere quod in se est* (thesis 33), Luther continues: "In sum, nature possesses neither a right dictate [of conscience] nor a good will" *(breviter, nec rectum dictamen habet natura nec bonum voluntatem)* (thesis 34). From this condemnation of nature, Luther passes to polemical statements on philosophical ethics and logic (theses 35-53).

Between thesis 54 and thesis 57 *contra Occam,* we again find reference to Biel, II *Sent.,* q.u., art. 3, dub. 2—this time regarding his proposition III: "Although that which is called the love of God *ex naturalibus* is naturally prior to *caritas* and infused grace in the order of nature, *caritas* is first in the order of merit" *(Quamvis dilectio Dei ex naturalibus quae dicta est sit prior natura caritate et gratia infusa in esse naturae, caritas est prior in meriti ratione).* We find the development of thought, its clothing in a new guise, if you like, typical of this passage from the *Collectorium.* The order of nature, or the love *ex naturalibus,* which, because of its natural disposition, precedes infused charity, is reversed in the order of merit, i.e. in the order where its worthiness for salvation is tested, where it is before God. "An act which is meritorious presupposes grace, and it is through grace that the act becomes meritorious" *(Actus qui fit meritorius praesupponit gratiam et ratio meriti convenit actui per gratiam).* Gabriel Biel specifies that the *habitus* of grace must concur, or actually join in the production of the act. "It is required that grace effectively concur" *(requiritur gratia concurrat effective).* Therefore: "for every meritorious act, the coexistence or sheer presence of grace does not suffice" *(ad actum enim omne meritorium non sufficit coexistentia gratiae).* Could these last words be those which provoked thesis 54 of the *Disputatio,* where Luther says: "The coexistence of grace *is* sufficient for a meritorious act; otherwise, coexistence means nothing. Against Gabriel" *(Ad actum meritorium satis est coexistentia gratiae, aut coexistentia nihil est. Contra Gabrielem)*. Biel said "coexistence is not sufficient, but it is necessary" *(. . . non sufficit coexistentia . . . sed requiritur)*. For Luther, this was to have no understanding of what the presence of God's grace was: "God's grace is never present as something idle, but it is a living, moving, and active spirit" *(Gratia Dei nunquam sic coexistit ut otiosa, sed est vivus, mobilis et operosus spiritus)* (thesis 55). Furthermore, it is absolutely impossible for one to love God without His grace being present. "It is not possible through God's absolute power to love God as one's friend where God's grace is not present. Against Gabriel" *(Nec per Dei absolutam potentiam fieri potest, ut actus amicitiae sit et gratia Dei praesens non sit. Contra Gabrielem)*. This proposition 56 of the *Disputatio* is presented as a retort to Biel's hypothesis, stated a few lines above, that: "if the one who loves God above all things has not received an infusion of grace, this act can still be performed through God's absolute power" *(Si amanti Deum super omnia non infunderetur gratia, quod fieri posset per Dei potentiam absolutam. . .)*.

Let us briefly underline the importance of this hypothesis, which touches on the very distinction between nature and grace. On its validity rests the theological equilibrium of Ockhamism. The believer lives in an order of salvation where loving God never occurs without the possession of grace. But when his faith entertains the idea of God's omnipotence, he can consider all things in the light of the absoluteness of divine power. From this point of view, he conceives that it is possible, apart from grace, to achieve the highest of purely natural acts, this love of God *ex puris naturalibus,* which appears to constitute the fullness of morality. "That act of friendly love is morally good and sufficiently clothed in all moral qualities—even the ultimate quality" *(actus ille amoris amicitiae: moraliter bonus et omnibus circumstanciis moralibus (etiam circumstancia finis) sufficienter vestitus. . .)*.

It is by the absolute power of God *(potentia Dei absoluta)* that purely natural things *(pura naturalia)* are separated from the natural order, where they are engaged according to God's ordained power *(potentia Dei ordinata)*. The hypothesis of a "pure nature" manifests how thoroughly arbitrary the entire order of grace is. High as the moral value of natural love of the divine object may be *(summe diligible, summe diligendum)*, it is yet not worthy of eternal life. "Although this act of friendly love is morally good, etc., it is neverthe-

Distinguish

    Florentine humanism

    Humanistic influences

    on reformers

less not meritorious" *(Actus ille amoris amicitiae, licet esset moraliter bonus, etc. . . . non tamen esset meritorious).* Truly, the latter is of another order, absolutely "supernatural," to which revelation alone provides access. Only by faith can we know the possibility of eternal life, which is bound to the vision of God. Only by faith can we know in fact that this God, who is perfectly free to remain hidden, offers Himself as an object for man to behold and love. Only by faith can we know, in the end, what way, what conditions of merit, have been freely chosen by God in order to guide us to salvation.[8] Whatever the price that reason must place upon our actions, it still remains less than the ultimate value of the act which saves. Morally to act rightly *(moraliter recte agere)* is not the same as to act simply and absolutely rightly *(recte agere simpliciter et absolute).* The fullness of the act which merits beatitude for man is only possible *secundum legem statutam* as a consequence of a free acceptance by God of conditions that He freely determines when He institutes "positive" religion. This perspective on eternal life, the Biblical "if you want to enter into life. . . . ," gives a new meaning to human acts which transcends their natural ethical significance and responds to the creative intention of the deed. Here, in our opinion, is the meaning of the famous opposition of goodness according to the substance of the act *(quantum ad substantiam facti)* and according to the intention of the lawgiver *(quantum ad intentionem praecipientis).* It was taken up by Gabriel Biel in the explanation of his fifth and last proposition, to which Luther opposed his thesis 58, the thesis which introduces into the *Disputatio* the themes of the Law and Grace (up to thesis 93).

Thesis 57 *contra Occam* is viewed in this context: "God cannot accept a man who does not have His justifying grace" *(Non potest Deus acceptare hominem sine gratia Dei justificante).* Having examined Biel's explanation of his proposition I, we already know that for Luther, "to will that God be God" *(velle Deum esse Deum)* means that "an act of friendship toward God is not from nature but from prevenient grace" *(Actus amicitiae non est naturae, sed gratiae praevenientis)* (theses 17 and 20). Again, against Biel's exposition of his proposition III, Luther has reminded us that grace, which never simply coexists but moves and acts (thesis 56), is present in every act of love toward God. We cannot suppose it to be otherwise, even *de potentia Dei absoluta* (thesis 57). Of course, we should remember here that the Ockhamist supposition that man's love of God emanates from a "pure nature" does not presuppose only a Power which is capable of causing to exist separately that which, without contradiction, can be conceived separately. Even to apply this force presupposes a human nature that is essentially good—a soul whose will, which is not distinct from its substance, would not know how to be naturally bad (cf. theses 8 and 9). It is with regard to this substantial goodness of human nature that Ockhamism affirms the transcendence of the merits of grace, the essential Grace, which coincides with the *acceptatio divina,* and which would alone be necessary if redemption were not superabundant. Human nature for Ockham, though incapable of meriting salvation, still seemed acceptable to God as it was—it was good in itself.[9] *Acceptare hominem sine gratia iustificante,* "to accept man without justifying grace," is a normal possibility in Ockhamism. It is rejected by Luther, who logically must assign to Grace a task commensurate with the natural and inevitable evil and corruption of human nature *(naturaliter et inevitabiliter mala et vitiata natura)* (thesis 9), which Ockham ignored. One might say that man, as Luther conceived him, posed a problem for justifying grace *(gratia justificans)* quite different from that posed by man as Ockhamism saw him.

To what text of Ockham does thesis 57 relate? Perhaps to question 8 of Book III of the *Sentences* where the *Venerabilis Inceptor* deals with the necessity of the theological virtues and the infused *habitus.* "The fact," he tells us, "that I believe beatitude to be accessible by way of merit does not logically imply that I consider infused virtues necessary." This is an evident conclusion from the analyses of Book I, distinction XVII, which relate to charity: "The second conclusion is evident in the first book on charity, viz. that God can accept someone *in puris naturalibus* as worthy of eternal life without any habit of charity . . ." *(Secunda conclusio patet in libro primo de caritate, quia Deus potest aliquem acceptare in puris naturalibus tanquam dignum vita aeterna sine omni habitu caritatis. . .).* Some lines later we are reminded that, in Ockhamism, divine acceptance actually is grace, which is God, so that *de potentia Dei absoluta* we can envision the Holy Spirit as present and accepting the natural act *(Spiritus Sanctus coexistens acceptans actum naturalem),* by which is meant an act which does not imply an infused *habitus* inherent in its *pura naturalia.*[10] If it means the exclusion of this possibility, thesis 57 follows thesis 56 to reject hypotheses that are realizable through God's absolute power *(per Dei potentiam absolutam).* First it was a question only of purely natural love; now it is a question of the acceptance of the pure nature from which the act emanates.

In our interpretation, this possibility implies a whole perspective on God and man and their relationship. Luther's rejection of it is based on an argument from the absoluteness of divine Power that isolates a fundamentally good human nature. Denifle's point of view, of course, prevented him from seeing the meaning of this proposition in the *Disputatio*. "According to Luther," he writes, "it is not only an hypothesis but a reality that God accepts us without sanctifying grace." [11] Unfortunately for Denifle's conception of an apparently logical transition from the Ockhamist doctrine of divine acceptance to the non-imputation theory of justification in the Reformation, we know that in 1510–1511, commenting on Peter Lombard (I *Sent.*, d. XVII), Luther actually set aside the hypothetical speculation *de potentia Dei absoluta*, which is hardly evoked in the statement: "charity (whatever it may possibly be) is in fact . . ." *(caritas— quicquid sit de possibili—de facto. . .)*.[12] These speculations by Biel and Ockham are rejected by Luther expressly in theses 55 and 57 of the *Disputatio* of 4 September, 1517. The marginal notes on the *Sentences* retained a concept of salvation by charity, asking if the philosophical category of *habitus* agreed with a theological virtue. Here Luther maintained that an act of love constituted this bond with the Eternal which saves us.[13] What we have said about the *Disputation Against Scholastic Theology*, notably about the criticism that it contains of Biel (III *Sent.*, d. XXVII), indicates the place occupied by the problem of loving God. Would not some research on the relation between Luther and Ockham and his school begin with an analysis of *caritas de facto*? Thesis 94 seems to extend the invitation: "It is a subtle evil to say that the same act is both enjoyable and useful. Against Ockham, the Cardinal of Cameria [Pierre d'Ailly] and Gabriel" *(Subtile malum est dicere: eundem actum esse fruitionem et usum: contra Occam, Cardinalem Cameracensem, Gabrielem)*.

The three theses preceding thesis 94 are aimed at Gabriel Biel, III *Sent.*, d. XXVII, q.u., art. 3 m, dub. 4 m—a passage annotated by Luther.[14] It is always a question of "charity," a concept which, before being fixed in the conclusion of article 2, had been prepared for by Biel's preliminary remarks in article 1. The first analysis provoked a lively reaction from the Augustine of Wittenberg.[15] Biel first aired the notion of acts of rational love which emanate from liberty, and then presented these acts differentiated into friendly and concupiscent love, according to the ways in which they approached their object. Biel makes this distinction clear when he compares the intentionality of the will with that of the intellect—which adheres to one truth by reason of first one, then another truth. To love the object for itself *(propter se)* defines friendship, and to love it for something else *(propter aliud)* is concupiscence. But in the second case, even before this something else is loved, we are necessarily referred to an object which is loved for its own sake, out of friendship. To these two differently loved objects, Biel asks whether there are two corresponding acts of love. His answer: "not always." A single love is sometimes sufficient for the will to direct itself simultaneously to what is an end in itself and to what it ordains as a means to this end. We see here the terms that Luther's *Disputatio* will take up: "And then," Biel writes, "this act is simultaneously friendly love and concupiscent love. The act is, at the same time, enjoyable and useful: enjoyable insofar as it tends toward its end; and useful insofar as it moves along the chosen way for the sake of its end" *(Et tunc ille actus est amor amicitiae et concupiscentiae simul. Sicut simul est fruitio et usus. Fruitio in quantum tendit in finem. Et usus in quantum tendit in media propter finem ordinata.)* [16] This is Ockham's teaching, which is rooted in the comparison of reason and will: the former has no less power over its objects than the latter, and the will can draw a conclusion by performing an act.[17]

The act which is at the same time enjoyable and useful *(actus simul fruitio et usus)* is found in the explanation of the seventh conclusion to the same distinction XXVII of the *Collectorium*. With this thesis Biel makes clear, following Pierre d'Ailly, that the commandment to love God above all things does not in his opinion necessitate an act of a higher degree of intensity of being than the love of self or of another created object; the conclusion speaks of an act more perfect in degree or essence *(actus perfectior gradualiter vel essentialiter)*. But a *notabile* of article 1, citing the same Cardinal, says: "perfection according to degree of intensity or essential perfection" *(perfectio secundum intensionem gradualem sive perfectionem essentialem)*. Here is the proof that Biel presents: because the same act can love God and love creatures for God's sake *(quia eodem actu potest diligi Deus et creatura propter Deum)*—God loved for Himself, the creature loved for God, the same act enjoyable and useful—this act is neither in degree nor in essence more perfect or more imperfect in itself *(Idem actus fruitio et usus—idem autem non est gradualiter aut essentialiter perfectius et imperfectius seipso)*. According to this opinion the commandment to love God does not, therefore, require a more intense act. To the contrary, let us read some lines further on. It is a question not of degree of intensity in the act but of what one desires in the object, and the manner in which the will is directed toward its end—*potest licite quis diligere creaturam actu quantumcumque gradualiter intenso seipsum vel aliam, dummodo tamen non velit sibi summa bona, nec bona quaecumque propter seipsam tanquam finem ultimum.* In demanding that one not treat the creature as a supreme end, that one not desire it as God, the commandment to love does not ask that one love the creature less intensely. There we touch on Luther's thesis 95: "it is a subtle evil to say that the love of God is, even in intensity, the same kind of love as that for creatures"—*item (sc. subtile malum est dicere), quod amor Dei stet cum dilectione creaturae, etiam intensa.*

Why was this subtlety rejected as evil? Thesis 96 indicates the reason: "To love God is to hate oneself and to know nothing beyond God" *(Diligere Deum est seipsum odisse et praeter Deum nihil novisse).* The love of God is exclusive of all other loves. Therefore, it is an evil to consider, in the subtle manner of Ockham and his disciples, the same act as going to God *propter se,* and to the creature *propter Deum.* We have undoubtedly found the context of proposition 94. We can recognize its importance when it is emphasized that charity is understood by Luther as knowing nothing but God.

The theme, "Luther and Ockham," is not unprofitable if, in these seductive reconstructions, one pays attention to the texts. They suggest to us that, in order to confront the Reformer with the celebrated Franciscan and his school, we must study, within the history of post-Scotist theology, the analysis of the adhesion of love to the divine Being: *velle Deum esse Deum*—a formula simultaneously so abstract and so full of meaning.

NOTES

1. *WA* 1, 224–228.
2. Karl Holl, *Gesammelte Aufsätze zur Kirchengeschichte,* 1: *Luther* (Tübingen, 1927), 123.
3. "Nostri propositi est dogmata et scripta venerabilis inceptoris Guilelmi Occam Anglici, veritatis indagatoris accerrimi, circa quattuor sententiarum libros abbreviare." *Epitoma pariter et Collectorium circa quattuor Libros Sententiarum, Prologus* (Basel, 1508).
4. *Luthers Randbemerkungen zu Gabriel Biels Collectorium in quattuor libros sententiarum und zu dessen Sacri Canonis missae expositio* (Lyon, 1514), ed. Hermann Degering (Weimar, 1933).
5. We plan, in a later study, to take up an analysis of Biel's teaching in this

distinction XXVII and to deal with Luther's reading of it. One will find a first draft, in relation to the problems that Biel's text presents for doctrinal history, in our review of Carl Feckes' edition of the *Quaestiones de Iustificatione* in: *Revue d'Histoire Franciscaine*, 6 (1929), 417–419. The interpretation Feckes has given to the "nominalist" concept of grace in *Die Rechtfertigungslehre des Gabriel Biel und ihre Stellung innerhalb der nominalistischen Schule* (Münster, 1925), in our opinion, must be confronted with that of J. Rivière, article on *Mérite* in the *Dictionnaire du Théologie Catholique*, x, col. 701ff.

6. Cf. our work, *Nominalisme au XIVe Siècle* (Montréal, 1948), pp. 22–24.

7. *Randbemerkungen zu Gabriel Biel*, p. 13.

8. This whole view of Biel, III *Sent.*, d. XXVII, art. 3, dub. 2 m, is based on our earlier studies: *Justification et Prédestination au XIVe Siècle* (Paris, 1934), chap. 3; *Luther Commentateur des Sentences* (Book I, d. XVII) (Paris, 1935), pp. 82–85; Note on "esse beatificabile: passio theologica" in *Franciscan Studies*, 9 (1949), 404–416.

9. *Justification et Prédestination*, esp. pp. 104–105, 119, 123–124, 130–133.

10. III *Sent.* q. 8, especially G. Cf. *Luther Commentateur*, p. 83, nn. 1 and 2; p. 86, n. 2.

11. *Luther et le Luthéranisme*, trans. J. Paquier, III (Paris, 1912), 224. Cf. Denifle, *Luther und Luthertum*, I (Mainz, 1904), 585.

12. *Luther Commentateur*, p. 42, n. 2 and p. 92.

13. *Ibid.*, pp. 93–94.

14. *Randbemerkungen zu Gabriel Biel*, p. 16.

15. *Ibid.*, p. 11–12.

16. III *Sent.*, d. XXVII, q.u., a. 1, notabile 2 m, D.

17. I *Sent.*, d. 1, q. 1, K (Lyon, 1695).

5

HEIKO A. OBERMAN

Facientibus Quod in se est
Deus non Denegat Gratiam:
Robert Holcot O. P. and the
Beginnings of Luther's Theology *

Heiko A. Oberman, Professor of Church History and director of the Institut für Spätmittelalter und Reformation at the University of Tübingen, is author of The Harvest of Medieval Theology: Gabriel Biel and Late Medieval Nominalism *(1963) and coeditor of the critical edition of Biel's* Exposition of the Canon of the Mass, *a major textbook for the young Luther, and* Defense of Apostolic Obedience. *In addition to an earlier monograph on Thomas Bradwardine (1958), Oberman has more recently published a collection of key documents by medieval theologians in English translation:* Forerunners of the Reformation: The Shape of Late Medieval Thought *(1966). He is represented in this volume by two articles, relating Luther to medieval nominalism and to medieval mysticism.*

In this first selection, "Facientibus Quod in se est Deus non Denegat Gratiam: Robert Holcot O.P. and the Beginnings of Luther's Theology," Oberman weighs the appearance of the key nominalistic concepts of the facere quod in se est *and the* meritum de congruo

* HThR 55 (1962), 317–342.

*in the young Luther. According to nominalist theologians, a truly
merciful God could be expected to give grace as a "fitting reward"
(meritum de congruo) to the man who "does his very best" (facit
quod in se est). Oberman distinguishes two versions of this formula:
a* facere quod in se est *between reason and revelation (he who* thinks
his very best can expect divine illumination as a fitting reward) and a
facere quod in se est *between the will and grace (he who* does *his
level best can expect an infusion of grace as a fitting reward). Oberman maintains that even in Luther's very earliest work, the traditional
commentary on Lombard's* Sentences *(1509–1510), he breaks decisively with the first version, yet appears to retain the second well
into 1516. The young Luther is, ironically, both critic and advocate of
the semi-Pelagianism of nominalism.*

"In manu enim illius et nos et sermones nostri, et omnis sapientia
et operum scientia, et disciplina." *Liber Sapientiae* vii:16

1. *Sola fide tenetur:* HOLCOT'S SCEPTICISM

WHEN THE English nominalist and Dominican friar Robert Holcot († 1349) reaches the sixteenth verse of the seventh chapter in his
Wisdom commentary, he seizes the opportunity to underscore the
main theme which he had so passionately presented on the preceding
pages as well as in his *Sentences* commentary: Wisdom is a gift of
God; man's claim, therefore, that he can have a natural knowledge
of God is false.

We should not be tempted to regard this statement as the solution
of a Christian obscurantist who, bewildered by the challenging claims
of philosophy, *scientia,* withdraws into the safe citadel of theology,
sapientia. The riddle of Holcot's place in the medieval history of the
relation of faith and reason forces itself upon the reader when, in this
one lecture, both the inaccessibility of true knowledge of God and
the accuracy of the natural knowledge of God on the part of the
great philosophers are brought out.

It is first emphasized that the wisdom of God stands over against
the wisdom of man since "we preach Christ crucified, a stumbling-
block to Jews and folly to Gentiles." [1] Nevertheless at the climax of
this same discussion Holcot introduces an extensive quotation from
the source of all pagan philosophy, Hermes Trismegistos. He gives as
his reference the eleventh book of the *De Natura Deorum,* and cites

a passage which forms the last part of Asclepius in the *Corpus Hermeticum*.[2] Holcot's purpose is to show that Hermes knows that God is self-sufficient. For Hermes, God has no need to receive anything from man, and so it makes no sense to burn incense for him. On the contrary, man depends on God for everything, including his wisdom; thanksgiving is therefore the best incense man can offer God.[3] Notwithstanding the fact that Hermes is a pagan, Holcot observes, he returns his thanks to God in everything.[4]

It is not the choice of Hermes Trismegistos which is the surprising element here. Holcot's contemporary Thomas Bradwardine († 1349), who had a career remarkably similar to that of Holcot, also likes to quote Hermes and regards him as "Father of the philosophers."[5] Both Bradwardine and Holcot in the thirties of the fourteenth century were part of the household of Richard de Bury, Bishop of Durham.[6] Arthur Darby Nock, in his introduction to the critical edition of Asclepius, has called attention to the familiarity with the *Corpus Hermeticum* which de Bury's important *Philobiblon* reveals.[7] In view of the fact that Holcot and Bradwardine had access to the same library, it does not surprise us that a part of Hermes' prayer at the end of Asclepius not only appears in Holcot's *Super libros Sapientiae* but also in Bradwardine's *De Causa Dei*.[8]

But here then arises the problem: it is by no means extraordinary that Thomas Bradwardine, whose first axiom is Anselm's ontological proof of God's existence, draws on the wisdom of pagan philosophers.[9] The consistent theme of the first book of *De Causa Dei* is the concordance of philosophy and theology,[10] and quotations from Hermes serve to show that philosophy provides a reliable natural theology.[11] Holcot, however, does not share Bradwardine's confidence in the capacities of natural reason, and he does not tire of showing that it is impossible to prove that God exists: "hec propositio est mere credita"[12] or "sola fide tenetur."[13]

This denial of the possibility of a natural knowledge of God has earned Holcot the reputation of a sceptic.[14] Gordon Leff, limiting his investigation to the *Sentences* commentary, concluded that "Robert Holcot well illustrates how fruitfully Ockham provided for his followers along the path to scepticism."[15] Beryl Smalley broadens the basis of judgment when she concludes that "Holcot admitted as an exegete to the scepticism that he professed as a theologian."[16] The implications of this charge of scepticism may appear from Miss Smalley's general conclusion: "Consistency was not Holcot's outstanding virtue as a thinker, unless it may be that he was true to his scepticism in his being inconsistent. Scepticism makes it difficult to hold a clear-cut theory in politics as in theology, witness William of Ockham." [17] Alois Meissner goes merely one step farther when he suggests that Holcot stands for a stark agnosticism as regards the possibility of a natural knowledge of God.[18] Though we cannot discuss the problem in all its dimensions, we should at least note that the issue before us transcends the importance of the individual case of Robert Holcot, since the scepticism of Holcot has been seen as representative of nominalism as such and even as characteristic of the climate of the whole fourteenth century.[19]

If Holcot is indeed such a thoroughgoing sceptic and agnostic as hitherto has been claimed, one wonders of course why he values so highly the authority of Hermes—or for that matter the authority of Socrates, Plato, and Aristotle.[20] If there is such a radical cleavage between the realm of reason and the realm of faith, what then can philosophers, and especially pagan philosophers, offer to the field of natural theology? It is possible to answer this question by pointing out that Holcot holds the Augustinian [21] doctrine of an aboriginal revelation to Adam, his children, and the holy prophets, who handed this knowledge of God down in oral and written form. This revelation finally reached the Greek and pagan philosophers, who thus *received* but did not *produce* the knowledge of God.

Though this doctrine of "the splendid pagans" or of the philosophical cloud of witnesses is not exclusively Augustinian—we find it, e.g., also with Pelagius [22]—the fact that this revelation is a gift administered to the elect is a characteristic emphasis of Augustine.[23] In greater detail but true to Augustine's intention, Thomas Bradwardine shows that behind the natural theology of Hermes and Aristotle stands ultimately the gift of revelation given to Seth, Enoch, Noah, Abraham and Solomon.[24]

Holcot remains within this Augustinian tradition when he points out that all those who had knowledge of God without contact with Old Testament revelation were instructed by God rather than by their own rational argumentations. We are, however, forewarned that Holcot's position cannot simply be identified with that of Augustine by the fact that this gift of knowledge of God is not bestowed on the elect but on those who live according to the principles of natural law.[25] Unlike Augustine and Bradwardine, Holcot is not interested in an aboriginal revelation to explain the great insights of Hermes and Aristotle. He is more interested in the general ethical corollary that such knowledge of God is available to all who live according to the principles of natural law. It is this peculiar emphasis which throws a very different light on Holcot's understanding of the relation of faith and reason than the traditional charge of scepticism has led us to believe.

In *Lectio* 28 of his *Wisdom* commentary, Holcot explicitly asks the crucial question whether there are Christian doctrines which transcend the power of reason and yet still have to be revealed and believed since they are necessary for salvation.[26] Holcot first advances two arguments for the opposition: there are no such articles of faith which simultaneously transcend reason and are necessary for salvation since 1) nature does not fail in necessary things and, therefore, does not fail in establishing articles necessary for salvation; 2) certain doctrines such as those concerning the Incarnation and Transubstantiation are contrary to reason; since this implies a negation of the powers of reason, which is blameworthy, it is immoral to believe these articles of faith.[27]

It is not surprising that Holcot, along with the whole medieval tradition, rejects this concept of Christianity as a rational-natural religion.[28] What is important is the way in which he replies to the two arguments advanced.

In contrast to what one might expect of a radical sceptic, Holcot answers to the first point that God has so disposed nature that if man does what is in him, *facit quod in se est,* that is, uses his natural powers, he can acquire sufficient information about the articles of faith which are necessary for salvation.[29]

In his answer to the second argument Holcot points out that the supernatural articles of faith are *not contrary to* reason but go *beyond reason.* To deny reason is indeed blameworthy, but one does not deny reason if one grants that reason cannot reach beyond itself into the realm of supernatural faith which transcends the realm of the senses. The *facere quod in se est* means for Holcot that the act of faith is not merely the exercise of the theoretical reason but an exercise of the whole man: *sine discursu rationis et perceptione voluntaria veritatis, fides non habetur.*[30] The knowledge philosophers like Hermes and Aristotle possess is, therefore, not necessarily due to their acquaintance with the aboriginal revelation. They "have done what is in them" by using their natural powers and have thus reached enlightenment, though this does not exclude the possibility that they made use of the available tradition of truth.[31]

Actually it is only the latter possibility in which Holcot, the moralizing exegete, is interested. The philosophical pre-Christian tradition is not a live option any more; it has been absorbed by the Church and only there is the true tradition to be found. One should not turn therefore to the philosophers but to Christ and his Church, since, compared with Christ, the philosophers' wisdom is stupidity.[32] Holcot does not refer here explicitly to Augustine, but the parallel with Augustine's letter to Dioscorus, *Epistula* 108, is obvious and striking: the true members of the *Plotini schola* recognized in Christ the personification of truth and went over to the Church. So it came about that only within the Church truth is to be found.[33]

Holcot proclaims, indeed, on every page of his *Wisdom* commentary the insufficiency of philosophy.[34] He holds with Augustine that only the authority of the Church can provide a solid basis for the understanding of supernatural truths.[35] Yet to embrace this authority does not mean a negation of reason or a blind jump. This indeed would substantiate the charge of scepticism. Holcot makes quite clear that the God to which the Church witnesses can to a degree be known from his creation.[36] Miracles are probable reasons which engender the act of faith.[37] The same kind of reasonable consideration, which one may call a common-sense argument or *ratio de congruo*, is admitted by Holcot when he tells the story of how a heretic who did not believe in the immortality of the soul was converted by a lay brother who argued that one cannot lose anything in believing this, but only gain eternal bliss if this proves to be true.[38]

The main reason, however, why one should be doubtful about such charges as agnosticism, fideism and scepticism is that, whereas Holcot consistently enough emphasizes that all these semi-arguments as such are insufficient without revelation on the part of God, this revelation is granted only to those who use their rational capacities to the utmost to seek and understand God. To clarify Holcot's use of the *facere quod in se est* as regards the problems of faith and understanding, we turn to his doctrine of predestination and grace which provides us with an elucidating parallel.

II. *Sola gratia salvatur:* HOLCOT'S PREDESTINARIANISM

In the first part we have seen that Holcot does not believe that man through his own power can acquire a saving knowledge of God: *sapientia* is a free gift of God. The transcendence and sovereignty of God is preserved and posited beyond the reach of man's *scientia*.[39] This "scepticism" is considerably mitigated, however, by the concept of the *facere quod in se est.* Man can not only acquire some knowledge of God from creation, but he can also acquire the gift of enlightenment if he makes the best possible use of his natural capacities. Since exactly the same structure of arguments reappears in Holcot's discussion of the relation of free will, grace, and predestination, we can now be more concise in our discussion.

Just as we found strong indications which seemed to support the claim that Holcot be regarded as a full-fledged sceptic, so we find explicit documentation for the claim that Holcot holds an Augustinian doctrine of unmerited grace and predestination without cause. Again God's transcendence and sovereignty are established and posited beyond the reach of man.[40]

Especially if one accepts the view that Holcot is one of the *Pelagiani moderni,* so bitterly attacked by Thomas Bradwardine, the *sola gratia* theme is striking. Though man's responsibility is not denied, all good works are clearly said to be effects of God's predestination.[41] The famous question whether God's predestination is based on foreknowledge of future good works is answered in the negative.[42] Several times the prevenience of grace is clearly enunciated; the beginning of the process of justification is said to be due to the initiative of the Holy Spirit.[43] One can therefore very well understand that it has been argued that Holcot does not deviate from the theology of Aquinas and the Dominican order in his doctrine of grace and predestination.[44]

But again, as was the case with Holcot's "scepticism," we are confronted with a series of statements which seem to contradict this emphasis on God's sovereignty as expressed in the uncaused nature of predestination and in the prevenience of grace. Holcot takes I Tim. 2:4 quite seriously: "[God] desires all men to be saved and to come to the knowledge of the Truth."[45] Yet with this general will for salvation goes the condition that God only wants those to be saved who live according to the laws established by him. This, then, man can and has to decide in all freedom.[46]

Now the question arises with a new urgency how man can be held responsible to live according to the established laws and thus lay claim to the promised salvation, while the actualization of his natural capacities depends on God's granting him the gift of prevenient grace. It is again the doctrine of the *facere quod in se est* which reverses the predestinarian trend and forms the bridge between the transcendent sovereignty of God and man's responsibility for his own salvation.

Holcot solves the problem in the same way as his fellow nominalists, William of Occam[47] and Gabriel Biel.[48] God is committed to give his grace to all who do what is in them. This does not detract from

His sovereignty since in eternity God was free to establish totally different laws; he was free to act with absolute power, the so-called *potentia absoluta,* subject only to the law of noncontradiction or the law of consistency. Out of sheer mercy and grace he freely decided in eternity to establish the law that he would convey grace to all who make full use of their natural capacities. Though the law as such is freely given, and therefore an expression of God's *potentia absoluta,* God is now committed to it, in the order chosen by him, the order of His *potentia ordinata,* and therefore gives his grace "necessarily." [49]

The dialectics of the two powers of God permits Holcot, as it did Occam and Biel, to hold an extreme predestinarian position which centers around the idea that God does not owe anything to any man. While this is true *sub specie aeternitatis et de potentia absoluta,* Holcot can now at the same time assert a doctrine, which one cannot but term Pelagian, according to which man can earn first grace and ultimately—in cooperation with grace—earn his salvation, *de potentia ordinata.*[50] The fact that God *accepts* this *facere quod in se est* as meritorious while this action as such has no intrinsic condignity or meritorious value, is expressed with the terminological differentiation between *meritum de congruo* and *meritum de condigno.*[51]

Holcot rejects the application of the potter and the clay simile of Rom. 9:21—which was so important for Bradwardine in his defense of justification by grace alone [52]—on the grounds that there is no pact or commitment binding the potter over against the clay,[53] while this is exactly the mark of God's relation with his creatures.

We may conclude that the commitment by which God in eternity obligated himself conveys to man's action a dignity which it would not have in itself: if man goes halfway, God will meet him with the gift of grace. Without this gift of grace man is *helpless;* but it is just as true that, without the full use of man's own natural powers, the offer of grace is *useless.*

When we now apply our findings with regard to the relation of free will and grace to the relation of reason and revelation we are in a position to assess the validity of the charge of scepticism. There can be little doubt that Holcot denies that man unaided by grace can with his natural reason prove the existence of God, or grasp the mysteries of the Holy Trinity and of the Incarnation. In view of the foregoing we may say that Holcot holds that man cannot reach the knowledge of faith *de condigno.* Only to this extent is Holcot a sceptic. It would perhaps be more appropriate to say that for Holcot man without revelation is subject to philosophical uncertainty and that therefore man is freed from scepticism by faith.[54] This form of scepticism, however, is not without precedent in medieval theology and can even be said to be rooted in the Augustinian tradition.[55] Holcot's emphasis on the intrinsic deficiencies of man's rational powers as compared with the confidence in natural reason on the part of Anselm, Aquinas, and Bradwardine tends to give his views an air of radicalism which places him on the left wing of the nominalistic tradition.[56]

Nevertheless, Holcot does not reject the possibility of acquiring *de congruo* the articles of faith which are necessary for salvation. Man can and therefore has to do his very best in going halfway in his search for God; thus he will receive enlightenment. Man's natural reason is *helpless* when confronted with the task of solving the mysteries of faith, but at the same time man's natural reason is the very presupposition and precondition for this enlightenment. Without man's effort to search out God with all his might, the offer of enlightenment is *useless*.

We may conclude that for Holcot the way to faith does not by-pass but presupposes the full use of natural reason. The doctrine of the *facere quod in se est* is the key to both Holcot's "scepticism" and "predestinarianism." What first seemed to be the contradictions and the inconsistencies of one who despairs of reason proves to be the reflection of the dialectic of the two powers, and the "unnecessary" but dependable commitment of God to man's serious efforts in thought and action.

III. *Theologia est celum . . . homo autem terra:* LUTHER'S EARLIEST POSITION (1509–1510)

One can contest the appropriateness of regarding the *De servo arbitrio* (1525) as representative of the young Luther. But his assertion there over against Erasmus' explicit approval of scepticism is the concise summary of his position from 1509 onward: "For the Holy Spirit is not a sceptic, nor are what he has written on our hearts our own doubts and opinions, but assertions far more certain and firm than life itself and all human experience." [57] One of Luther's chief objections to the prince of the humanists and his followers would always be that they moved in the realm of theology with the same scholarly attitude of uncommitted inquiry characteristic of and necessary in the field of philosophy, the arts, and the sciences.

This insistence on the essential difference between *scientia* and *sapientia* is not an argument especially construed to clarify a new position after the break with humanism in the mid-twenties. It can be traced back to Luther's earliest writings and perhaps best be summarized by the statement: "Smoke of the earth has never been known to lighten heaven; rather it blocks the stream of light over the earth. Theology is heaven, yes even the kingdom of heaven; man however is earth and his speculations are smoke. . . ." [58]

For the understanding of the positive and negative relation of Luther to the nominalistic tradition, the first works, the marginal comments of 1509–1510 on one volume of Augustine's *Opuscula, De Trinitate, De Civitate Dei* and Lombard's *Sentences,* are obviously of crucial importance. As is well known Luther was educated at Erfurt by such disciples of Gabriel Biel as Jodocus Trutvetter, Bartholomaeus Arnoldi of Usingen, and John Nathin. [59] Even if Luther later developed in a radically different direction, we might expect him to show here his indebtedness to the nominalistic teachers. In view of the widespread contention that Luther denies the validity of reason and constructs an even more radical contrast between reason and revelation than Occam and Biel, [60] it is proper to compare Luther with the radical Holcot rather than with the more moderate Biel. [61] The hypothesis that Luther, as *sententiarius* in 1509, is to be regarded as a nominalist is thus investigated under the most favorable conditions.

Two recent contributions to the understanding of Luther's concept of the relation of reason and revelation are particularly important for our investigation. Bernhard Lohse has paid careful attention to the young Luther in his monograph on faith and reason in Luther's theology. The lasting contribution of his study might well be that it will no longer be possible to be satisfied with the observation that for Luther reason is the whore, *Frau Hulda,* in order to prove that Luther is antirational. Lohse has further shown that the distinction between the use of reason *coram mundo* or *coram hominibus— scientia*—in contrast with its use *coram deo—sapientia*—is not adequate unless one insists that it is the same reason which operates on the levels of creation and redemption. [62]

As regards the study of Luther's sources, Bengt Hägglund has been the first to discuss in more detail the supposition that Luther is dependent on Occam and Occamism in the "divorce" of faith and reason. His conclusion is that for Occam and his disciples—in contrast with Luther—there exists an essential harmony between reason and revelation. This conclusion can be regarded as representative of the present state of scholarship. [63] Without mentioning him by name

Hägglund points out that Vignaux's separation of Holcot from the main current of nominalism cannot be maintained. Holcot's replacement of general logic by a special logic of faith does not imply the positing of the doctrine of double truth, nor does it bring Holcot closer than his fellow nominalists to Luther's thesis that theological truths are beyond the grasp of all logical speculation.[64]

If Hägglund's conclusion could be sustained, i.e., if it could be shown that nominalism operates on the presupposition of an essential harmony between reason and revelation,[65] it is possible to suggest that Luther, at least on this basic point, had, in 1509, as *sententiarius* at Erfurt, already broken with the nominalism of his philosophy and theology professors, since the only possible theme which one can discover in the series of unconnected comments on widely varying passages is the *disharmony* between faith and reason.[66] Such a conclusion, not drawn by Hägglund himself, runs counter to the present consensus of Luther scholars.[67]

In the following we want to argue that though Hägglund's thesis has to be reformulated, there is nevertheless good reason to believe that Luther at the end of 1509 has become independent of the nominalistic tradition as regards the relation of faith and reason, while retaining till 1515–1516 the doctrine of the *facere quod in se est* in its application to the relation of will and grace.

In our discussion of Holcot's position we have seen that the incompatibility of man's reason with God's revelation is not due to the fact that the articles of faith are *contrary* to reason, but to the fact that they are *beyond* the grasp of reason. Disharmony interpreted as irrationality is indeed rejected. But at the same time there is no basis for the supposition that metaphysics would provide a bridge between *scientia* and *sapientia,* as Hägglund has suggested. Metaphysics is contrasted with the authority of Holy Scripture and made responsible for the transformation of Catholics into schismatics and into unbelievers and for the change of doctors into sycophants.[68] The only bridge between the knowledge of man and the knowledge of God is the *facere quod in se est.* This is a dependable bridge insofar as it is sustained by the promises and the faithfulness of God.[69]

But this bridge should not be taken as a symbol of natural harmony between reason and faith since the range of man's rational powers falls short of the mysteries of faith. Bartholomaeus of Usingen, Luther's philosophy professor and a student of Aristotle, provides us with an illustration of how easily one is led astray on this point. He writes in his *Libellus contra Lutheranos* of 1524 that the importance of natural reason cannot be denied since it is the *rudimentum gratiae;* grace does not extinguish the light of reason but uses it as the driver uses his horse.[70] This does not imply, however, a harmonization of faith and reason but it shows the possibility and necessity of the *facere quod in se est.* Again, the bridge is not man's extension of a given natural structure, but it is erected by the intervening action of God.[71] The *facere quod in se est* allows the nominalist to posit at once the discontinuity of faith and reason and the moral and intellectual responsibility of the individual in search for God.[72]

In our presentation of Luther's relation to nominalistic theology as regards the *facere quod in se est,* we propose in lieu of the customary chronological sequence rather to take as our point of departure Luther's *Disputatio contra scholasticam theologiam* (1517), in which he clearly and openly attacks the medieval theological tradition. While this point is uncontested, it is not yet clear by what stages he arrived at the conclusions there formulated. From 1517 we shall search our way back towards the earliest evidence we have. This procedure makes it possible to avoid the usual "blind" approach to the marginals of 1509–1510 through the no-man's land between the last pertinent nominalistic sources and these first Lutheran documents.

There can be little discussion about the fact that Luther in 1517 in his *Disputatio contra scholasticam theologiam* has completely broken with those characteristic tenets of nominalistic theology which we have described above. He rejects here explicitly the doctrine of the *facere quod in se est,* as a liaison both between human will and grace and between human reason and revelation.[73] Applied to man's moral powers, this means that what precedes grace is not a disposition but indisposition and rebellion.[74] The proper disposition for the reception of grace is an effect of God's eternal election and predestination.[75] Applied to man's rational powers this means that ignorance of God is seen as a characteristic of fallen nature.[76] Aristotle does not help here; yes, one cannot become a theologian unless one breaks with Aristotle.[77] Not only syllogistic logic, but also the special logic of faith which we met with in Holcot is declared inadmissible in theology.[78] Luther sums up his conclusions with the statement: "All the works of Aristotle compare with theology as darkness with light." [79]

The 1517 disputation is not the first occasion on which Luther attacks both the moral and rational aspects of the *facere quod in se est.* When on September 25, 1516, he chairs a disputation of theses for which he himself is largely responsible,[80] one thesis is defended—the second conclusion—which states that the sinner cannot prepare himself for grace either *de congruo* or *de condigno*.[81] Inferred from this is the conclusion that the man who does what is in him—with his will or his reason—sins.[82]

This point Luther had already reached in his development while lecturing from November 1515 till September 1516 on the Epistle to the Romans. In his long exposition of Rom. 14:1 Luther designates the doctrine of the *facere quod in se est,* or rather the *fiducia* in this doctrine, as having overturned almost the whole Church.[83] Our point in citing this passage is not that it provides us with evidence of a remnant-ecclesiology.[84] Its import is rather that it assures us that in dealing with the problem of the *facere quod in se est,* we are not discussing a point which is alien to or even marginal for Luther's own frame of reference. He is explicitly and fully alerted to its significance.

In comparison with the quoted passages of the disputations of 1517 and 1516, there are two noteworthy aspects of the *scholion* to Rom. 14:1 of some months earlier. In the first place Luther restricts himself to a rejection of the *moral* implications of the *facere quod in se est*. It is only the "Pelagianism" of the will in relation to grace and not the "Pelagianism" of the reason in relation to revelation to which he addresses himself.[85] In the second place Luther leaves the impression that it is not so much the doctrine of the *facere quod in se est* as such which is objectionable, but rather its Pelagian interpretation, according to which man is able to prepare himself for the reception of grace.[86] This is a strange distinction since, as we have seen, this interpretation is the sole intention of this doctrine in the nominalistic tradition.

It is, of course, possible that Luther alludes here to the difference between the Thomistic and the nominalistic understanding of the sinner's preparation for grace.[87] In view of Luther's tendency to identify the various scholastic schools,[88] however, it is more appropriate in explanation to point to his exposition of Psalm 113:1, in the light of which the Romans passage affords us a glimpse of Luther in full transition. The Psalm passage dates most likely from the summer or fall of 1515. We reproduce this passage at length since here we find formulated in no uncertain terms Luther's adherence to and respect for the doctrine of the *facere quod in se est*. Again he discusses only that part of the doctrine which applies to the relation of will and grace; since he is silent in this context on the

relation of intellect and revelation, we shall pursue this issue separately below. But for the rest we find all the elements of the usual
nominalistic argumentation; such as that man's disposition is not
meritorious *de condigno* but *de congruo,* due to God's merciful
commitment.[89]

Thus in the period, probably as short as half a year, which lies
between the comments on Psalm 113:1 (c. 1515) and Rom. 14:1
(c. 1516), Luther has radically revised his position on a doctrine
which in 1515 he espoused but which in 1516 he attacks as responsible for perverting the Church. The fact that he attempts to
salvage the doctrine of the *facere quod in se est,* in the commentary
on the Letter to the Romans, by distinguishing between its Pelagian
interpretation and the doctrine itself is readily explained in the light
of his enthusiastic support of this doctrine so shortly before.[90] In
the slightly later disputations of 1516 and 1517, which we have discussed, this distinction has also disappeared and the doctrine is without qualifications rejected.

This investigation does not lead us to claim that we have thus
solved the riddle of the dating of Luther's *Turmerlebnis.* The discussion of this question has proved to be fruitless. The complexity
of Luther's thought makes for a plurality of levels on which his
development took place.[91] We nevertheless suggest that the search
for the occurrence of the doctrine of the *facere quod in se est* has
led us to a decisive transition between two stages in Luther's
development.

When we return now to the second aspect of the nominalistic
doctrine of the *facere quod in se est,* the relation of reason and
revelation, and investigate its place in the thought of the young
Luther, we find new evidence for the plurality of levels on which
Luther's development took place. While in the disputations of 1516
and 1517 both aspects of the *facere quod in se est* are mentioned
and rejected, we were surprised to find that in his exposition of
Rom. 14:1 Luther is silent about the relation of reason and
revelation.

This situation can be readily explained now that we know that
this exposition probably harks back to and certainly is the reversal
of his position taken in the exposition of Psalm 113:1; and in this
latter passage the *facere quod in se est* is upheld only as applied to
the relation of will and grace.

Luther's silence in 1515–1516 on the second aspect of the *facere
quod in se est* should not be taken as an implicit allegiance to it. The

best evidence for this assertion is perhaps Luther's comments on the *Collectorium* of Gabriel Biel since these were written, according to the editor Hermann Degering, in the crucial period of change under discussion, between the beginning of 1515 and the summer of 1516.[92] Luther here proves to be completely independent of Biel and highly critical of the main shape of Biel's theology. This criticism now is directed both against the relation of will and grace [93] *and* against the relation of reason and revelation as presented by Biel.[94] The fact that Luther in 1515 defines the *facere quod in se est* in a restricted sense is simply due to the fact that by that time he had already rejected the nominalistic application of this doctrine to the relation of reason and revelation. Actually we do not have evidence that he ever held it—though this is likely in view of his training—since in the first documents we possess, the marginals of 1509–1510, he has already rejected this point of view.

There can be no doubt that these marginals amply bear out Luther's repeated declaration that he belongs to the school of Occam.[95] Nevertheless, this observation proves to apply unambiguously only to the anthropology and epistemology of Occam and his school.[96]

There are various aspects of the fragmentary theology of the marginals which have in the past been designated as deviations from the nominalistic tradition, but it is fair to say that today they are not highly regarded as evidence for Luther's development.[97] Our investigation leads us to a different conclusion. When we restrict our purview to the relation of reason and revelation we note that on this point Luther derides his fellow schoolmen for their reliance on philosophy.[98] Though Luther once mentions the distinction between merits *de congruo* and *de condigno,* he refers here to actions of the will and not of the reason of man.[99] As we have seen, he will retain this distinction until his Commentary on the Psalms.

There is no trace in the marginals, however, of the *facere quod in se est* as applied to the human reason. Perhaps the most striking evidence is that the two main points in the frontal attack against the doctrine of the *facere quod in se est* in the *Disputatio contra scholasticam theologiam* (1517), which we mentioned above, are to be found in the marginals of 1509–1510: (1) the contrast between light and darkness to express the obstacle of philosophy for theology; [100] (2) the understanding of the preparation on the part of man as an effect of God's prevenient initiative.[101] The first time, then, that we encounter Luther, we find that he so stresses God's prevenience in the act of faith that there is no place any more for the nominalistic interpretation of the *fides ex auditu* as the faith man can acquire when he does what is in him.[102] For Luther *fides ex auditu* is a gift of God.

We may conclude, therefore, that Luther's statement "theology is heaven . . . but man is earth" [103] cannot be reduced to nominalistic proportions.[104] Whereas in 1515–1516 Luther finally rejects the doctrine of the *facere quod in se est* as a Pelagian reliance on the capacities of man's unaided will, we find that in 1509–1510 Luther has already discarded the other nominalistic inference from this doctrine which we encountered with Holcot, but also with Occam and Biel, as the thesis that the man who does what is in him acquires all information necessary for salvation. Not merely the "young Luther," but the "youngest Luther," even *before* beginning his career as a professor, as a biblical exegete, and eventually as a Reformer, has on points which later prove to be cornerstones in the structure of his thought become independent of the nominalistic theological tradition in which he was reared.

NOTES

[Prof. Oberman includes the citations from the primary sources to which his notes refer. Since it is not practical in a volume of this nature to reproduce these extensive Latin quotations, the interested student is referred to the apparatus in the *HThR*. The notes below are complete save for certain of these quotations.—ED.]

1. 1 Cor. 1:23; RSV. *Super Libros Sapientie* (Hagenau, 1494) [abbreviated as *Sap.*] Lect. 97 A. [Selections from these lectures are translated into English in H. A. Oberman, *Forerunners of the Reformation: The Shape of Late Medieval Thought* (New York, 1966), pp. 142–150.—ED.]

2. *Sap.* Lect. 97 B=Asclepius 41; *Corpus Hermeticum*, II, Texte établi par A. D. Nock et traduit par A. J. Festugière (Paris, 1945), pp. 352–355.

3. *Sap.* Lect. 97 B. The most radically different reading in the critical edition is that of the first sentence: "Melius, melius ominare, Asclepli;" *ed. cit.*, p. 352.

4. *Ibid.*

5. "Pater philosophorum," *De Causa Dei contra Pelagium et de virtute causarum. Opera et studio Henrici Savilii* (London, 1618), I. 1.142 C; I. 2.149 D. Cf. Heiko A. Oberman, *Archbishop Thomas Bradwardine: A Fourteenth Century Augustinian. A study of his theology in its historical context* (Utrecht, 1957), p. 24.

6. *Archbishop Thomas Bradwardine*, p. 43.

7. *Ed. cit.*, p. 273. On the connection between Holcot and de Bury, see J. de Ghellinck, "Un évêque bibliophile au XIVᵉ siècle," *Revue d'histoire ecclésiastique* 18 (1922), 495. On the long debated possibility of Holcot's authorship of the *Philobiblon* see *Philobiblon: Richard de Bury*, ed. Michael Maclagan (Oxford, 1960), pp. xxxvff. Since no clear evidence is available Maclagan

makes the plea "It seems simpler to suppose that Richard de Bury was in fact himself the author of the work which has so long borne his name; and it is certainly more agreeable to do so," *ed. cit.*, p. lxxvi. On Holcot's life and works see Beryl Smalley, "Robert Holcot O.P.," *Archivum Fratrum Praedicatorum* 26 (1956), 7–28. Cf. also "Some Latin Commentaries on the Sapiential Books in the Late Thirteenth and Early Fourteenth Centuries," *Archives d'historie doctrinale et littéraire du moyen âge,* 18 (1950–51), 117–121.

8. *De Causa Dei,* 1.6.182 A.

9. *De Causa Dei,* I. 1.2 E.

10. I. 12.200 E. Cf. I. 4.172 B; I. 9.194 C.

11. I. 2.154 C/D; I. 2.155 B; I. 2.157 B; I. 10.195 E/196 A; I. 12.201 C; I. 19.226 D.

12. I *Sent.* q. 4 art. 3 M. The edition used is *Quaestiones super quatuor libros Sententiarum* (Lyon, 1497)

13. I *Sent.* q. 4 art. 3 M. cf. ib. R.

14. C. Michalsky, "Les courants philosophiques à Oxford et à Paris pendant le xive siècle," Présenté 19 Jan. 1920, *Bulletin de l'Académie Polonaise des Sciences et des Lettres* (Cracow, 1920), p. 70; David Knowles, *The Religious Orders in England,* II (Cambridge, 1955), 80ff.

15. *Bradwardine and the Pelagians* (Cambridge, 1957), p. 216. Leff seems to qualify his judgment when he observes (p. 218): "The human intellect can, by its own powers, believe that God is the highest good. . . ." Leff has, however, misunderstood I *Sent.* q. 4 art. 3 M where Holcot categorically denies this possibility. Only when *assuming* that God exists can one show that He is to be loved above everything else.

16. "Robert Holcot," p. 82; *English Friars and Antiquity in the Early Fourteenth Century* (Oxford, 1960), pp. 183, 185f.

17. "Robert Holcot," p. 93; *English Friars,* p. 198.

18. "Holkot vertritt in der behandelten Frage einen schroffen Agnostizismus, Fideismus und Traditionalismus," *Gotteserkenntnis und Gotteslehre nach dem Englischen Dominikanertheologen Robert Holkot* (Limburg a.d. Lahn, 1953), p. 30.

19. Gordon Leff, *Gregory of Rimini: Tradition and Innovation in Fourteenth Century Thought* (Manchester, 1961), p. 19. Cf. however, Damasus Trapp: "The many among the moderni [in the 14th century] never despaired of reaching eventually universal truth; at least such a general despair has never been proved." "Clm 27034. Unchristened Nominalism and Wycliffite Realism at Prague in 1381," *Recherches de théologie ancienne et médiévale* 24 (1957), 321.

20. III *Sent.* q. 1 TT. Beryl Smalley quotes the parallel passage *Sap.* Lect. 156 A (in her numbering 157 A), "Robert Holcot," pp. 84f.; *English Friars,* Appendix I, pp. 327f.

21. Holcot refers to *De Civitate Dei* 18.28; his inclusion of Job makes it likely that instead he has in mind *De Civitate Dei* 18.47; *PL* 4.609. Cf. *Epistola* 102.2, 12; *PL* 33.374, *Epistola* 102.2, 15, and *PL* 33.376.

22. *Epistola Pelagii ad Demetriadem* 3; *PL* 30.19.

23. *De Civitate Dei* 18.47; *PL* 41.610.

24. *De Causa Dei* I. 1.74 E–76 D.

25. I *Sent.* q. 4 art. 3 Q ad7.

26. *Sap.* Lect. 28 B.

27. *Ibid.*
28. *Ibid.*
29. *Ibid.*
30. *Sap.* Lect. 28 B.
31. *Sap.* Lect. 156 A.
32. *Prol. Sap.* E.
33. *CSEL* 34.2 (Vindobonae, 1898), 697.
34. Cf. E. Gilson: ". . . la doctrine d'Augustin proclame à chaque page l'insuffisance de la philosophie." *Introduction à l'étude de Saint Augustin* (Paris, 1949), 3rd ed., p. 311.
35. *Prol. Sap.* F.
36. *Sap.* Lect. 122 A; cf. *Sap.* Lect. 82 B.
37. I *Sent.* q. I art. 6 J.
38. *Sap.* Lect. 14 B; *Sap.* Lect. 18 A. Beryl Smalley concludes: "This is real scepticism. It goes with fideism." "Robert Holcot," p. 85; *English Friars*, p. 187. To the *facere quod in se est* belongs *prudentia*, and this plays a part in missionary efforts, not as demonstration but as persuasion. Christ himself is the example. *Sap.* Lect. 197 B.
39. *Sap.* Lect. 123 A.
40. Holcot makes explicit the parallel between the problem areas of faith and reason on the one hand and will and grace on the other. *Sap.* Lect. 118 B.
41. II *Sent.* q. I U.
42. II *Sent.* q. I X; *Sap.* Lect. 79 D. See the more elaborate treatment by Bradwardine in *De Causa Dei* 1.35–1.46 and in *De Praedestinatione et Praescientia* published in *Nederlandsch Archief voor Kerkgeschiedenis* 43 (1961), 195–220.
43. *Sap.* Lect. 149 A. *Ibid.* Cf. *Sap.* Lect. 148 D.
44. "Der Grund der Prädestination liegt nur in Gott, in seinem Willen, die Prädestination ist letztlich Gnade." Alois Meissner, *Gotteserkenntnis und Gotteslehre*, p. 102. "Holkot folgt also in seiner Prädestinationslehre der allgemeinen thomistischen Ansicht," *ibid.*, p. 104.
45. RSV; *Sap.* Lect. 144 A.
46. II *Sent.* q. I D; II *Sent.* q. I CC.
47. I *Sent.* d. 41 q. I G.
48. Biel, I *Sent.* d 41 q. I art. 3 dub 3. We note also that Biel and Occam exactly like Holcot insist that nevertheless God's predestination is to be regarded as uncaused. *Ibid.* art. 2 concl. 3; Occam, *ibid.* q. I H.
49. "Necessitas coactionis nullo modo cadit in deo, necessitas vero infallibilitatis cadit in deo ex promisso suo et pacto sive lege statuta et hec non est necessitas absoluta sed necessitas consequentie. . . . Concedendo quod ex misericordia et gratia sua pro tanto quia talem legem misericorditer statuit et observat. Sed statuta lege necessario dat gratiam necessitate consequentie." *Sap.* Lect. 145 B. These two kinds of necessity reflect the distinction between the two powers. The *statuta lege* makes clear that also for Holcot God is committed to the order *de potentia ordinata*, which is therefore dependable. Cf., however, Leff, who assigns to Holcot an "extreme scepticism, which allows anything to be possible," *Bradwardine and the Pelagians*, p. 223. Though Leff has retracted some of his earlier statements he still regards the order *de potentia ordinata* as an unreliable whim of God, constantly threatened by God's *potentia absoluta:* "its [the potentia absoluta] purpose was not the emancipation of man from his limits *in*

statu isto but of God from His obligation to abide by those limits. . . ." *Gregory of Rimini*, p. 22.

50. *Sap.* Lect. 48 c.

51. ". . . opera nostra ex sua naturali bonitate non merentur vitam eternam de condigno sed de congruo tantum quia congruum est quod homini facienti secundum potentiam suam finitam deus retribuat secundum potentiam suam infinitam." *Sap.* Lect. 25 B. Cf. *Sap.* Lect. 116 B; IV *Sent.* q 1 art. 3.

52. *De Praedestinatione et Praescientia* [69], *ed. cit.*, p. 210.

53. *Sap.* Lect. 145 B.

54. *Sap.* Lect. 122 B. Cf. *Sap.* Lect. 118 A.

55. "Il n'y a pas d'augustinisme sans cette présupposition fondamentale: la vraie philosophie présuppose un acte d'adhésion à l'ordre surnaturel, qui libère la volonté de la chair par la grâce et la pensée du scepticisme par la révélation." E. Gilson, *Introduction à l'étude de Saint Augustin*, p. 311.

56. Cf. Occam: ". . . alique veritates naturaliter notae seu cognoscibiles sunt theologice, sicut quod deus est, deus est sapiens, bonus, etc. cum sint necessarie ad salutem." *Prol. Sent.* q. 1 F. Philotheus Boehner calls attention to a revealing observation by Peter of Candia: "Alii doctores quos videre potui, tenent quod talis propositio non est per se nota, sed est bene demonstrabilis. Et huius opinionis fuerunt beatus Thomas, Doctor Subtilis, Ockham, Adam (Wodham), Johannes de Ripa. . . ." Ms. Vat. lat. 1081, fol. 42 vb; *Collected Articles on Ockham*, ed. E. M. Buytaert (St. Bonaventure, 1958), p. 413.

57. *WA* 18, 605; quoted by Gordon Rupp, *The Righteousness of God, Luther Studies: A reconsideration of the character and work of Martin Luther* (London, 1953), p. 272.

58. Comment on Lombard, 1 *Sent.* d. 12 c 2; *WA* 9, 65.

59. Cf. the survey by Robert H. Fife, *The Revolt of Martin Luther* (New York, 1957), pp. 32–65.

60. See the survey of literature by Bernhard Lohse, *Ratio und Fides: Eine Untersuchung über die ratio in der Theologie Luthers* (Göttingen, 1958), pp. 7–21.

61. Paul Vignaux misses in Holcot what he finds in Occam, d'Ailly and Biel: "un dernier écho de la *fides quaerens intellectum.*" *Luther commentateur des Sentences* (Paris, 1953), p. 100.

62. *Ratio und Fides*, p. 135. Arnold Lunn explains the two aspects of Luther's understanding of the function of reason as "the conflict between Luther the Catholic and Luther the anarchist. . . ." *The Revolt Against Reason* (New York, 1951), p. 48. Though it is regrettable that the 19th century Roman Catholic Luther-image has apparently not yet completely disappeared, it should be pointed out that the difference between "Catholic reason" and "anarchist reason" is precisely the one intended by Luther when he distinguishes between reason *coram deo* and *coram mundo*. See also the appropriate comment by Roland Bainton in "Probleme der Lutherbiographie," *Lutherforschung Heute, Referate und Berichte des I. Internationalen Lutherforschungskongresses* (Aarhus, August 18–23, 1956), ed. Vilmos Vajta (Berlin, 1958), pp. 28f.

63. "Hier [in Occamism] . . . waltet eine ungestörte Harmonie zwischen Theologie und Philosophie, zwischen Glaubenserkenntnis und rationaler Erkenntnis," *Theologie und Philosophie bei Luther und in der Occamistischen Tradition: Luthers Stellung zur Theorie von der doppelten Wahrheit* (Lund, 1955), p. 40; cf. p. 86.

64. *Ibid.*, pp. 93, 53.

65. Cf. also Hägglund, "Was Luther a Nominalist," *Concordia Theological Monthly* 28 (1957), 441–452; esp. 449.

66. *WA* 9, 66: "Major est enim huius scripturae authoritas quam omnis humani ingenii capacitas." Cf. *WA* 9, 27; 9, 43; 9, 47; 9, 65; 9, 84.

67. Otto Scheel's careful analysis has been most influential, *Martin Luther: Vom Katholizismus zur Reformation*, II (Tübingen, 1930), 430ff. Herbert Rommel, *Über Luthers Randbemerkungen von 1509/10* (Kiel, 1930), esp. p. 85. Reinhold Seeberg is an exception: ". . . so wüsste nichts in den Bemerkungen zu nennen, was die Ansätze zu der evangelische Heilserkenntnis bei ihrem Urheber ausschlösse," *Lehrbuch der Dogmengeschichte*, IV. 1 (Basel, 1953), 5th ed., 72. Bernhard Lohse finds a departure from Occamism in the epistemological parallel Luther draws between reason and will, *Ratio und Fides*, p. 27. As we noted in the discussion of the *facere quod in se est* this parallel is characteristic for nominalism. See further Biel, II *Sent.* d. 27 q. 1 art. 2 concl. 4 and *Sacri canonis misse expositio* (Basel, 1515) [abbreviated Lect.] Lect. 23 F.

68. "Ita sacra scriptura omnium facultatum domina dici debet et non illa vana metaphysica quam dicta scientiarum et dominam Aristoteles vocat seu estimat. . . ." *Sap*. Prol. c. "'Hoc enim catholicos in scismaticos et infideles, et doctores in adulatores convertit. . . ." *Ibid*. D. The reference to Aristotle is an allusion to *Metaphysicorum*, Lib. I, cap. 2; *Scriptorum Graecorum Bibliotheca Arist. Opera Omnia*, II (Paris, 1850), col. 471.

69. Cf. Biel: Lect. 59 P. See also IV *Sent*. d. 9 q. 2 art. 1 nota 1 B; IV *Sent*. d. 16 q. 2 art. 3 dub. 4. The first explicit formulation of this doctrine is by Alexander of Hales: "Numquam deest facienti quod in se est ad esse gratuitum et spirituale. Facere quod in se est uti ratione per quam potest comprehendere deum esse et invocare adiutorium dei." *Sum*. II q. 129 me 8; II *Sent*. d. 22 q. 2 art. 3 dub. 1. For the first implicit statement see *Glossa ordinaria*, super Rom. 3:22, *PL* 114.480 and Ambrosiaster, *PL* 17.79. A survey of its late medieval use is found in John Altenstaig's *Vocabularius Theologie* (Hagenau, 1517), fol. 85.

70. *Libellus . . . in quo respondet confutationi fratris Egidii . . . contra Lutheranos* (Erphurdiae, 1524) fol. h 3. On the use of the image of driver and horse with Augustine and Luther, see Alfred Adam, "Die Herkunft des Lutherwortes vom menschlichen Willen als Reittier Gottes," *Luther-Jb*. 29 (1962), 25–34. This should be complemented by references to its peculiar use by Scotus, Occam and Biel; see my *Harvest of Medieval Theology* (Cambridge, Mass., 1963), Chapter VI.2.

71. Caspar Schatzgeyer, like Usingen a nominalist and one of the first opponents of Luther, is as explicit as one might wish. *Scrutinium divinae scripturae*, ed. Ulrich Schmidt, *Corpus Catholicorum* 5 (Münster i. W., 1922), 18.

72. Holcot goes even so far as to explain the geographical boundaries of the *corpus christianum* on grounds of a lack of earnestness in the search of the unbelievers. *Sap*. Lect. 28 A/B; *Sap*. Lect. 15 B; *Sap*. Lect. 145 B.

73. "Falsum et illud est, quod facere quod est in se sit removere obstacula gratie." *WA* 1, 225.

74. "Ex parte autem hominis nihil nisi indispositio, immo rebellio gratiae gratiam praecedit." *Ibid*.

75. "Optima et infallibilis ad gratiam praeparatio et unica dispositio est aeterna dei electio et praedestinatio." *Ibid*.

76. ". . . ignorantia dei et sui et boni operis est naturae semper invincibilis." *WA* 1, 226.

77. "Error est dicere: sine Aristotele non fit theologus; immo theologus non fit nisi id fiat sine Aristotele. . . ." *Ibid.*

78. "Frustra fingitur logica dei. . . . Nulla forma syllogistica tenet in terminis divinis." *Ibid.* See exactly the opposite thesis in Biel, III *Sent.* d. 7 q. 1 art. 3 dub. 1. Cf. I *Sent.* d. 5 q. 1 art. 2, 3.

79. "Breviter, totus Aristoteles ad theologiam est tenebrae ad lucem." *WA* 1, 225.

80. *WA Br.* 1, 65.

81. "Homo Dei gratia exclusa praecepta eius servare nequaquam potest, neque se vel de congruo vel de condigno ad gratiam praeparare, verum necessario sub peccato manet." *WA* 1, 147.

82. "Homo quando facit quod in se est, peccat, cum nec velle aut cogitare ex seipso possit." *WA* 1, 148.

83. "Ideo absurdissima est, et Pelagiano errori vehementer patrona, sententia usitata qua dicitur 'Facienti quod in se est, infallibiliter Deus infundit gratiam,' intelligendo per 'facere, quod in se est,' aliquid facere vel posse. Inde enim tota Ecclesia pene subversa est, videlicet huius verbi fiducia." *WA* 56, 503.

84. Thomas Bradwardine, a faithful son of the medieval Church, wrote in his preface: "Totus etenim paene mundus post Pelagium abiit in errorem." *De Causa Dei,* Praefatio, fol. 2; cf. II.31.602 D.

85. *WA* 56, 502.

86. See *WA* 56, 503, quoted above, note 83.

87. Only in his early Sentences Commentary does Thomas teach the *facere quod in se est* as sufficient disposition for the infusion of grace. II *Sent.* d. 28 q. 1 art. 4. Yet even the mature Thomas does not always avoid ambiguity. The use of the Dionysian sun-image, applied to the operation of grace, neutralizes the *auxilium gratiae.* This is the case in *Summa contra Gentiles,* III, cap. 159.

88. "Luther zag Thomas nu eenmaal door de bril van het Occamisme. Met de theologie van Thomas was hij niet voldoende vertrouwd." Maarten van Rhijn, "Kende Luther Thomas?" *NAK* 44 (1961), 156; cf. Stephanus Pfürtner, *Luther und Thomas im Gespräch* (Heidelberg, 1961), p. 52.

89. "Hinc recte dicunt Doctores, quod homini facienti quod in se est, deus infallibiliter dat gratiam, et licet non de condigno sese possit ad gratiam preparare, quia est incomparabilis, tamen bene de congruo propter promissionem istam dei et pactum misericordie. Sic pro adventu futuro promisit, 'ut iuste et sobrie et pie vivamus in hoc seculo, expectantes beatam spem' [Tit. 2:12f.]. Quia quantumvis sancte hic vixerimus, vix est dispositio et preparatio ad futuram gloriam, que revelabitur in nobis, adeo ut Apostolus dicat: 'Non sunt condigne passiones huius temporis etc.' [Rom. 8:18]. Sed bene congrue. Ideo omnia tribuit gratis et ex promissione tantum misericordie sue, licet ad hoc nos velit esse paratos quantum in nobis est." *WA* 4, 262.

90. Less radical but connected with the reevaluation of the *facere quod in se est* is another shift in Luther's thought in the same period. In his exposition of Rom. 4:7 Luther rejects the claim that the sinner can obey the commandments insofar as the substance of the act is concerned. *WA* 56, 274. Contra Biel, III *Sent.* d. 27 q. 1 art. 3 dub. 2. His earlier exposition of Ps. 68:17, however, still leaves room for this; here the distinction between the substance and quality of

an act is still employed, though used to expose sin. *WA* 3, 430. The humility
theme in the Lectures on Romans (e.g. *WA* 56, 259: ". . . a Deo iustus repu-
tatur, quia respicit humiles") is characteristic for nominalistic theology where
it appears as a refined form of the *facere quod in se est.* See Biel, Lect. 8 B; IV
Sent. d. 17 q. 2 art. 3 dub. 7.

91. See the survey by Wilhelm Link, *Das Ringen Luthers um die Freiheit
der Theologie von der Philosophie* (Munich, 1955), pp. 6–77. F. Edward
Cranz places the reorientation of Luther's thought on justice, law, and society
toward the end of 1518. *An Essay on the Development of Luther's Thought on
Justice, Law and Society* (Cambridge, Mass., 1959), pp. 41–71. Ernst Bizer
adduces convincing arguments for the thesis that the beginning of 1518, e.g.
Luther's exposition of Hebrews 7:12, marks a decisive change in his concept
of faith: *Fides ex auditu: Eine Untersuchung über die Entdeckung der Gerechtigkeit Gottes durch Martin Luther* (Neukirchen, 1958), pp. 74f. A. F. N.
Lekkerkerker's own presupposition of a single-level development—the concept
of the punishing righteousness of God—led him to charge Bizer with "terrible
onesidedness." "Notities over de rechtvaardigingsleer bij Luther en Trente," *Kerk
en Theologie* 9 (1958), p. 161.

92. *Luthers Randbemerkungen zu Gabriel Biels Collectorium in quattuor
libros sententiarum und zu dessen Sacri canonis missae expositio* (Weimar,
1933), p. XII.

93. Comment on Biel's statement: ". . . nullus peccato mortali obnoxius
habet dilectionem dei." III *Sent.* d. 27 art. 1 nota 4 G: "Si hec vera sunt, quomodo potest ex naturalibus diligere deum? An potest ex peccato mortali per se
ipsum venire? Igitur hoc vero destruuntur omnia sequentia falsa." *Ed. cit.*, p. 13.

94. Comment on Biel's statement: ". . . appetitus rationalis presupponens
iudicium intellectus. . . ." III *Sent.* d. 27 art. 1 nota 1 B: "Sed non in fide." *Ed.
cit.*, p. 12. On man before the reception of grace: "Non est intelligens, non est
requirens deum. . . ." *Ed. cit.*, p. 16.

95. "Sum enim Occamicae factionis. . . ." *Adversus execrabilem Antichristi
bullam* (1520), *WA* 6,599; *WA* 6,195; *Tr* II, Nr. 2544; *WA* 38,160 (1533).

96. E.g. *WA* 9,9; 9,33; 9,40; 9,54; 9,83; 9,91.

97. See the survey by Herbert Rommel, *Über Luthers Randbemerkungen von
1509/10* (Kiel, 1930), pp. 2ff. Rommel regards all these claims as fallacious,
ibid., p. 85.

98. Comment on Lombard's statement that God is more true than can be
conceived, I *Sent.* d. 23 c 4: "Hoc verbum olim erat verum: nunc tanta est
philosophorum subtilitas, ut etiam si verum esset, falsum esset: quia nihil est
nostris [!] incomprehensibile et ineffabile." *WA* 9,47. Cf. ". . . nostri [!]
subtiles magis quam illustres." *WA* 9,29.

99. On Lombard's observation "Hac voluntate concupiscitur. . . ." II *Sent.*
d. 26 c 8: ". . . tanquam merito de congruo, non condigno." *WA* 9,72.

100. *WA* 1,226: ". . . Totus Aristoteles ad theologiam est tenebrae ad
lucem." *WA* 9,65: ". . . nunquam est compertum fumos terrae illustrare
celum, sed magis impedire lucem super terram."

101. *WA* 1,225: ". . . praeparatio et unica dispositio est aeterna dei electio
et praedestinatio." *WA* 9,92: "Invocatio fit de fide. Unde per contrarium est
iste ordo: mittitur, praedicatur, auditur exterius. . . ."

102. Gabriel Biel, III *Sent.* d. 23 q. 2 art. 2 concl. 1. Cf. von Usingen. *Liber
Tertius* (Erphurdiae, 1524), Q Iᵛ; quoted by Nikolaus Häring, *Die Theologie*

des Erfurter Augustiner-Eremiten Bartholomaeus Arnoldi von Usingen (Limburg an der Lahn, 1939), p. 120. Cf. Holcot, 1 *Sent.* q. 1 art. 6. It is regrettable that Ernst Bizer does not start his inquiry before Luther's commentary on the Psalms; *Fides ex auditu,* pp. 15ff.

103. *WA* 9,65.

104. Nominalism has been claimed by Roman Catholic scholars as the cradle of Luther's theology. Its alleged un- or anticatholic nature would then explain Luther's "defection." See H. Denifle, *Luther and Luthertum,* 1 Abt. 2, pp. 522, 536, 587; Willem van de Pol, *Het Wereld Protestantisme* (Roermond, 1956), p. 36. Louis Bouyer, *Du Protestantisme à l'Eglise* (Paris, 1954), p. 176. Josef Lortz, *Die Reformation in Deutschland,* 1 (2 ed. Freiburg i. Breisgau, 1941), 176.

6

STEVEN E. OZMENT

Homo Viator:
Luther and Late Medieval Theology [*]

Steven E. Ozment, Assistant Professor of History and Religious Studies at Yale University, has published Homo Spiritualis: A Comparative Study of the Anthropology of Johannes Tauler, Jean Gerson and Martin Luther (1509–16) *(1969) and a Latin-English edition of selections from Jean Gerson (1969). "Homo viator: Luther and Late Medieval Theology" is an assessment of certain traditional assumptions about the originality of Luther's Reformation discovery. In both popular and scholarly treatments of this issue, it has been argued that medieval theology made the believer an uncertain pilgrim, suspended between present hope and fear of future judgment, and that Luther, having discovered the unity of God's judgment and mercy in Christ, overcame this anxious pilgrim status. Ozment maintains that this description oversimplifies both medieval and Reformation theology. Especially in the medieval mystical traditions one finds not only a reconciliation of divine judgment and mercy, but a reconciliation strikingly similar to that which supposedly characterizes the uniqueness of Luther's discovery. This suggests, on the one hand, a motive for Luther's early preoccupation with and praise of mystical writings. On the other hand, it indicates that the most important*

[*] *HThR* 62 (1969), 275–287.

distinction between Luther and medieval theology may not be found in the problem of divine judgment and mercy. Ozment argues that the decisive differences do not lie in the suspension of the pilgrim status (since Luther and medieval theology can both do that easily enough), but in the way in which that status is overcome. For the medieval theologian it could be suspended only in direct proportion to the degree to which man himself was no longer human and sinful. The medieval mystical traditions go furthest in overcoming man's pilgrim status precisely because they go furthest in "deifying" man. Luther, on the other hand, overcomes the pilgrim status "by faith alone"—a feat theologically impossible for every medieval theologian, since such faith leaves man fully human and sinful in himself.

I

DESPITE THE persistence of significant differences over the interpretation of *humilitas* in Luther's early works,[1] there is an apparent consensus on both the nature of the problem which drove him to his Reformation theology and the nature of the discovery which forms the heart of it. As the picture now comes into focus in the secondary literature, the problem Luther apparently confronted so despairingly might be summarized as the *viator*-status of Christian life within the traditional medieval *ordo salutis*.

In the order of salvation to which Luther was heir, the Christian must, in this life, remain existentially suspended between God's future judgment and a past and present exhibition of God's mercy and goodness. In the past God was merciful, sending His Son to die for sinful mankind. In the present His mercy is no less evident in the grace of the sacraments. When one looks to the future, however, the situation is somewhat changed. For this same Christ who was incarnate for man's salvation in the past and who is spiritually present to effect this salvation now will come in judgment upon all people in the future.

While the Christian can look to the past and to the present with joy and security, he can look to the future only with fear and unrest. As the traditional *locus classicus* for this existential situation put it: "nescit homo an odio vel amore dignus sit" (Eccl. 9:1). The situation can be summarized graphically as follows:

Present *misericordia Dei*   Future *iudicium Dei*
a) *Christus incarnatus*   c) *Christus Iudex*
b) *Christus in corde (gratia infusa)*

←Christian→

Hope and security   Fear and unrest

Luther's resolution of this *Anfechtung*-producing dichotomy between divine mercy and judgment is presented in contemporary scholarship as the discovery that, in Christ and in the faith which con-
forms one to Him, the mercy and the judgment of God are never
divided but simultaneously present and reconciled. Christ past, present,
and future is the judgment and the mercy of God simultaneously.
He is both crucified sinner and resurrected Lord, and the believer
who is united with Him in faith is both crucified sinner and resurrected lord. The *viator*-status of a Christian who must live between
fear-inspiring judgment and hope-creating mercy is existentially and
theologically overcome. "Judgment [= *iudicium Dei*] and righteousness [= *misericordia Dei*] occur in the *existentiell* Now of the
Word"; [2] "God sends righteousness [= *iudicium Dei*] simultaneously with peace [= *misericordia Dei*]"; [3] the gospel is the "Word
from Christ" as "judgment" and "righteousness"; [4] there is a "realized
eschatology"; [5] "the heart of the gospel [as Luther discovered] is
that the *iustitia Christi* [= *misericordia Dei*] and the *iustitia Dei*
[= *iudicium Dei*] coincide and are granted simultaneously." [6]

The variations in terminology notwithstanding, each of the above
descriptions of Luther's Reformation discovery is materially heir to
the research and conclusions of Erich Vogelsang.[7] After a thorough
analysis of the *scholia* to Psalm 70/71 of Luther's *Dictata super
Psalterium* (1513–1516), Vogelsang summarized his findings in the
following way: "God's heart is not divided: once in the past, mercy;
once in the future, wrath. No, God's will is from eternity to eternity
united and unchangeable"; "What is new lies in the fact that Luther
now says that *iudicium Dei est Christus in persona sua,* i.e., that
Christ has Himself borne the judgment, which He now executes
upon [the believer] in faith"; "Here lies the heartbeat of Luther's
doctrine of justification and his Christology: two focal points, justification and the forgiveness of sins, *iustitia et iudicium, opus proprium
et opus alienum Dei,* are held together by Christ as their midpoint." [8]

The reconciliation of the *misericordia* and the *iudicium Dei* which
is, in Vogelsang's (hermeneutical) terms, accomplished *literaliter*
or *historice* in Jesus Christ is now accomplished *moraliter* or *tropo-*

logice in the believer conformed to Him in faith.[9] Graphically sum-marized, the situation appears as follows:

Christus incarnatus (praesens, futurus)

Misericordia Dei	↑	*Iudicium Dei*
	Fides (Conformitas Christi)	

II

Assaults on the *viator*-status of Christian life are certainly not without precedent, heretical and orthodox, in the late Middle Ages. This becomes especially clear when one leaves the exegetical and scholastic medieval traditions proper and enters the domain of medieval spirituality and mysticism. Indeed, should the above inter-pretation of Luther's Reformation theology become an absolutely definitive one, then it may be possible not only to align this theology with late medieval mysticism more closely than has been done pre-viously, but also to align it with medieval mysticism at a heretofore unemphasized point: the suspension of the *viator*-status of Christian life. For, although it is only momentarily achieved (and therefore something always to be sought), the goal of the mystic (if not already the penultimate stage to it) intends nothing other than the suspension of the *viator*-status of the Christian who finds himself between God's fear-inspiring wrath and judgment and His love-inspiring mercy and goodness.

The *communio voluntatum* and *consensus in charitate,* which mark the mellifluous spirituality of Bernard of Clairvaux († 1153), are an initial case in point. In his familiar treatise, *De diligendo Deo,* Bernard presents an order of salvation which consists of four stages of love. In the first stage, man knows and loves himself alone, and only for his own sake *(diligit seipsum homo propter se).* As he be-comes aware of his inability to persist through himself alone, how-ever, man begins to seek God through faith. Although, in this second stage, man begins to know and love God, he does not do so for God's sake, but for what he can get from God *(diligit in secundo gradu Deum, sed propter se, non propter ipsum).* After prolonged worship, meditation, reading, prayer, and obedience—full participation in the life of the Church—familiarity and love of God increase to the point where God becomes an object of love for His own sake *(diligit Deum non iam propter se sed propter ipsum).* Bernard is frankly doubtful whether, in this life, man ever progresses further, to the fourth and final stage: the mystical and apparently strictly

eschatological union in which the human spirit, having lost all awareness of self, knows and loves only God and simply and solely for
God's sake *(tantum propter Deum)*.[10]

Parallel to this presentation, and something of a commentary on
it, is Bernard's distinction in the same treatise between the love of a
servant, of a mercenary, and of a son. He points out that the servant
loves and obeys because he fears the power of his lord; the mercenary,
because he knows the lord is good and will reward him. The son,
however, loves neither out of fear nor out of a desire for gain; he
loves because he finds the father to be "absolutely good" *(bonus
simpliciter)*.[11]

For Bernard, then, loving God not for one's own sake but for His
sake (loving God because He is understood to be absolutely good)
is not the ultimate stage to which the Christian aspires. Yet, even at
this penultimate point of the *ordo salutis,* fear of God's power is
effectively overcome and a form of sonship with Him established.
In via the *viator*-status of the Christian who must live between fear-
inspiring power and judgment and love-inspiring goodness and mercy
is existentially overcome: to the Christian *in charitate,* God is *bonus
simpliciter.*

A later parallel to Bernard's description is found in the work of
the Chancellor of the University of Paris and mystical theologian,
Jean Gerson († 1429). Gerson defines the mystical union, which is
in principle democratized and deeschatologized, on the model of
friendship.[12] Its chief defining characteristics are *quies, satisfactio,*
and *stabilitas* [13]—a state in which the soul, united with God as with
the One who is "most highly its good, center, goal and complete
perfection," is so sated that it neither requires nor desires anything
further.[14]

Still more relevant are the descriptions of the *unio mystica* presented by John Tauler († 1360) and Nicholas of Cusa († 1464).
Here we find the Neoplatonic concept of the divinity and simplicity
(*einvaltikeit* [Tauler], *simplicitas* [Cusa]) of infinite being developed theocentrically (Tauler) and Christocentrically (Cusa) in order
to overcome the *viator*-status of Christian life. According to Tauler,
God is not only the Being which grants and preserves the life of
created things, but also the Unity of being in which all multiplicity
and opposition are overcome. Tauler summarizes as follows:

> Let man behold the character of the pure unity of being. For
> God is infinite simplicity and in Him all multiplicity is united

and purified in a simple being. His being is His activity—His knowing, rewarding, loving, judging—all one, His mercy and His righteousness. Enter [this pure unity of being] and take your inconceivably great multiplicity therein so that He can "simplify" it in His simplified being.[15]

Despite the important terminological differences, the parallel with Luther is remarkable. In place of Luther's *Christus incarnatus* we find the simplicity of God *(einvaltikeit gottes)*, and in place of Luther's *fides* we find the *unio mystica* drawing the Christian into the simplicity of divine being where all opposition is overcome. The existential and theological result is identical with Luther's Reformation discovery as presented above: the *in via* suspension of a *viator*-status which places the Christian between the judging righteousness and the forgiving mercy of God and grants him no peace.[16] In the mystical union the mercy of God and the judging righteousness of God coincide and are granted simultaneously. Graphically represented, Tauler's position is as follows:

An almost identical picture can be found in Nicholas of Cusa. He writes: "For all divine attributes come together in God and the whole of theology is placed in a circle, so that righteousness *(iustitia)* in God is goodness *(bonitas)* and goodness righteousness. . . . All the saints who have had regard to the infinite simplicity of God agree about this." [17]

Where Cusa appears to part company with Tauler is in the Christocentric conclusion which he draws from the theocentric reconciliation of the opposition between the righteousness and the goodness of God. One enters this reconciliation of opposites only through Christ. For Cusa, to be "in Christ" means to be in the simplicity of divine being where all contrasts and oppositions—and that means the opposition between God's judging righteousness and His forgiving goodness—are overcome. The sonship which one receives through union with Christ is nothing other than placement within the simplicity of divine being.[18]

Finally, we call attention to the Christocentric application of the same Neoplatonic motif of the *coincidentia oppositorum* in divine being as presented by Bonaventura († 1274). He writes that "in Christ," who is our reconciliation with God,

> being is united with consummation, God with the man who was formed on the sixth day [Gen. 1:26], the eternal with temporal man (i.e., man who was born in the fullness of time from a Virgin), the simplest with the most complex, the most impassible with the one who suffered and died most intensively, the most perfect and immeasurable with one who is small, the most highly unified and all-embracing with a composite individual who is distinct from all others, namely, with the man Jesus Christ.[19]

And, Bonaventura continues,

> he who fully turns his face to Him who is our reconciliation, by beholding Him suspended on the cross through faith, hope, and love, and through devotion, admiration, exaltation, appreciation, praise, and joy, makes a passover with Him, i.e., a crossing, so that by the rod of the cross he may pass through the Red Sea [Exod. 12:11], out of Egypt, and into the desert, where he may taste the hidden manna [Apoc. 2:17] and rest with Christ in the tomb as if he were outwardly dead, yet still experiencing, to the extent that it is possible in this life, what was said on the cross to the thief who united himself with Christ: "today you will be with me in paradise." [Luke 23:43] [20]

III

In the medieval mystical traditions the ability, theologically and indeed Christocentrically, to overcome the *viator*-status of the Christian who must live between God's past and present mercy and His future judgment is, as we have seen, by no means absent. If there are uncompromising differences between Luther and late medieval theology, they are not to be found here.

Where, then, is the point of distinction? This point and the point of perhaps permanently irreconcilable difference is to be found not in the goal, but rather in the way in which both Luther and late medieval theology reach that goal. The difference lies in the *sola fide*.[21] And it lies here not because the *sola fide* denies the necessity of good works for salvation, for this is quite secondary, but rather because the *sola fide* suspends the *viator*-status of Christian life while at the same time leaving the Christian sinful *in re*.[22] This is a position maintained by no medieval theologian, whether scholastic or mystic, Dominican or Franciscan, Thomist or nominalist. And it is the point at which the most conciliatory Catholic ecumenist finds he must back away from Luther's Reformation.[23] For the medieval theologian, it is axiomatic that the *viator*-status of Christian life is suspended only in direct proportion to the degree to which the Christian is no longer sinful *in re*. The reason why the *viator*-status can be so completely overcome in the medieval mystical traditions is that these traditions go furthest in making man righteous and, indeed, even godly *in re*.

No opponent of Luther recognized and attacked this aspect of the *sola fide* as keenly as did the grand Dominican inquisitor of Cologne, Jacob Hochstraten († 1527).[24] In a 1526 *Disputatio*, Hochstraten cites and proceeds to refute eight Lutheran blasphemies, the first of which is thematically definitive for the entire discussion: it is blasphemous to teach that "faith alone justifies the unrighteous." [25] Why, in Hochstraten's opinion, is this a blasphemous teaching?

The answer to this question rests initially on the familiar distinction between the roles played by "faith alone" or—the same thing for Hochstraten—"unformed faith" *(fides informis)*, and by love or "faith formed by love" *(fides charitate formata)*, within the order of salvation. For Hochstraten, it is not the function of faith alone but exclusively of faith formed by love to justify the unrighteous. This is because the latter uniquely applies the passion of Christ to the whole man.[26] Taken alone, the act of faith is simply the apprehension *(assensus)* and adherence *(inhaesio)* of the mind to the articles of faith; it is correct knowledge *(recta cognitio)* of all the good things which are to be expected from God.[27] Hence, faith alone is the foundation, not the edifice: it is the "prior part of righteousness," to which the more noble part, *charitas*, is added.[28]

This, however, is not the major reason for the inadmissibility of faith alone as the agent of justification. This reason is found in the fact that, in Hochstraten's interpretation of the order of salvation, the stage of faith is a stage of insufficient self-reformation. Man is not yet absolutely cleansed of the guilt of infidelity.[29] Without the purification of the heart through *charitas* there can be neither righteousness, merit, nor eternal life.

Just as love is the gift of God by which one merits the gift of eternal life (so faith is the gift of God) by which one attains love or righteousness. Why, therefore, do we not confess that the gift of faith merits love, as love merits eternal life? The reply to this forceful question is not difficult. The man who has received faith but not yet obtained love is impious and unrighteous; he is a rebel against God in his heart, and hence he is in God's displeasure. Accordingly, he is unable to merit anything from God, for he is a debtor to Him. The situation is otherwise when love has been obtained and one is established in grace as a friend and a son of God. Then, one can, through the good works which are rewards of God, merit eternal life. . . .[30]

This critique is now applied directly to Luther's treatise *De libertate christiana* (1520). Hochstraten focuses on one of Luther's most "mystical" passages—the description of the union of the soul with Christ, as a bride with her bridegroom, "through the pledge of faith" *(per arram fidei)* [31]—as he casts a *"sola charitate"* against Luther's *"sola fide."* [32] The case against Luther is summarized as follows:

> That rash advocate [Luther] lists no preconditions for the spiritual marriage of the soul with Christ except only that we believe Christ, who promises all good things, and trust that He will bestow all the good things [He has promised]. Not a single word is said about the mutual love by which the soul loves Christ, who is love, above all things. Nor do we hear anything about the other divine commandments, to the keeper of which eternal life is both promised and owed. Now what else do those who boast of such a base spectacle [as the marriage of the soul with Christ by faith alone] do than make of the soul, which is wedded to Christ in spiritual marriage, a prostitute and adulteress, who knowingly and wittingly connives to deceive her husband and, daily committing fornication upon fornication and adultery upon adultery, makes the most chaste of men a pimp and a cowardly patron of her disgrace? As if Christ does not take the trouble to distinguish and choose, but simply assumes even the most foul bride and is unconcerned about her cleanliness to such an extent that He neither cares nor desires to make her a pure and honorable lover! As if He requires from her simply those two internal acts of believing and trusting and does not care about her righteousness and the other virtues which righteousness produces! As if, with the attainment of those two acts, He does not at all abhor her in-

volvement in other vices! As if a certain mingling of righteousness with iniquity and of Christ with Belial were possible![33]

Hochstraten's case against Luther is quite forcefully expressed here: Luther permits a foul and dirty bride to enter spiritual matrimony with Christ. When faith and trust alone are the agents of union, righteousness and iniquity intermingle and embrace. The man who is still *peccator in re* becomes one with Christ.[34]

Hochstraten's reaction to the *sola fide* represents the best medieval theological thinking. He works with very traditional tools. He understands the order of salvation in orthodox Thomistic categories; indeed, he follows the logic of Thomas's order of salvation almost verbatim.

According to Thomas, faith without love *(fides informis)* is faith which, although capable of correcting particular intellectual sins, still retains the guilt of infidelity.[35] The faith which is formed by love, however, is faith which suffers no impurity whatsoever, for love covers every fault (Prov. 10:12).[36] From within this traditional framework, Luther's *sola fide* looks very much like an effort to harvest the fruits of the *fides charitate formata* with a *fides informis*. Such an effort can be viewed only as logically contradictory and theologically blasphemous by the standards of orthodox medieval Catholicism.[37]

Although Hochstraten perceives the major theological consequence of Luther's *sola fide*, the precise nature of the *sola fide* escapes his grasp and is seriously misjudged. For unlike the traditional *fides informis*, Luther's *sola fides* is a *viva fides;* it embraces and places the whole man in Christ and frees him to serve his neighbor unmeritoriously.[38] And unlike the traditional *fides charitate formata,* Luther's *sola fides* unites the believer with God in Christ while still leaving him sinful in himself. Luther, much to Hochstraten's chagrin, suspends the *viator-status,* yet, by the standards of medieval theology, leaves the Christian very much a *viator*.

We find ourselves led to the conclusion that, from the perspective of late medieval theology, the most revolutionary aspect of Luther's theology is not the suspension, but rather the retention, of the Christian's *viator*-status. This is not meant in the sense that the Christian remains in fear and trembling about a future judgment. That aspect of the Christian's *viator*-status is as effectively overcome by Luther as it was by late medieval mysticism. It is meant, rather, in the sense that the Christian receives a full humanity, which he can in no way—substantively, generically, or accidentally—identify either with God, Christ, or the Holy Spirit. He may be one with Christ *in fide et spe,* and he may join with his neighbor *in charitate.* Yet he does both while remaining simultaneously a confessed *peccator in re.*

NOTES

1. The alternatives are defined by Ernst Bizer and Heinrich Bornkamm. See Bizer's *Fides ex auditu: Eine Untersuchung über die Entdeckung der Gerechtigkeit Gottes durch Martin Luther* (Neukirchen, 1961), pp. 29f., 31, 51. Bornkamm's reply: "Zur Frage der Iustitia Dei beim jungen Luther," I, *ARG* 52 (1961), 23f.; II, *ARG* 53 (1962), 20, 24. Recent contributions to the debate are Heiko A. Oberman, "Wir sein pettler. Hoc est verum: Bund und Gnade in der Theologie des Mittelalters und der Reformation," *ZKG* III/IV (1967), 232–252, esp. 249f., and my own study, *Homo Spiritualis: A Comparative Study of the Anthropology of Johannes Tauler, Jean Gerson and Martin Luther (1509–16)* (Leiden, 1969), 159–183.

2. Albert Brandenburg, *Gericht und Evangelium: Zur Worttheologie in Luthers erster Psalmenvorlesung* (Paderborn, 1960), p. 141.

3. Regin Prenter, *Der barmherzige Richter: Iustitia Dei passiva in Luthers Dictata super psalterium 1513–1515* (Copenhagen, 1961), p. 73.

4. Reinhard Schwarz, *Fides, Spes und Caritas beim jungen Luther* (Berlin, 1962), p. 171.

5. B. A. Gerrish, *Grace and Reason: A Study in the Theology of Luther* (Oxford, 1962), p. 126. Cf. F. Edward Cranz, "Martin Luther," in *Reformers in Profile: Advocates of Reform, 1300–1600,* ed. B. A. Gerrish (Philadelphia, 1967), pp. 95f.

6. Heiko A. Oberman, " 'Iustitia Christi' and 'Iustitia Dei': Luther and the Scholastic Doctrines of Justification," *HThR* 59 (1966), 19. Oberman's article now appears with other classical statements on the nature of Luther's Reformation discovery in *Der Durchbruch der reformatorischen Erkenntnis bei Luther. Wege der Forschung,* CXXIII (Darmstadt, 1967). Included in this collection are statements from H. Denifle, H. Grisar, E. Hirsch, E. Stracke, G. Pfeiffer, R. Prenter, A. Peters, and H. Bornkamm.

7. Oberman's technical terms, *iustitia Christi* and *iustitia Dei,* set the discussion systematically within its late medieval context but do not make a material advancement beyond Vogelsang in the interpretation of the nature of Luther's Reformation discovery.

8. Erich Vogelsang, *Die Anfänge von Luthers Christologie nach der ersten Psalmenvorlesung* (Berlin, 1929), pp. 64, 103, 119.

9. The importance of this hermeneutical combination for Luther's Reformation discovery, especially as interpreted by Gerhard Ebeling, is critically assessed by James S. Preus, "Old Testament Promissio and Luther's New Hermeneutic," *HThR* 60 (1967), 145–161.

10. *PL,* 182, 998 C–999 A; cf. *ibid.,* 991 A–B for the *deificatio* effected in the *unio mystica,* and *PL,* 183, 1125 A–B, 1126 A–B.

11. *PL,* 182, 995 C–D.

12. "Haec vero unio amantis cum amato ab Aristotile in Ethicis tangitur ubi ait: 'Amicus est alter ego,' [*Ethica,* IX, 9] cuius unionis ratio exprimi videtur cum ab eodem dicitur: 'Amicorum est idem velle et idem nolle' [*Ethica,* IX, 12;

Rhetorica, II, 4]." *De mystica theologia speculativa, cons.* 40, 104.20ff., in *Ioannis Carlerii de Gerson. De mystica theologia,* ed. André Combes (Lugano, 1958).

13. *Ibid., cons.* 42, 113.5ff.

14. *Ibid., cons.* 42, 113.14ff.

15. "Denne sehe der mensche an die eigenschaft der einiger einikeit des wesens, wan Got ist an dem lesten ende der einvaltikeit und in ime wirt alle manigvaltikeit geeiniget und einvaltig in dem einigen ein wesende. Sin wesen ist sin wurken, sin bekennen, sin lonen, sin minnen, sin richten alles ein, sin barmherzikeit, sin gerechtekeit; dar in gang und trage din unbegriffelichen grosse manigvaltikeit, das er die einvaltige in sinem ein valtigen wesende." *Die Predigten Taulers,* ed. Ferdinand Vetter (Berlin, 1910), 277, lines 14ff.

16. That significant differences between Tauler and Luther still remain despite this parallel is not denied. See *Homo Spiritualis,* pp. 44f., 197ff.

17. "Nam omnia attributa divina coincidere in Deo et totam theologiam esse in circulo positam, sic quod iustitia in Deo est bonitas et e converso . . . et in hoc concordant omnes sancti, qui ad infinitam Dei simplicitatem respexerunt." From the *Apologia doctae ignorantiae* (1449) in *Cusanus-Konkordanz,* ed. Eduard Zellinger (Munich, 1960), p. 91, §45.

18. *Ibid.,* p. 147, §85: "Filiatio igitur est ablatio omnis alteritatis et diversitatis et resolutio omnium in unum, quae est transfusio omnium unius in omnia." Cf. Ernst Hoffmann, *Nikolaus von Kues: Zwei Vorträge* (Heidelberg, 1947), pp. 51f.

19. *Itinerarium mentis in Deum,* VI, 5.

20. *Ibid.,* VII, 2.

21. In the Schmalkaldic Articles, that article over which there can be absolutely no compromise, "es falle Himel und Erden," is the *sola fide. Luthers Werke in Auswahl,* 4, *Schriften von 1529–1545,* ed. Otto Clemen (Berlin, 1959), 296f.

22. The *locus classicus* in the early Luther is the passage in the lectures on Romans: "Nunquid ergo perfecte iustus? Non, sed simul peccator et iustus; peccator re vera, sed iustus ex reputatione et promissione Dei certa, quod liberet ab illo, donec perfecte sanet. Ac per hoc sanus perfecte est in spe, in re autem peccator. . . ." *WA* 56,272.16ff. Later (Sept. 1538), Luther summarizes this situation as follows: "Quomodo concordant sanctum esse et orare pro peccato? Mira profecto res est. Es ist warlich ein fein ding. Reim da, wer reimen kan. Duo contraria in uno subiecto et in eodem puncto temporis." *WA* 39/1, 507.20ff.

23. Otto H. Pesch, Professor of Dogmatics and Ecumenical Theology at the Albertus Magnus Academy in Walberberg near Bonn, concludes: "Für [Thomas] Gottes Gnade dem Menschen nicht nur seinen sündigen Willen *verzeiht,* sondern diesen Willen selber *wandelt.* Wegen dieses gewandelten Willens, oder pointiert formuliert: wegen dieses nicht nur begnadigten, sondern begnadeten Willens kann Thomas keinen *peccator in re* zugeben." As a footnote to these words, Pesch adds: "Dann steht Thomas näher bei Paulus als Luther, denn auch Paulus kennt keinen *peccator in re." Die Theologie der Rechtfertigung bei Martin Luther und Thomas von Aquin,* in *Walberberger Studien der Albertus-Magnus-Akademie,* 4 (Mainz, 1967), 529.

24. For a brief sketch of the main issues raised by Luther's early opponents, see H. Jedin, "Wo sah die vortridentinische Kirche die Lehrdifferenzen mit

Luther," *Catholica* 2 (1967), 85–100; H. A. Oberman, "Roms erste Antwort auf Luthers 95 Thesen," *Orientierung* 20 (1967), 231ff.

25. *Iacobi Hoocostrati Disputationes contra Lutheranos*, in *Primitiae pontificiae theologorum Neerlandicorum Disputationes contra Lutherum inde ab a. 1519 usque ad a. 1526 promulgatae, Bibliotheca reformatoria Neerlandica*, III, ed. F. Pijper (The Hague, 1905), 546.

26. *Ibid.*, p. 566.

27. *Ibid.*, pp. 582, 589.

28. *Ibid.*, p. 589.

29. *Ibid.*, p. 588.

30. *Ibid.*, pp. 590–591.

31. *Ibid.*, p. 607; *WA* 7,54f.

32. "Charitas, non sola fides est, quae animam sponsi sui Christi, connubio iungit." Hochstraten, *ibid.*, p. 609; cf. pp. 593f.

33. *Ibid.*, pp. 609–610.

34. Cf. *WA* 7, 25.26ff.; 54,36ff.; 55,17ff.

35. *Summa Theologiae*, II-II[ae], q. 6, art. 2, ad 3.

36. *Ibid.*, II-II[ae], q. 7, art. 2, ad 3.

37. A. M. Landgraf argues that Thomas summarizes the position of early and high Scholasticism when he maintains that *charitas* and not *fides* is the indispensable bond between man and the mystical body of Christ. "Grundlagen für ein Verständnis der Busslehre der Früh- und Hochscholastik," *Zs. f. katholische Theologie* 45 (1927), 161–194; esp. 192–194. In this connection see Duns Scotus, I *Sent.*, dist. 17, q. 3 in *Joannis Duns Scoti opera omnia*, X, ed. Vives (Paris, 1893), 74.

38. Cf. Gerhard Ebeling, "Glaube und Liebe," in *Martin Luther: 450 Jahre Reformation* (Bad Godesberg, 1967), pp. 69ff. On the horizontal, nonmeritorious nature of Christian charity in Luther's theology, see Gustaf Wingren, *Luther on Vocation*, trans. C. C. Rasmussen (Philadelphia, 1957), pp. 37–50. It is perhaps pertinent to point out that, in his commentary on canon 9 of the decree on justification, Calvin opposed Trent's interpretation of the Reformation's *sola fides* as not being a *viva fides*. "This canon is very far from being canonical. . . . They imagine that a man is justified by faith without any movement of his own will, as if it were not with the heart that a man believeth unto righteousness." *Antidote to the Council of Trent, Calvin's Tracts*, III (Edinburgh, 1851), 151.

PART THREE

MEDIEVAL
SPIRITUALITY
AND THE
REFORMATION

7

R. R. POST

The Windesheimers after c. 1485: Confrontation with the Reformation and Humanism *

Regnerus Richardus Post (1894–1968), late Professor of Church History and the History of the Middle Ages at the Catholic University of Nijmegen, gained acclaim with his editions of primary sources and detailed historical syntheses such as Scholen en onderwijs in Nederland in de Middeleeuwen *(1954),* Kerkelijke Verhoudingen in Nederland voor de Reformatie *(1954),* Kerkgeschiedenis van Nederland in de Middeleeuwen *(1957), and, most recently,* The Modern Devotion: Confrontation with Reformation and Humanism *(1968). It is from the concluding chapter of this last work that "The Windesheimers after c. 1485: Confrontation with the Reformation and Humanism" comes. The Windesheimers, the most widespread and active of the Modern Devotionalists, represented the strictest form of late medieval monastic piety and reform. Post asks whether they can be considered genuine forerunners and allies of the Reformation and Humanism. The test case for the "confrontation" is the young Erasmus, who for some nine years knew at firsthand the educational methods and religious ideals of the* Devotio moderna. *Post gives special attention to Erasmus'* Epistola de contemptu mundi, *which he compares in style and content with other treatises on this popular*

* The Modern Devotion: Confrontation with Reformation and Humanism, in Studies in Medieval and Reformation Thought, III (E. J. Brill, Leiden, 1968), 653–680.

topic, a topic which found an audience within the brotherhouses of the Devotionalists. It is argued that Erasmus recommends the life-style and values of the Devotionalists at precisely those points where they promote scholarly freedom and leisure: "The arguments employed in recommending the monastic life are those of a Humanist." And, in larger perspective, Post maintains that the "optimism" of Erasmus and the Renaissance and the "evangelical freedom" of Luther and the Reformation are more a reaction against than a continuation of the measured "pessimism" of the Devotionalists. The confrontation reveals irreconcilable antagonism.

L IKE THE Brethren of the Common Life, the Windesheimers in this period were confronted with Humanism and with the Reformation, and various questions therefore arise to occupy the historian. Did the Windesheimers pave the way for this new phenomenon in the domain of culture, Church, and Christianity or did they foster it? Did they actively take part in it, since their ideas coincided with the new ideals and aspirations? In order to answer these questions one must form some idea of the extent of the Windesheim monastic community at the beginning of this period, when the first signs of a humanistic culture could be detected in the regions where the Windesheimers had their monasteries. These included the greater part of the northern and southern Netherlands, the Rhineland, Westphalia, and southern Germany. The farther from Windesheim the fewer the number of monasteries; the most distant were in Zürich, Basel, and Halberstadt. The influence of the Windesheimers on monasteries, however, extended far beyond those which were incorporated in the congregation, since many Regular Benedictine and Cistercian monasteries and convents also experienced the beneficial effects of their reform work. Toward the end of the century even French houses in and near Paris were affected.

The Windesheimers were not pioneers in this observant movement, nor were they alone in supporting and promoting it. In certain periods, however, and in particular regions, they may well have been the most successful leaders. Even where they were not directly involved, for example in the Observant movement of the Franciscans, Dominicans, and Augustine Hermits, the Windesheimers contributed to producing a spiritual climate which required a strict observance, and to keeping it alive.

In this way they helped to further such observantist reform movements, just as they also enjoyed the ideals which these latter orders put into practice. This may be said to constitute the sum of their outside work. They undertook no pastoral duties, had no parishes, preached only in their own monastery churches for their brethren and other persons associated with the monastery, such as the novices and *donati*. Their ascetic works, however, especially those written in the second period, reached various other people over a wide area: men or women in different monasteries, members of the clergy, and very many of the laity. In this the Windesheimers certainly surpassed the Brethren, even though their works formed only a small part of the considerable body of pious literature published toward the end of the Middle Ages and in the beginning of the sixteenth century.

The Windesheimers were directly concerned with the pastoral care of the nuns in convents belonging to the congregation, but this was the limit of their pastoral activity. They found it difficult enough to organize and maintain this work so as to care for the religious needs of the nuns without losing that monastic spirit which was so desired and considered so necessary. Life outside their own monastery and their work among the nuns could easily lead to independent comfort and superfluity, to the acquiring of personal possessions, to friendly relations with the Sisters, and to infringement of the rule of enclosure. Their exalted monastic ideals, on the other hand, which included contempt for the world, were conducive to retreat, to enclosure after the model of the Carthusians, and hence to the blocking of any channels by which they might exercise a religious influence on the world. An important factor is that they had no schools; they obtained their recruits either through personal contact, through family relations, or through the Brothers' hostels. Sometimes, however, the initiative came entirely from the boys and their parents, since the monastery and monastic life not unnaturally held a great attraction for the people.

Was there any link between the ideas, doctrinal concepts, and piety of the Windesheimers and of Lutheranism—in other words, with those of the leaders of the Reformation with whom they were first and most closely confronted? To my mind there was not sufficient similarity either in the field of dogma or of moral theology or indeed in the quality of their spiritual life, except, of course, for the fact that both were Christian. Like the Brethren, the Windesheimers did not believe in justification by faith alone, or in underestimating the value of human cooperation in the process of salvation. They accepted no certainty of faith other than that accepted by their contemporaries. They esteemed the Bible certainly, but no more than it was esteemed in other theological circles and they certainly did not rely on the spirit of the Bible alone. So far as the spiritual element is concerned, there was a considerable contrast between the spirituality of the Windesheimers and that of Luther. This is true indeed of most of the people of the late Middle Ages. The Windesheimers held the office, and the Holy Mass, in high regard. They stressed the value of a large number of prayers, despite their continued emphasis on inner prayer, on meditation and the constant awareness of the good intention. Just as Luther finally rejected observantism in his own order, and was driven to opposition by the opinions of his fellow Brothers when the rigid observantists did not help him in his moral conflicts, so must those who felt any sympathy for the new theology have viewed the Windesheimers with a critical eye. The latter may indeed have felt the attraction of Lutheran principles from time to time, but precisely because they were so opposed to the Windesheimers' own ideals and not because they resembled them.

It goes without saying that some of the hundreds of canons defected to Lutheranism, but they constituted only a tiny percentage. There were also a couple of priors who went over to the Reformers, either from a spirit of sympathy toward the new doctrine or from pure religious indifference. Some, in order to earn a living for themselves and the Brothers, may have come to an agreement with the city council whereby they received an annuity in return for handing over the monastery buildings and their incomes to the city. Among such houses were St. Leonard in Basel in 1525, Frankendaal in the Palatinate,[1] and Domus S. Christophori at Ravensberg in the Palatinate, in the archdiocese of Mainz.[2] The number, however, was so small as to be negligible.

In the sixteenth century the Windesheim monasteries experienced harmful effects from the Reformation in two ways. In the first place, several of the houses were vacated or destroyed because regional or city authorities either forbade the practice of the old religion or rendered it impossible by confiscating church property and especially that of the monasteries. In other words, the monasteries suffered the effects of violent action by the authorities or by the forces of war. Here and there they were the victims of revolutionary activities among the citizens. Second, there prevailed at this time a sort of religious malaise, a coldness toward the old foundations of the Catholic

Church. This phenomenon was apparent in an expressed contempt for monastic authority and monastic customs and in a desire for renewal in prayer, liturgy, training, novitiate, and dress. There was also a decline in the prosperity of the monasteries, coupled with an unprecedented burden of taxation and a progressive struggle against any increase of goods or property held in mortmain. Strong criticism was voiced against the ownership of land by the monasteries, land which was claimed by the nobles for their sons and, especially, for their daughters. In addition, there was aversion to the feudal rights of landed proprietors. All these developments were accompanied by a sharp drop in the number of vocations, the results of which can be clearly noted around 1540. This turning away from monastic life and criticism of monastic practices and authority led to desertion by some of the monks, either to join the Reformers or, more usually, to seek freedom in the world or become secular priests. This resulted in their forcible recapture and incarceration, widespread discontent and rebellion, and neglect of the rules concerning personal possessions, enclosure, and perhaps also celibacy. This degeneration, this decline, was surely promoted by the religious conflict, the dogmatic disputes, the attacks on the Church. It is a phenomenon which also appeared in the Lutheran church, and even among several of the first Calvinist ministers. A new era brought improvement, and various Windesheim monasteries were quick to seize the opportunity. But this section of the Modern Devotion was certainly no preparation for the Reformation, except perhaps to some degree in the negative sense—insofar as the Reformation signified a reaction against all that was inherent in the religious life of the time, and Windesheim was an important part of this religious life. Besides being a dogmatic renewal and a reaction against the relaxation of all religion, the Reformation was also a reaction against a very particular expression of religion, and one found among the Windesheimers.

The problem of the relationship between Windesheim and Humanism brings up the question: did the *Devotio moderna* promote the rise and success of Humanism in those regions where it was widespread, and if so to what extent? In using the term *Devotio moderna,* one thinks first of the Brethren, who are considered to have had a great influence on education. We have therefore discussed this question in relation to them and have arrived at a negative conclusion. Was it different with the Windesheimers? Can these, the most widespread, the most active, the most literary, and the most productive of the Modern Devotionalists be said to have fostered Humanism? Did any of their members win fame as Humanists in the first period of Humanism? Were they the pioneers of this new culture? Since they kept no Latin schools it is not possible to approach this question by way of teaching and the schools. Moreover, the first gatherings of Humanists from the Netherlands and the region of Münster took place, not among the Windesheimers or the *fraters* but in the Cistercian monastery in Aduard after 1480. These meetings were attended by rectors and teachers from the city schools and by some aristocrats, but not by Brethren of the Common Life and still less by Windesheimers. Nevertheless it was not long before individual Humanists or persons inclined toward Humanism began to emerge in the monasteries of Windesheim, as had John Veghe in Münster, James Montanus in Herford, and Massaeus in Ghent for the Brothers. One such man was from Lopsen near Leiden, a certain Cornelius Gerard or Cornelius Aurelius, a native of Gouda, from which town he derived his name Aurelius (from *aurum* = *goud* [gold], a word which was presumed to be concealed in the name of Gouda). There were also two other Canons Regular, the contemporaries Desiderius Erasmus of Rotterdam, who had spent his childhood in Gouda, and William Hermans. Both were members of the house of Stein near Gouda. This monastery was not incorporated in the congregation of Windesheim but in the small chapter of Sion near Delft. Sion subscribed to the ideas and methods of Windesheim, but remained independent. The congregation, however, can be considered as forming part of the *Devotio moderna;* it proceeded from the same spirit, just as did the many houses of the Third Order (which developed differently from the large group of Modern Devotionalists and have therefore not been dealt with in this book). Nor did the members of the congregation of Sion add anything new to the Modern Devotion.

The three men just mentioned, who worked together during Erasmus' period in the monastery and kept up a flourishing correspondence, exemplify the problem of Erasmus and the *Devotio moderna.* This is a complicated question and much literature has been devoted to it. Did Erasmus, in his formative years in Deventer and 's-Hertogenbosch, and during his first years in the monastery, come into contact with, and absorb the combination of devotion and Humanism, enriching both and deriving from them an individual outlook on life which may perhaps be characterized by the general term *philosophia Christi?* Or did Erasmus absorb the principles or the spirit of the devotion in Deventer, Zwolle, and Stein, and later add the Humanism which scarcely existed in these circles—the Humanism which entered the Netherlands as a new culture, to some extent supplementing the existing school training? Must we assume that Erasmus, by his own efforts and utilizing what he already knew from the school, assimilated the new culture, afterward developing it considerably, molding it into a coherent system of thought, the *philosophia Christi?* It might also be that what he had seen with the Brothers of Deventer, found out to his cost in 's-Hertogenbosch, and experienced somewhat reluctantly in Stein, had but little influence on him, since in all these places he retained his intellectual independence. He may indeed have assimilated the Humanistic culture, as it was revealed in the Netherlands in this period, through his own great mental efforts and exceptional talent, and he may have developed it without fusing it with the devotion which had been more or less imposed upon him in the early period. Only later would the link with Christian piety and the theological choice have occurred to him, inspired by conversations with John Colet during his nine months' stay in England (May 1499–February 1500). It is certain that he there became acquainted with a philosophical Humanism after the model of Ficino, and with a pious and learned theology. It was undoubtedly this stay in England which led him to resolve henceforward to devote his life to the study of the Bible and of theology.[3]

Not all students of Erasmus resolve the problem of his relationship to the Modern Devotion in the same manner. The whole matter indeed is rather nebulous, although some facts are certain. The school of Deventer, which Erasmus attended at least from the beginning of 1478 until far into 1483, and where he learned Latin, was not run by the Brothers. It happened, however, that one of the *fraters,* John Synthen, taught at Deventer during this period. He had a good reputation as a teacher, and despite his use of the old-fashioned grammar of Alexander de Villa Dei, was conscious of the need for improvement in the teaching of Latin. Since he taught in the *fraters'* own school, Erasmus was never one of his pupils, nor does he often mention Synthen later. There are no data to suggest that Erasmus lived in the Brothers' hostel in Deventer—in contrast to his stay in 's-Hertogenbosch, he never speaks of it. In any case he would not have fitted in, since the *fraters* really only took boys who wished to enter a monastery or become priests, neither of which vocations appealed to Erasmus at that time. Nevertheless it was in Deventer that Erasmus acquired his taste for the classics and his high opinion of the Humanistic culture—a fact which appears clearly in letters to Cornelius Gerard[4] and to an unnamed friend.[5] His feelings in this period were expressed by a desire for a better Latin, for more Latin authors to read, and by criticism amounting to a complete rejection of most of the medieval schoolbooks. This opinion he shared with most other northern Humanists in this first dawn of 1480–1500. It was probably Alexander Hegius, a prominent pupil of Rudolf Agricola, who introduced the new spirit to Deventer after his appointment as rector of the school in 1483. Although these ideals were put into practice only slowly and gradually at first, the change in the general outlook, which aroused both admiration and criticism, signified a revolution in the whole concept of education. It is therefore understandable that Erasmus held the rector Alexander Hegius in particular esteem, especially in the first years after his school days in Deventer. Later, however, his opinion changed. In 1523 Erasmus wrote in his *Spongia* that he owed little of his education to Alexander and Rudolf Agricola.[6] Apart from the fact that Erasmus left Deventer shortly after Alexander Hegius' appointment, there are other reasons for assuming that he is unlikely to have been taught by Hegius. The rector traveled a good deal, gave only a few lessons in the first class, and sometimes addressed the boys on Sundays. Erasmus, however, would presumably have heard these addresses, which would have been exhortations to love study and esteem the Latin writers.

Nothing is therefore known of any particular contact between Erasmus and the Brothers or the Modern Devotion in Deventer, although there is always the possibility that he heard the Brothers' Sunday sermon, that he received the sacraments there, and even that he chose one of the *fraters* as his spiritual adviser. The only basis for this supposition, however, is the fact that the Brothers were responsible for the pastoral care of the schoolboys. The boys, for their part, were not obliged to make use of their spiritual guidance, except insofar as they went "in crocodile" from the school to the Brotherhouse on Sunday afternoons to hear the sermon.

While the situation in Deventer is uncertain, there can be no doubt about what happened in 's-Hertogenbosch (1484–1487). There Erasmus lodged in the *fraters'* hostel, but unlike the other youthful inmates, did not attend the city school. He was thus dependent upon what he was able to learn from either of the two Brothers in charge of the hostel. He seems to have been unlucky in his masters. One of them he considered the ultimate in stupidity, while the other, in his opinion, was merely a recruiting agent for the monastery. He wrote as much in 1516 in his extremely tendentious letter to

Grunnius [7] and repeated the same view in 1528–1529.[8] Yet despite this exaggeration, his comments clearly describe the actual situation. Erasmus had been better taught, and completely surpassed his master in his knowledge of Latin. It was for this reason that he later considered the years spent in 's-Hertogenbosch as wasted. He would have liked to go to the University, but his guardians sent him to the Brothers. Is the devotion of these *fraters* likely to have had much effect upon this sensitive boy, who was completely, and rightly, convinced that he far excelled his masters in his knowledge of Latin and in his talents as a writer—who indeed despised these masters? Would he not have seen their pious exercises and the perpetual renewing of their good intention as a hindrance to the development of his talents, rather than as objects of admiration and imitation?

His sojourn with the *fraters* and his monastic life offered various possibilities for penetrating more deeply into the ideals and practices of the Modern Devotion. Did Erasmus make use of these opportunities? His frame of mind during the monastery years of 1487–1493 must be deduced from the works which he wrote at that time, notably the prose works *De contemptu mundi* and the *Antibarbari,* the verses and the letters.

In *De contemptu mundi* his aim is to persuade one of his friends, a certain Jodocus, to accept the monastic life, as he had done himself. He is well satisfied with his choice, and since he wishes others to share in this felicity he writes a treatise on the subject. He himself calls it an epistle. He hereby joins the ranks of ascetic writers, from Cassian to Dionysius the Carthusian, who have dealt with the same subject either in separate treatises or more or less incidentally in other works. These include Ambrose, Augustine, Gregory I, Peter Damian, Anselm, Bernard, Innocent III, Bonaventure, Geert Groote, Thomas à Kempis, John of Schoonhoven, Dionysius of Rickel (the Carthusian), and several others. These writers influenced one another, and it is fortunate that, after many monographs on individual authors, a comprehensive work is being compiled on the majority of them under the general title *Christianisme et valeurs humaines; A. La doctrine du mépris du monde en occident de S. Ambroise à Innocent III. B. Le thème de la dignité de l'homme au moyen âge et à la Renaissance.*[9] Two sections of Part A have appeared; they have already clarified the problem considerably and have contributed important, although of course not entirely new, information concerning the persons discussed. These works could be of great assistance to us in appreciating at their true value the *contemptus mundi* ideas of the

Modern Devotionalists, as well as the particular book by Erasmus. It is curious, however, that those responsible for this publication have drastically curtailed its scope with reference to the late Middle Ages. They no longer intend to deal with the contempt for the world of the aescetic writers, but only that of the literary ones, and even here they confine themselves to France. Was their decision to introduce this limitation inspired by a conviction that the late medieval ascetic writers—including the Modern Devotionalists—the Carthusian Dionysius of Rickel, and the Windesheimer John of Schoonhoven, have really nothing fresh to contribute to this subject? In this opinion, of course, they would not be entirely wrong, yet even if these writers dealt with the same theme in a manner not strikingly original, it would still be important to round out the general picture. It is indeed already obvious from this study that the Modern Devotionalists, and also the Carthusian Dionysius, were able to draw upon an abundant heritage from Church Fathers and medieval writers in dealing with this subject. The material was there for the taking and many will have availed themselves of it. If, therefore, in *De contemptu mundi* Erasmus sets down thoughts similar in style or content to those found in Thomas à Kempis or in other Devotionalists, this does not necessarily mean that they were borrowed. Erasmus wrote in a monastery which, while not belonging to the Windesheim congregation, was fired by similar ideals. In every monastery he visited he must have experienced something of this contempt for the world —which may have come straight to these canons from the followers of Geert Groote, but at the same time may simply be considered as the common property of the medieval monasteries. It may indeed be directly derived from or motivated by certain Bible texts; such pious expressions are not lacking in Erasmus' treatise, but they constitute only a small part compared with themes derived from literature and examples taken from antiquity.

It follows from this that Erasmus' treatise might be included among the "thèmes de la dignité de l'homme au moyen âge et à la Renaissance." In my opinion the work must be attributed to the Renaissance, but it gives no theory of the dignity of man, which in any case only evolved slowly in the Renaissance period. The Middle Ages too were aware that there were degrees in the imitation of Christ. They knew that some of the Apostles were married, while others were not, that some lived from what the faithful collected, and that the bachelor St. Paul provided for himself. Some admired Paul for this, but did not feel themselves obliged to imitate him. St. Thomas Aquinas valued human powers as natural gifts which had to be developed, and thus to some extent supplied the man of the Renaissance with the grounds for his appreciation. Was the preoccupation with the salvation of souls and love for one's fellow not a lack of appreciation of the great contempt for the world as formulated in particular by Peter Damian and his twelfth century contemporaries? They interpreted everything referred to in the New Testament by the terms "flesh," "secular," and "world," as sinful, or at least as obstacles to the love of God. In so doing they obliged themselves to make the choice: the world, or the monastery. The choice was not a difficult one in theory, but in practice to choose Christ was to be compelled to renounce the world, marriage, family ties, and all possessions, an ideal in fact which could only be realized in the monastery. Certain texts of Peter Damian and Anselm show that they wished to impose this burden of choice upon some of their relations or upon well-loved persons living in the world. They considered these losses not as deprivations but as joys, and certainly as means to acquire the greatest or heavenly joy. Thus in the practical sense the choice was extremely difficult. Only a few could bring themselves literally to leave the world, which is perhaps just as well, or how would the world carry on? In actual fact the people of the Middle Ages did not embrace this stern conclusion *en masse,* yet they were certainly not persuaded that they were past redemption and would necessarily be relegated to the Lord's left hand on the last day.

The difficulty of the dilemma as propounded led to many treatises on the *contemptus mundi,* depicting on one hand the world with its problems and dangers, and on the other the monastery with its spiritual joys. The world was a sea full of dangers—all was uncertain and short-lived. Of what significance were honor, riches, health, the family, office, when all could be lost in a moment through failure of crops, rebellion, war, or death, which is the end of all? The monastic, on the other hand, performed the service of God, was a stranger to fame and wealth, and was always prepared for death. The life hereafter was merely a continuation of his life on earth. The author needed less imagination to describe the first than the second and, as the term *contemptus mundi* indicates, devoted more attention to it. Anyone could testify to the brevity and precariousness of many things in the world, and the classical writers were in as good a position to do so as the Christians. These latter, however, were able to contribute fresh concepts: original sin and personal sin; will of God, love for God and for one's neighbor; reward and punishment; good works and merits. Jerome had already pointed out that it was not sufficient to abandon all. Had not the philosopher Crates also done this? Many others despised wealth, but one must also follow Christ, and this was the privilege of the Apostles and the faithful.[10]

It seems to me that on this point Erasmus' *De contemptu mundi* differs from the works of his predecessors, including the Netherlanders Dionysius the Carthusian and John of Schoonhoven.

John of Schoonhoven deals only with the first question, the reasons for despising the world, and not with the attractions of the monastic life. Nevertheless, in giving the five reasons why it is comparatively easy to renounce the world, the love of God recurs again and again. The five reasons are: the effort, which tires the lover of the world. He considers this effort vain, to a certain extent, unless it includes the knowledge of God. Only those who despise the world have the true knowledge of Christ.[11] The second reason for despising the world is the neglect of the better; in other words, he who chooses to love the world neglects the love of the eternal, hence the conclusion: take the way of Christ, serve Christ Jesus.[12] The third reason for fleeing the world is its vanity, which contrasts with a love for Christ and life in eternity.[13] Considering the transience of the world (fourth reason) the motto must be: follow Christ.[14] The world is a dangerous sea, and only the grace of Christ is of any avail (fifth reason),[15] so he continues: to the burdens of the world is opposed the attraction of the service of Christ. The mention of this attraction may perhaps be attributed to the fact that, in those chapters which give reasons for despising the world, the author makes no separate recommendation of the service of Christ. He has combined what Erasmus dealt with in two separate sections. This is acceptable if one remembers that for Erasmus the monastic life is attractive not because its principal aim is the service of Christ, but for completely different reasons: for the liberty, the peace, and the *voluptas* which can be found there.

The form of Erasmus' book [16] diverged from that of all preceding works. In the first place he wrote a different Latin, less flexible than that of John of Schoonhoven, but completely classical. Furthermore, he does not argue in general, but employs the form of a letter to a certain Jodocus whom he wishes to persuade to enter a monastery. This renders the question more concrete, more adapted to a particular person. It is especially evident in the introduction, but most of the true motives which are intended to lead to a decision to enter a monastery are of a general nature. In his introduction he explains how he has finally overcome his reluctance to write. He was impelled by his love for Jodocus, the necessity of the matter, their youthful friendship, common study, and affinity. He wishes to dissuade him from the noise and life of the world and lead him to the solitary and peaceful life of the monastery. He is confident that his effort will be well received by Jodocus. All sorts of dangers threaten him, which become more menacing the more he ignores them or denies their existence. He compares the dangers of the world with those of the sea and refutes a supposed remark by Jodocus. The comparison is not valid: "I feel safe on earth." Erasmus: "As a young man you do not perceive what dangers threaten you. David, Solomon, and others also suffered shipwreck. See what measures Ulysses takes to avoid being enticed by the sirens. For you, Jodocus, there is little hope, since much contributes to your downfall; your exuberant youth, seductive beauty, wealth, freedom, dreams by night, and songs by day. All this is endangered by the rocks, Charybdis, Syrtes; favourable and unfavourable winds, storms." Erasmus does not mean that the monks are saved while all others perish, but that he who loves danger will perish in it (Chap. II). "Seek therefore the safest way. As Virgil has already said, men are blind to such dangers. The world holds many attractions for you, but look to the example of Ulysses. What could the world give you?" (Col. 1243). "Wealth? But the Holy Scriptures call this the root of all desires (theft, sacrilege, robbery). *Incestus:* see what Flaccus Horatius has to say on this subject, and how Eutrapelus renounced everything." Again he quotes a text from Horace and an example from antiquity, Vultreius. It seems that no one is satisfied with what he has, but always desires more, just as a dropsical man is always thirsty. But if the wheel of fortune spins, you are no longer a Croesus but an Irus, as has happened with many kings. But even assuming that your fortune stays constant, when you die you will have to leave it to another. Here he quotes the words of our Lord: *Matth.* 6:19-20. "Lay not up for yourselves treasures upon earth, where moth and rust doth corrupt and where thieves break through and steal: but lay up for yourselves treasures in heaven, where neither moth nor rust doth corrupt and where thieves do not break through nor steal."

He ends the third chapter: it is very scandalous for a Christian man to seek along evil paths for that which endangers his salvation—something which it was not difficult for even the pagan philosophers to despise on account of their learning and fame.

The fourth chapter deals with the theme: the pleasures of the flesh are deadly and bitter. Erasmus proves the first by referring to Plato and the (almost Christian) *ethici* like Cicero and Cato, who spoke on the basis of what they had learned from Pythagoras. Erasmus considers this pleasure a foolish joy. Compare it with the eternal punishments. But, you will say: I am thinking of a lawful marriage. Erasmus is unwilling to condemn this: *Melius est nubere quam uri.* Marriage is not evil, but it is unfortunate. A celibate life undertaken out of love for *pietas* is much better and in many respects much happier.

In the fifth chapter Erasmus points out that honor is vain and uncertain. All the applause of followers means nothing, but even the honor which comes from the practice of virtue is uncertain. Consider Sisyphus who is condemned to roll a rock uphill forever. Hear what Juvenal says. And then death threatens! Where are the former tyrants? Where are Alexander, Paulus Aemilius, Julius, Pompey, where the princes of Greece, Rome, or of the Barbarians? He introduces Alexander, who laments and says that all his fame has passed away. "What use to me now are the marks of honour, the gilded monuments, the laboriously constructed pyramids?"

Erasmus devotes a separate chapter to the necessity of death, which renders everything short-lived (Chapter VI). He introduces this well-known fact, which is given so little thought, with Cicero's words and with a verse from Horace. Jodocus defends himself by saying: "I am still young, why should I trouble myself?" which provides Erasmus with material for the argument that many die extremely young or in middle age, and frequently just as they are on the verge of some important undertaking, for instance, marriage. In conclusion Erasmus refers to the seer (Vates) who says: "Dispone domui tuae, morieris enim," and to the Gospel: "Stulte, hac nocte animam tuam a te tollent et ista quae parasti cuius erunt?" The words of Rudolf Agricola, "omnia mors sternit, quod naturae est occidit. Una fine caret virtus, et bene facta manent" (Death fells all and kills everything born; only virtue has no end and good deeds remain), give Erasmus the opportunity to describe the thoughts of a person on his deathbed: Where is my wealth gone? Where my beauty? It is then that the uses of virtue appear.

That the world is unfortunate and evil is the theme of the seventh chapter. That it is unhappy is already evident from the many wars and calamities which Erasmus has already experienced, though he is not yet twenty-four (his birthday fell at the end of October, 1493). Everything is so dear that one would need to be a Croesus to pay. This thought is clarified by a choice of texts. The world is not only unhappy but also evil, full of perjury, deception, robbery. It is thus that St. Paul says: "Totus mundus in maligno positus est." Jodocus, who evidently had means at his disposal, runs great moral danger in drinking bouts and gatherings. Hence the advice to flee the world.

With the eighth chapter begins the second and positive section of the work, which is roughly the same length as the first, negative section. To the evil, unhappy, and ephemeral world is contrasted the good, happy monastery, directly concerned with attaining the permanence of heaven.

The eighth chapter is a warm, ardent, and utterly convinced exhortation to Jodocus to decide now and quickly to enter a monastery. He mentions the service of God, which is so different from the service of the devil. The monastic places his faith in the word of our Lord· "Take My yoke upon you and you shall find rest for your soul, for My yoke is sweet and My burden light." According to Erasmus the monastic life possesses three qualities which elevate it above the life in the world: it is free, it is peaceful, and it has its "pleasure," *voluptas*. He elaborates the first in Chapter IX by refuting an objection based upon a definition of liberty given by Cicero: "Freedom consists in the power to live as one wishes." In the monastery, however, one may do nothing without the consent of the abbot, not even cough. Erasmus refutes this remark simply, but not very convincingly. The monk wishes for nothing that is not permitted, therefore he may do everything that he pleases. The remainder of his argument merely describes the lack of freedom in the world (authorities, married partners, passions, habits) without dealing in more detail with freedom in the monastery.

Chapter X bears the title: those who retire from the world *(solitarii)* enjoy a double peace, outward and inward. The first is the freedom from the noise and bustle of the world, which Erasmus skillfully describes. According to Biblical and profane history, those who are accustomed to lead withdraw from the cities to mountains, caves, lonely or quiet places. Thus did Moses, John the Baptist, Christ, three Apostles, Pythagoras, Plato. A line from the philosopher Crates leads Erasmus to see in this withdrawal the danger of laziness or crime.

Erasmus considers inner peace important, but he scarcely pauses to describe it. Again he confines himself to proving that the people in the world, whose evil ways he assumes, are deprived of this inward peace, since they are tormented by various fears. Here he refers to a text of Juvenal and to the example of Orestes, from the fables, to Lucius Sylla from Roman history and Cain from Biblical history.

The monk need not fear either the human judge or God. He has his treasure in heaven, the thought of which imparts a great sense of peace. The monastery makes the bad good and the good better. The world, on the other hand, makes evildoers of the good and rogues of evildoers.

Chapter XI is taken up with the "pleasure" of the monastic life. This was originally the last chapter. It is strange that Erasmus employs the term "voluptas" for the joys of the monastic life and that he defines these pleasures with reference to the ideas of Epicurus. He may have done so under the influence of Laurentius Valla, whose works he was already studying or had studied. Those in the world hate the monasteries, since they consider life there to be horrible, inhuman, and devoid of all pleasures. According to Erasmus it is nothing of the sort, so that he would dare to invite all Sardanapalici to learn to know our joys. Epicurus himself thinks that one must not accept pleasures if the difficulty of attaining them is too great. In any case we [in the monastery] renounce various worldly pleasures— unchastity, drunkenness—for they bring more difficulties than joys. So it is with us. We keep vigil, we rest, we keep silence in order that we may be spared greater pains. We do not drink to the point of drunkenness, we do not dance, we do not go where our fancy impels us, but anything we lack we receive again with interest. Our pleasures far surpass those which resemble those of the animals. We renounce the pleasures of the body, receiving instead those of the soul (this is essentially the same as what Epicurus advises). The contemplation of the heavenly and immortal pleasures for which we hope already surpasses the pleasures of the body which the worldling esteems so highly. It is true that here we receive only a small foretaste of the joys of heaven, but this is so great that we gladly abandon all other pleasures for their sake. Here Erasmus mentions the rapture of the mystics to which contemplation can lead. He himself has not yet received this gift, but he has often heard those so privileged confess with tears that worldly pleasures signified nothing in comparison with what they had experienced. Erasmus then describes the parting meal of a certain Margaretha, whom he loved as a sister. Here he shows his talent in capturing such little scenes. He went to lend his assistance in persuading the girl's father to give his consent. They succeeded, but at the end they were all, except Margaretha, crying like children, as if she were on the point of being laid in the grave. Well, Erasmus concludes, the joys which the parents offered Margaretha could not have been overcome, had not greater joys awaited her in the convent.

Finally he quotes St. Jerome, who says that in the desert he felt the joys of Rome, even the presence of the choirs of angels. That is the supreme *voluptas*. For the scholar there is, in addition, the opportunity for the *studia sacra,* the time and the library where the following books are to be found: books of the Old and New Testaments; the Fathers Jerome, Augustine, Ambrose, Cyprian; the Christian Cicero, Lactantius Firmianus, and for those who desire a more sober repast, St. Thomas and St. Albert the Great. There too he will find various commentaries on the Holy Scriptures, and writings by philosophers and poets. You are completely free to use these as you will, and you have also at your disposition a park, a garden, delightful for walking in and musing. He therefore urges Jodocus to enter the monastery.

In an epilogue Erasmus briefly summarizes his argument, urgently repeats his message to Jodocus, and attempts to clear up his last difficulties.

Erasmus first published the book in 1521. But in two editions of 1523 he added a twelfth chapter, which is so different that he now proposes that Jodocus can best achieve the monastic ideal by living in the world. Suffice it to say that Erasmus strongly advises Jodocus against entering a monastery, for the monasteries have completely changed. They are no longer the places where a pure Christianity is practiced, but where fugitives from the world often give themselves up to all kinds of sin and attempt to satisfy their own desires.

Erasmus' *De contemptu mundi* follows the pattern of previous works on the same subject to the extent that, like his predecessors, he speaks of the dangers of the world, of the vanity of honors and fame, of the precariousness and uncertainty of possessions, and of the brevity of all in the face of certain death which can cut down the young and healthy without warning. He does not, however, define exactly which human qualities or spiritual possessions are threatened by the dangers he depicts. He seems to have been referring especially to human virtues, and thus this work is an expression of Erasmus' moralism. There is no mention of any threat to man's belief or faith in God or attachment to the Church. Where this work does diverge completely from earlier, similar ones is in the fact that Erasmus derives many of his examples and illustrative texts from classical antiquity.

The second section is the weaker and at the same time the more distinctive, for the arguments employed in recommending the monastic life are those of a Humanist. The monastery offers freedom and tranquillity, not for introspection, meditation, or prayer, but for study, of the classics as well as of the Bible and the Fathers. These last are mentioned even before the medieval theologians. The joys of the monastic life are described according to the views of Epicurus. Erasmus is, however, convinced that mystical rapture can constitute the greatest happiness of the monk, the highest peak attainable in this world of which meditation is a foretaste. Even the hope of gaining this privilege is such a great joy that it compensates for all the deprivations. Here Erasmus' description touches the monastic life itself, which is more than can be said for his eulogies of freedom and tranquillity. In this connection he devotes more attention to the lack of liberty, the noise and clamor in the world, and to the inner distraction of the worldling. No matter how much he urges Jodocus to choose the monastic life, there is no attempt to describe this life. He gives scarcely one religious motive for entering; the love of God or of one's neighbor is not mentioned, nor is there any question of monastic virtues such as obedience, humility, poverty. He ignores the devotional exercises, such as the hours, singing, the Holy Mass, and the holding of the chapter. It is as though he is entirely oblivious to all this, and his whole day is devoted to his Latin and his Latin histories. One can detect few characteristic traits of the Modern Devotion. The flight from the world and the eulogy on monastic life are commonplaces in the Middle Ages. Erasmus' innovation is his motivation from the classics.

Plato and Cicero are religious authorities for him. In the classics and in the Bible Erasmus feels the presence of those who wrote them. According to Kohls this was the basis of his program—back to the sources—and of his zeal for the study of the classical languages.[17]

There is, however, no trace of the Humanistic praise of the world, condemnation of the *contemptus mundi,* or glorification of human powers the development of which contributes not only to joy in this world and to the progress of civilization, but even to the attainment of man's supernatural goal. In the eyes of Erasmus, human intellectual activity is a virtue, but not of more value than humility and mortification.

At about this same time Erasmus must have been working on

his *Antibarbarorum liber*,[18] which seems to have been almost completed shortly after his departure from Stein but which, like the previous work, was not published until later (1521). In a conversation among four gentlemen, the new practice of Latin and poetry among the Dutch Humanists is defended against the attacks of ignorant schoolmasters and magistrates, various members of the mendicant orders, and the theologians. His criticism of the schools and teachers is sharp, sharper than that of the other groups. All opponents are donkeys and ignorant clods. The Humanists defend themselves by rejecting any accusation of heresy and by referring to history, for it appears that Augustine, Jerome, Lactantius, and Ambrose are on their side. There is thus, in Erasmus' opinion, no conflict between his Humanism and Christianity, between erudition and knowledge. On the contrary, the old culture had prepared for Christianity and has now made it young again. But we have no certainty about the text of 1493.[19]

There is also a trace of this fusion in Erasmus' poems.[20] Like many other Humanists, Erasmus began his humanistic career, if one may call it such, as a poet, and it was as a poet that he experienced "for the first time the joy of seeing himself in print." [21] As a poet he obtained admission to Gaguin and Faustus Andrelini, and as such he was received and honored for the first time in England. During the first year of his monastic life, 1487–1488, he celebrated profane subjects, but in 1489 his attitude changed.[22] Probably at the urging of Cornelius Aurelius, Erasmus resolved henceforward to sing only the praises of the saints and of sanctity. Huizinga considered this statement to be a spontaneous youthful pious resolve.[23] C. Reedijk on the other hand thinks that it "has a ring of sincerity, but it remains difficult to establish to what extent Erasmus was subconsciously seeking both protection and justification under the banner of piety for purely aesthetic ambitions." [24] For the most part Erasmus kept to this resolution, notably in the monastic years which ended in 1493–1494. Since he made this resolution either at the urging of Cornelius Aurelius, the Canon Regular of the Windesheim monastery of Lopsen near Leiden, or following his example, this change of heart might be attributed to the influence of the *Devotio moderna*. William Hermans, who lived in the same monastery as did Erasmus, also sang the praises of the saints and of holy things. It was certainly the expression of a pious mentality, but this did not exist only among the Modern Devotionalists. It may be considered as a general late-medieval attitude of mind. As early as 1489 Erasmus had composed a poem in which he had laid down the requirements of a truly Christian humanistic poetry:

> Huc si quem pia, si pudica musa
> Delectat; nihil hic vel inquinatum
> Vel quod melle nocens tegat venenum
> Christum tota sonat chelis guielmi.[25]

It is the pious, pure muse which pleases, not uncleanness; and nothing which conceals the hurtful poison with honey; Christ is the object of praise. According to Reedijk a similar attitude is also apparent from other texts: "Here we have a strong reaction against those who maintain that literary refinement cannot but endanger Christianity and that a clumsy style is a guarantee of impeccable piety." Here Erasmus takes very much the same attitude as Gaguin.[26] Pure poetry is not necessarily a vehicle for impure and godless thought; bad Latin is not a guarantee of true piety; one can praise God and at the same time aspire to a classic purity of form.[27]

Erasmus' correspondence with his friends does not treat of the life in the monastery, but rather of the school program, the training which he and his friends enjoyed in Deventer, the unsuitable school books in use there which all ought to be discarded; the best authors, the eventual dangers associated with the reading of some of them, the value of these for molding their own style, the modern Italians like Valla and Poggio.[28] For these first Dutch Humanists, the purity and elegance of Latin and the form of prose and poetry are the burning questions of the day, the essence of the new culture, and the subject of conflict between old and new. It was a struggle for the schools. Teaching too thus came under discussion, but only insofar as the Humanists insisted on suitable, easy-to-use grammars, adapted to the children's needs, and reliable dictionaries. This is the full extent of the preoccupation with teaching in their letters. They make no mention of training the boys to be upright young men, or to the practice of the Christian virtues. Later, however, Erasmus went further in his *Antibarbari*,[29] but only after he had made contact with the English Humanists in 1499, and particularly with John Colet. The transition took place gradually and erratically and was never complete. There was no violent crisis and no road to Damascus. "For many a long year yet, without our being able to reproach him with hypocrisy, Erasmus can play the litterateur or the theologian at will

and as it best suits him." [30] Reedijk, too, notes a development. Up
to this time it was Erasmus' dearest wish to be a poet among his
peers, but just as his poetry gradually makes way for the prose writer,
so "literature for its own sake lost his interest." [31] His didactical
ambitions are the first to be roused, the *Familiarum colloquiorum
formulae, De conscribendis epistolis,* and similar works begin to take
shape, although they will not appear in print for some years to
come. His defective knowledge of Greek must be improved, theology
begins to attract him, even if this attraction is not primarily due to
the lectures at the Sorbonne. The poet is on the way to becoming
one of the most original thinkers of the Renaissance era.

With Erasmus, however, the impulse for this transition had to
come from outside. This impulse he received in England. Huizinga
explains it clearly. In all the years preceding the first journey to
England, a worldly way of thinking which only leaves him in moments of sickness or weariness can be detected in Erasmus' writings,
and especially in his letters. Colet's words and example were the first
to transform Erasmus' inclination toward theological studies into a
firm and lasting resolve, a life purpose.[32] A more penetrating study
of the Holy Scriptures leads him to his *philosophia Christi* as the
basis for his view of life. This emerges for the first time clearly
in his *Enchiridion militis Christiani.* It is more than the "Reform"
depicted by Paul Mestwerdt: "Reform which at least did not
stand in contradiction to Erasmus' customary humanistic literary
interests." [33] On the contrary, humanistic literary interests constitute
the best means of arriving at the desired reform. This reform embraces theology in the first place, Bible study methods and hence a
simpler dogmatic, ethic, devotion, liturgy, and spirituality. Mestwerdt
finds it difficult to abandon the theory of the influence of the Modern
Devotion upon Humanism and Erasmus, since he still believes that all
schools in cities where the Brothers had their houses were actually
run by the Brethren. But this was so only in isolated cases and certainly not in Deventer and 's-Hertogenbosch, where Erasmus lived or
went to school.

On the other hand Cornelius Gerard or Aurelius (i.e. from Gouda),
who corresponded with Erasmus from 1489 onward, was a person
well known in the circles of the Modern Devotionalists. There are
indications that he attended school in Deventer and knew Erasmus
there. In any case he was a relative of William Hermans who had
certainly gone to school in Deventer, at which time he became
friendly with Erasmus. They met again in the monastery of Stein,

both Canons Regular of this monastery which belonged to the Sion chapter, and both fired with similar humanistic ideals. It appears that Cornelius Gerard too had been in a monastery, in Hieronymusdal or Lopsen near Leiden. He left it in 1497 in order to join others in reforming the abbey of St. Victor in Paris, an activity in which Erasmus took a lively interest and in fact visited his friend there. When it became apparent that the goal was not achieved, Cornelius Aurelius returned to his monastery, after having first described the catalogue of the abbey. (This work is now lost, but became known about forty years later from Rabelais' *burlesque catalogue*.) He wrote Latin verses *(Alphabeticum Redemptorum,* and *Mariad),* and received the poet's crown from Emperor Maximilian I in 1508.[34] Cornelius Aurelius was deeply interested in the history of the Netherlands and wrote the following historical works: *Defensio gloriae Batavinae, Elucidarium Variarum quaestionum super Batavina regione et differentia, Die cronycke van Hollandt-Zeelandt ende Vrisland,* the so-called *divisie-kroniek.*[35] The fact that he wrote this last in the vernacular is extremely significant for a Dutch Humanist in this early period. In his *Apocalipsis Adriani VI,*[36] written after the election of this pope who was a native of Utrecht (1522–1523), he shows a certain predilection for the pure Gospel and a critical attitude toward conditions existing in the Church. Among other things he disapproved of Church benefices being given to uneducated persons. The *Conflictus Thaliae et Barbarei,* usually attributed to Erasmus, may also be his work. It is indeed found under the name of Aurelius in the library of the canon Jan van Der Haer, who was transferred to the court of Holland in 1531.[37] Cornelius Aurelius had much earlier lost all contact with Erasmus. He died after 1523 (perhaps in 1529).[38]

Cornelius' cousin, the older William Hermans or Goudanus, a fellow student of Erasmus in Deventer and his fellow Brother in the monastery at Stein, joined Erasmus in studying Latin and ancient history in the monastery. Apart from his historical interests—he wrote the *Hollandiae Gelriaeque Bellum* 1507–1510—he also shared Erasmus' love for Latin verse. But his friendship with Erasmus was not based solely on their similar ideals; there was also a close personal relationship. William was childishly hurt by Erasmus' sudden departure from Stein, but the correspondence continued. Together they wrote: *Certamen Erasmi atque Guilielmi de tempore vernali, quod per viridantia prata alternis ex tempore luserunt anno eorum decimo nono* (i.e. 1487). Erasmus made William Hermans one of the participants in the conversation at Halsteren in defense of the new culture, later published as the *Antibarbarorum Liber,* and visited him at Stein in 1496–1497. He took away with him the *Silva odarum,* which he published in Paris on January 20, 1497, with an introductory letter he had succeeded in obtaining from Gaguin. However, as Erasmus' circle of friends grew wider his relationship with William Hermans cooled off. Hermans died in 1510.[39]

C. Reedijk has compiled a list of Dutch Humanists who flourished between 1520 and 1540. To this might be added a preceding generation from around 1480 (or 1485) to 1520. We should then see that with the exception of Erasmus and the cousins Cornelius and William, it contained no names which could conceivably be linked with the Modern Devotion as it had then developed. Georgius Macropedius, who entered the Brotherhouse in 's-Hertogenbosch in 1502 and whom we have already mentioned, would certainly find a place on it,[40] but Humanists associated with and proceeding from the foundations of the Modern Devotion are very few in number.

In the case of Erasmus and William Hermans the concept "Modern Devotion" must be very loosely interpreted. Erasmus had no further connection with the Brothers after his departure from 's-Hertogenbosch. They are scarcely mentioned in his letters, in fact one could almost count the references on the fingers of one hand. Apart from the well-known attacks in his autobiographical letters of 1516 and 1524 [41] and the statement made in 1517 that they in no way resemble Jerome, whose name they often bear,[42] there are only three instances. On December 18 Gerard Listrius, the recently appointed rector of the Zwolle school, wrote that the prior of St. Agnietenberg had openly declared himself a supporter of Erasmus, and that John Koeckman, rector of the Brotherhouse at Zwolle, sent greetings to Erasmus.[43] In addition John Goswin of Halen, rector of the Brotherhouse of Groningen, conveyed a letter and present to Erasmus in 1521, in the name of William Frederiks, parish priest of St. Martin in Groningen. He also carried back Erasmus' letter of thanks to the parish priest.[44] Finally, Conrad Goclinus, attached to the trilingual college of Louvain, informed Erasmus that according to current rumors Theodore of Heze, a former assistant of Pope Adrian VI, had, after a thorough investigation, ordered all Erasmus' books to be removed from the hands of the pupils of their school, which was the principal school in Liège (August 28, 1530).[45]

One must not take it for granted that everyone who showed any signs of piety at the end of the Middle Ages, or who was assumed to be devout, belonged to the Modern Devotion, or that any pupil from the schools of Deventer or Zwolle who achieved something in later life was a product of the Brothers.

GENERAL CONCLUSIONS

Geert Groote, the founder of the Modern Devotion, reveals himself in his letters as a very erudite and extremely active man, preoccupied with various questions of the day, a dauntless preacher with a rigoristic turn of mind. The later *Vitae* have a tendency to forget his academic work, making him a simple monastic or an ascetic, a somewhat scrupulous and rather small-minded *frater* who is an example of what the author of the *Vita* himself considers to be the most exalted attitude to life. Groote's three foundations, the Brethren and Sisters of the Common Life and the congregation of Windesheim, continued his work, but only up to a certain point. The Brothers were the closest to him. Some of the earliest of them preached in the parish churches, but lacked their master's élan. Soon they confined their attentions to two groups, the schoolboys and the Sisters, and undoubtedly the first group had their especial affection. From beginning to end, in all the places where the Brothers settled, they devoted themselves to the schoolboys. Some they admitted to their hostels, a privileged group whom they prepared for the monastic life and for the priesthood. It was from these that they drew most of their recruits. Apart from providing them with board and lodging, they attempted to train them in religious matters and help them with their studies, supplementing and going over the lessons which these boys received at the city schools. Until about 1480 this was the limit of their work as teachers. Around this time, however, their attitude changed, probably as a result of the menacing competition from the printing houses, which to a large extent rendered the copying of books impractical. Until this time they had devoted the greater part of the day to copying, with three purposes in mind: to earn their living by their own work, to have a change from their pious exercises, and to further the distribution of religious literature. Some of the Brotherhouses even started printing themselves, while others sought to expand their educational activities, but neither of these undertakings was entirely successful. Only in a few towns (Liège, Utrecht, and Trèves) did the Brothers' school flourish, and then due to favorable circumstances beyond their control. Even in these towns they lacked enough well-trained teachers of their own. Several attempts to found schools had to be abandoned because of civic ordinances against the schools, and their printing houses were no match for the competition. The schools would in fact be the only means by which the Brothers might have fostered Humanism in the early period. Since these educational institutions were not completely under their control, however, their influence on the origins and development of this new culture was negligible.

The flourishing schools of Liège, Utrecht, and Trèves already mentioned were indeed run in the humanistic spirit, but they were too late to count as pioneers. Since the Brothers did not attend universities, they were completely outside the academic world and accordingly their theological training was not of the slightest significance. Academics like John Pupper [von Goch], Wessel Gansfort, and Gabriel Biel cannot in fact be considered as exceptions to this general rule. The first was a secular priest, and the second was only on friendly terms with the Devotionalists—he acquired his learning in circles far removed from them. His ascetic writings agree with those of some of the Devotionalists, but more with those of the Windesheimers than the Brothers. Gabriel Biel entered the Brotherhood only after he had already received his academic training, i.e. as an adult man who had already been a preacher in the cathedral. Those houses he did live in, moreover, had a somewhat peculiar character. The members of his Brotherhouses were canons and formed chapters, while retaining the communal life and community of possessions. From 1440 onward this form had been recommended from Rome to all the Brothers and most of the German houses and several in the Netherlands adopted it in the course of time; those of Deventer, Zwolle, Doesburg, and others, however, did not. This new method facilitated the transition to the secular state, as happened in Delft and Doesburg before the Reformation. If the Brothers cannot be called pioneers of Humanism, still less can they be considered as having furthered the Reformation. Admittedly the inmates of a couple of houses did go over to Lutheranism, more or less under compulsion, but nearly everywhere else they opposed this new doctrine and perished on that account in many German cities. In general they ceased to attract the young people and in the sixteenth century they declined, so that it was easy to commandeer their houses for use as seminaries. In some places the Brothers' communities survived the Reformation. Apart from their pastoral work among the schoolboys and the Sisters, they derive their historical importance from their inner devotion, which they had in common with the Sisters and the Windesheimers, and they converted many outsiders by their example.

From the very beginning the Sisters of the Common Life, who

received their special character only c. 1392, attracted many young girls. The rapidity with which their various foundations sprang into existence is very striking, as is also the number of members they comprised, many more than the Brotherhouses had. However, with the exception of a few houses, particularly in the Yssel region, they had already changed in character around 1400. Most of the houses adopted the Third Rule of St. Francis and became incorporated in a separate union, the chapter of Utrecht. It is remarkable to note in this connection that several friends and adherents of Geert Groote promoted this aspiration to the monastic life. The Brothers too did not entirely escape this trend. Throughout the entire century, however, the Sisters displayed a desire for a stricter life, so that several groups, having adopted the Order of St. Francis, went on to take that of St. Augustine, afterwards demanding the "enclosure" after the model of the Carthusians.

The Windesheimers, the congregation (or chapter) of houses of Canons Regular, with the rule of St. Augustine, owed their existence to the Brothers insofar as the latter, on the advice of Geert Groote, founded a monastery at Windesheim three years after his death. This was quickly followed by others. The first fact of importance is the rapid spread of their monasteries over a wide terrain, which recalls the great orders of the previous century, although several existing monasteries also joined this congregation. Evidently general opinion was still more in favor of the monastic life, in preference to communities without vows. Their especial character consisted in the strict observance of the rule and the custom they had adopted. They were thus in sympathy with the move toward observantism, which to some extent characterized the monastic life of the time. This was largely a reaction against what had gone before, and against what was customary in many institutions in that period. The desire for an *artior vita,* a stricter life, which we have noted among the Sisters, also motivated these Canons Regular, who attempted to introduce it as much as possible, and often indeed by force, into other monasteries and even other orders. In this work they often obtained the support of the civil authorities. No particular influence on Humanism or the Reformation has ever been attributed to the Windesheimers, except, with regard to the latter, in a negative sense. Observantism could lead to what is called legalism and thus provoke a reaction from Luther, helping to render his doctrine acceptable.

All these groups practiced what they called inner devotion. It is from this that their name is derived. By this they understood, in general, deep consciousness of the personal relationship with God and a perpetual and intensive striving to direct all their work, prayer, and spiritual exercises to God. This presupposes, however, the practice of the virtues of humility, obedience, purity, mutual love, and mortification out of love of God. With two of the Windesheimers this latter was intensified to an exalted mysticism, a "contemplation" of God, insofar as this was possible in this world. The imitation of Christ helps us to make progress along this road, hence the constant meditation on Christ's life and passion. In the beginning this meditation consisted of a brief reflection, repeated several times during the day whenever a new activity was embarked upon. But it developed with Wessel and Mombaer into a complicated system of meditation methods designed to focus the mind on the desired subject. This more resembles meditation in the modern sense. The *fraters*, Sisters, and Windesheimers attempted to put these religious ideals into practice. In addition, they described them in various treatises of which one, the *Imitation of Christ* by the Canon Regular Thomas à Kempis, has achieved world renown.

Their emphasis upon "inward fervor, conscious inner devotion" did not, however, lead these Modern Devotionalists to reject or criticize the oral prayers such as the hours, the rosary, the psalms, and vigils. They also held the Holy Mass in high esteem, although they strove, through their inward meditation, to prevent these exercises from becoming too formalistic. "It is our highest duty to meditate on the life of Christ" (Cor. I:1.1).

In all this they made use of the traditional Christian heritage which they collected in their *rapiaria*, without imparting to it any new character, unless by the intensity of their experience. Their devotion was modern only in the manner in which they put it into practice, reacting against the prevailing spirit of relaxation. In this way the Devotionalists brought a most necessary renewal to a wide area. They may indeed have propagated the *contemptus mundi* over too wide a field, permeating religious life with a pessimism against which the optimism of the Renaissance and the evangelical freedom of the Reformation came as a reaction.

NOTES

1. J. G. R. Acquoy, *Het Klooster te Windesheim en zijn invloed*, III (Utrecht, 1880), 168.
2. *Ibid.*, p. 173.
3. J. Huizinga, *Erasmus*, German trans. by Werner Kaegi (Basel, 1936), pp. 38–44.
4. P. S. Allen, *Opus Epistolarum Desiderii Erasmi Roterodami*, I (Oxford, 1906), 23, lines 60, 95.

5. *Ibid.*, I, 31, lines 37, 48.
6. Leclerc, ed., *Lugduni Batavorum* (Leiden, 1703; repr. 1963) X 1666, A.
7. Allen, II, 295–296.
8. *Lugduni Batavorum*, I, 921.
9. R. Bultot, IV: Le XIe siècle, *Hermann de Reichenau, Roger de Caen, Anselme de Canterbury*, 2 (Louvain and Paris, 1963).
10. Hieronymus, *Liber 3 in Mattheus*, chap. 19.
11. Albert Cruys, *Jean de Schoonhoven, De contemptu huius mundi* (Brussels, 1963), p. 51; *Jean de Schoonhoven* (Nimègue, 1967).
12. *Ibid.*, p. 55.
13. *Ibid.*, p. 56.
14. *Ibid.*, p. 63.
15. *Ibid.*, p. 65.
16. *Lugduni Batavorum*, V, 1239–1262.
17. E. W. Kohls, *Die Theologie des Erasmus*, I (Basel, 1966), 30–32.
18. *Opera omnia*, X, 1261–1744. A. Hyma has found a manuscript at Gouda that probably goes back to the first version of Erasmus. He has edited this in *The Youth of Erasmus* (Ann Arbor, 1930), pp. 229–331. It is not entirely clear how far Erasmus revised the first text in 1520.
19. Kohls, pp. 35–68.
20. C. Reedijk, *The Poems of Desiderius Erasmus* (diss. Leiden, 1956).
21. *Ibid.*, p. 61.
22. *Ibid.*, pp. 54, 58.
23. Huizinga, p. 43.
24. Reedijk, p. 58.
25. *Ibid.*, p. 56.
26. *Ibid.*, p. 58.
27. *Ibid.*, p. 9.
28. Allen, I, nos. 1–40.
29. Kohls, pp. 68–198.
30. Huizinga, p. 42.
31. Reedijk, pp. 62–63.
32. Huizinga, p. 43.
33. P. Mestwerdt, *Die Anfänge des Erasmus, Humanismus und "Devotio Moderna"* (Leipzig, 1917), p. 303; see Kohls, pp. 68–198.
34. Reedijk, p. 50.
35. J. Romein, *Geschiedenis van de Noord-Nederlandsche geschiedschryving in de middeleeuwen* (Haarlem, 1932), p. 208,
36. C. Burmannum, ed. (Ultrajecti, 1727), pp. 270–273.
37. M. E. Kronenberg, "Werken van Cornelius Aurelius in the library of canon Mr. Jan Dircsen van Der Haer," *Het Boek* 36 (1963), 69–79.
38. P. C. Molhuysen, Cornelius Aurelius in *Nederl. archief voor Kerkgeschiedenis*, nieuwe serie II (1903), 1–35 and IV (1907), 54–73.
39. Reedijk, pp. 54–57. Romein, p. 206.
40. *Analecta Gysberti Coeverincx*, II, 115.
41. Allen, *Opus epistolarum* II, no. 447, 295.
42. 16 September (1517), Allen, III, no. 665, 91.
43. Allen, II, no. 504, 422.
44. Allen, IV, no. 1200, 483.
45. Allen, IX, no. 2369, 17, r. 33–40.

8

ALEXANDRE KOYRE

Paracelsus *

[TRANSLATED BY JANET COLEMAN]

Alexandre Koyré (1894–1964), late Professor of History and Philosophy at the Ecole Pratique des Hautes Etudes in Paris and member of the Institute for Advanced Studies at Princeton, wrote prolifically in the history of philosophy, religion, and science. In the English-speaking world he is most widely known through his Discovering Plato *(1945),* From the Closed World to the Infinite Universe *(1957), and* Newtonian Studies *(1965). His biographical sketch of Paracelsus, which first appeared in 1933, comes from an earlier period of research on such kindred thinkers as Jacob Boehme (1929), Valentin Weigel (1930), Caspar Schwenckfeld (1932), and Sebastian Franck (1932). Koyré introduces Paracelsus to the reader with the (still recurring) question: was he a "profound scholar" or simply a "superstitious quack," a precocious precursor of the modern world or an unrepentant child of the occult and aberrant practices of the Middle Ages? It is a question of assessment which might well be asked about the sixteenth century as a whole, and, in a certain sense, that is exactly what Koyré does. He takes the measure of the sixteenth century by examining the world of ideas in which one of its most impassioned connoisseurs lived. The conclusions reached reveal how sixteenth century theology, theosophy, astrology, and alchemy—the full range of*

* *Mystiques, Spirituels, Alchemistes: Schwenckfeld, Seb. Franck, Weigel, Paracelse* (Paris, 1955), pp. 45–80. Reprinted from *Revue d'histoire et de philosophie religieuses* (1933).

the occult—when expertly interpreted by one with the talents of Paracelsus, produced a vision of man and his world which was as eminently sensible and humane as it was strange and provocative.

I N HIS TIME—a time so curious, so alive, so passionate—there were few men whose work had a more lasting effect or an influence which provoked more heated battles than the work and personality of Theophraste Paracelsus, or, as he sometimes called himself, Aureolus Theophrastus Bombastus Paracelsus,[1] doctor of medicine, doctor of theology, doctor *utriusque iuris*. Few men knew admiration so great and hostility so implacable as this disconcerting personality. And there are few men about whose work and thought we are so poorly informed.[2]

Who was this genial vagabond? A profound scholar whose battle against Aristotelian physics and classical medicine had laid the foundation for modern experimental medicine? A precursor of nineteenth century rational science? An erudite, affable physician? Or was he an ignorant charlatan, a superstitious quack, an astrologer, magician, and maker of gold? Was he one of the greatest minds of the Renaissance or simply a belated heir to medieval mysticism? "A Gothic remnant," a pantheistic cabalist, an adept of vague stoicizing Neoplatonism and natural magic, or on the contrary, "the doctor," the man who, in offering himself to suffering humanity, would have found and formulated a new conception of life, the universe, man, and God?[3] A profoundly Christian mind, which, in the solitude of the Swiss mountains, would have attempted a "reformation" and preached an evangelical religion without a clergy, without dogma and rites? Or, in the end, a Christian who, despite all his frequently heterodox or even heretical opinions, would remain faithful to his church and would have finally preferred Catholicism to the new Protestant churches?

One can find all these views in the enormous body of literature on Paracelsus—without counting the writings of theosophists and occultists of every kind, who see in him one of the greatest masters, one of the adepts of the secret knowledge, and look for a way to demonstrate the identity of his teachings with that of the "sages of India." The one thing missing is a precise and patient analysis of his ideas, of the world in which he lived, and of the world of ideas of which his thought was a part.

Obviously, in the few pages of this monograph we do not pretend to supply what is needed; we will only attempt a quick sketch of his *Weltanschauung*. So we will avoid emphasizing sources and influences, and only establish links and parallels as much as seems profitable.[4]

Since we are tackling the study of a way of thinking which is no longer our own, as a great historian has admirably shown, what is most difficult and necessary for us is not so much to learn what is not known and what the thinker in question knew, as it is to forget what we do know or believe we know. Sometimes it is necessary not only to forget the truths which have become integral parts of our own thought, but in fact to adopt certain modes and categories of reasoning, or, at least, certain metaphysical principles, which, for the people of a past age, were as valuable and as sure bases of reasoning and research as are for us the principles of mathematical physics and the fundamentals of astronomy.[5]

It is in forgetting this indispensable precaution and in seeking "precursors"[6] of our actual thought in Paracelsus and the thinkers of his epoch, in asking them questions about which they never thought nor sought responses, that one comes, we believe, to misunderstand their work profoundly and to lock them into dilemmas which, though contradictory for us, were perhaps not so for them.[7]

We asked above if Paracelsus was one kind of man or another. It seems he was neither, or if one prefers, both. Most certainly, he was profoundly influenced by the hylozoist naturalism and magic of the Renaissance and, most certainly, he was a devotee of German mysticism. He vigorously fought the medical science of his time and proclaimed the value and necessity of "experience." But the experience he praised so much had absolutely nothing in common with experience as we understand it today. He opposed alchemy and astrology,[8] but not because he did not believe in the influence of the stars or in the possibility of creating gold. Very much to the contrary, the influence of the stars was for him something as sure and indubitable as the life of the world. Moreover, it was the sole means of explaining rationally the production and propagation of epidemic illnesses. As for the transmutation of metals, how, as a disciple of Trithemius, could he doubt its possibility, he who had himself worked in the Fugger mines and seen how "metals grow and develop"?[9]

Alchemy and astrology, with their key-concepts of *Tinctur (tinc-*

tura) and *Gestirn (astrum)*, were the very bases of his science, the science of medicine, the two pillars which supported the edifice of *philosophia sagax.* We are not surprised by it. Paracelsus was a man of his time and epoch. Everyone then believed in the transmutation of metals, as well as in the influence of the stars; in our opinion, indeed, it was perfectly reasonable to believe these things at the time.[10] Paracelsus proved his critical acumen, however, by allowing the influence of the stars to explain only the most massive phenomena, such as epidemics. Those who refused to recognize any astral influence were not necessarily ahead of their time—in retrospect they had good sense, but for their time they were not truly scientific. Criticism of providential astrology rested on theological reasoning, on the idea of free will, on considerations concerning the identity of the place and hour of birth of diverse people, i.e. on commonplaces, repeated to the point of surfeit since antiquity.[11] Paracelsus, in fact, admitted the soundness of all this.

Theophrastus Bombastus was not very scholarly; nothing in his writings nor in his biography permits us to suppose that he was imbued with the bookish science of his time. Of course, he had studied; he had even been received as a medical doctor at Verona,[12] but he does not seem to have gone beyond this. In his professorship, as in his practice, he is an "empiricist." He himself said that what was clearest in his learning was derived from those old women, half-sorceresses, whom he met along the way, or from popular practices, traditional recipes, the ways of village barbers, laboratory methods used by miners and gold and silver smelters. He truly was a *chyrurgus*, a man of practice, of the trade, not a man of study. And it was not so much out of patriotism or modern conviction that in the course of his writing he abandoned Latin [13] and used a Germanic dialect. The simple explanation is that he could not do otherwise. Those who listened to him and followed him did not know enough Latin.

Paracelsus is one of the most curious phenomena in the history of thought: an abundant fantasy, even superabundant, a passion to know, and a passionate curiosity for the world and concrete reality. Living reality was inherent in his genius—a barbarous genius, but genius just the same—and the dissolution of medieval science had, for him more than for any of his contemporaries, provoked a renaissance and revivification of the most primitive superstitions. Part of what he teaches is only folklore decorated with bizarre names, names which, with a childish and naïve joy, he invents for every occasion (and even beyond the occasion) and to which he gives "Latin" and "Greek" roots and endings.[14] He delights in being able to oppose the scholarly terminology of his slanderers and rivals with an even more amazing terminology.[15]

The spirits of the Renaissance and of the Reformation were united in his soul. But it was not the spirit of the literary and scholarly Renaissance nor that of the theological Reformation. Instead the unity was that of the popular soul of the era. There was a perpetual restlessness which never allowed him to remain in one place, and we always see him as a traveler and vagabond. We see the quarrelsome, aggressive, and boastful humor,[16] the impassioned curiosity. He wants to see all, to know all—magic, astronomy, theology, the world and its people. He wants to know all the diversities of human creatures, to know the universe, man, the king and lord of creation. He wishes to learn everything, but not through books, not dead wisdom, the dated ideas of official scholars, the doctors with pointed hats. It is in the world, in reality, in life and nature that he wants to seek his lessons and his masters.

And do they not see that these doctors with their official hats know nothing, are saddled asses who only speak of Avicenna and Rhasis, of humors, and of qualities? They lounge in their professorships and wrap themselves in long cloaks. They do their business by attaching themselves to pharmacists, prescribing costly and complex remedies,[17] extorting money from poor people. Do they alone know how to cure? No! They do not have the cure. Do they alone know what nature is and how one uses its forces? No! The primitive peasant—what am I saying?—a dog knows more about the cures of nature than they. It knows that nature has wisely disposed specific remedies for all illnesses and that one must only know how and when to use them. These self-styled doctors are only heretics and infidels. By their remedies they want to dominate nature and do not know that nature cures herself, that the doctor's highest duty, his only duty, is to aid in the battle against sickness, to be an ally of life, not its master.

Life and Nature—these are the grand themes of Paracelsist philosophy, as well as of all Renaissance philosophy: life and nature, or even "life-nature," since nature is life and life is the deepest essence of nature.[18] The world is living, in all of its parts, small and great, and there is nothing in it which is not alive: stones, stars, metals, air, and fire. This stream spreads and divides into isolated multiple currents. The currents meet again, battle, struggle with one another, and everything proceeds from the same single source, and eventually loses itself in the same ocean of life.

It is not in books nor in the doctrines of classical philosophers that Paracelsus had learned his "feeling for nature." It is not Stoicism, nor the Cabala, nor the Neoplatonism of the Florentine Academy which were the sources of his "philosophy." It is not in Pico della Mirandola, Reuchlin, or Agrippa of Nettesheim that he sought its elements, although certainly he used all the readings, traditions, doctrines, in developing his world image. It was especially from within himself, as in fact was the case for the entire Renaissance, that he found the view of the world which haunted him.

For Paracelsus, and in this he is only a child of his time, nature is neither a system of laws nor a system of bodies ruled by laws. Nature, this vital and magical power which ceaselessly creates, produces, and casts her children into the world! Nature is able to do anything, for she is all, and all that happens and that is created in the world is nature and is produced by nature.[19] Nature is comparable to man, to the gushing interior spring, which causes thoughts, desires, and images to surge upward in our soul. Now our desires and thoughts, in profoundly differing from one another and battling against one another in the soul, are nevertheless all produced by her. Everything bears her mark, all contribute to the soul, and yet these different parts are not nature. In precisely the same way living beings—and all beings are such—are "natural products," "children" of a single and unique vital and magical power which is present everywhere in each "product," and yet is none of them.

We believe it was not speculative reasoning which led Paracelsus to his magical panvitalism, any more than was this the case for most of his contemporaries. On the contrary, it was the exuberant life whose pulsations they felt within themselves; it was the new attitude toward this life, which, alone among all the disorder and the collapse of institutions, doctrines, and beliefs, in spite of everything and against everything, maintained its power and vitality. It made them seek speculative arguments in order to base, in reason, what was above all only an attitude of the mind. An attitude of the mind—or was it of the soul?—which was not opposed to the world but lived with it, which *felt* kinship with it, which above all viewed itself as part of the world, of the universe, and which, even in opposing itself to this world with which it was connected, could not forget the vital links which attached it to the world. In other words, this was

an attitude of a soul which lived more than it thought, and lived as
much in the body as in the mind.[20]

Speculative arguments are not missing if one takes the trouble to
look for them. One has only to use the venerable principle of argument by analogy in a vitalistic sense. For, by proceeding according to
good logic from the known to the unknown,[21] one arrives at the
no less ancient nor less venerable doctrine of man as a microcosm,[22]
the center, image, and representative of the world. He is the book
which contains and wherein one reads the secrets and marvels of the
macrocosm or *macranthropos*.[23]

From this point of view one has only to recover the classical doctrine of man as the image and likeness of God. For, in arguing by
analogy, one forms a coherent image of the universe, the visible
body of the invisible spirit, a tangible expression of immaterial
powers.[24] Indeed, how does one know something to which one is a
complete and perfect stranger? Does not to know mean to assimilate?
Does it not become in a way identical with the object or with the
person one wants to know? Here, again, tradition agreed perfectly
with popular wisdom: no one could understand what he himself had
not experienced. No one could understand another if he could not,
to a certain extent, identify himself with him and revive within himself the other's feelings, put himself in his place and feel in the
way he feels. There is no knowledge without sympathy and no sympathy without similitude. Like knows like. It is by what is within us
that we can know what is similar outside ourselves.

Man understands everything,[25] the sensible and material world, the
stars, and God. Therefore, he must have within himself these parts—
the constitutive elements—which correspond to the three stages of
the universe: the material universe, the astral universe, and God.[26]
Then, in fact, man is threefold: composed of body, soul, and mind
(esprit). He is a true microcosm as Scripture itself affirms. Is it not
said, in effect, that man was created from the mud of the earth, and
is it not evident that, by this word "earth," Genesis means the
world and the entire universe?[27] So man, in reality, occupies a
privileged position; he is, says Scripture, created in the image and
likeness of divinity. He is also created in the image and likeness of
the world. And, if one looks more closely, one will see that the image
and likeness of God is none other than the mind, while the soul
and body represent the universe from which they were made. They
correspond quite exactly. It is possible to establish a precise link
between the components of the human organism and the organism

of the world. One can determine the human organs to which the planets correspond, since it is evident that the planets and constellations play the same role in the universe that the internal organs play in the human organism. Just as one set rules and directs the movement of the universe, so the other rules and directs life, development, and even the growth and death of the individual.[28]

We must not forget, however, that everything in this world is twofold: on the one hand, visible and tangible and, on the other, invisible and intangible.[29] Thus, in man there is (for the moment passing over the mind) the invisible soul, which governs, directs, and inhabits the visible and tangible body. It is the same for the universe. Behind this universe of bodies, this visible and tangible world of the earth and heavens, there is an invisible and intangible entity: *Gestirn* or *Astrum,* which plays the same role in regard to the universe that the soul plays in regard to the body. We must go further. The *Astrum,* the *Gestirn,* is, in effect, the world soul which inhabits, directs,[30] and leads the universe, and which is expressed in the position of the "stars," just as the human soul is expressed or expresses its interior states by the intermediary of its body. Therefore, it is the body of the universe that we see, just as it is the body of our fellow men that we perceive through our exterior senses. Now, while perceiving the body we "read" the soul—which is expressed by this body—because the entire universe is but a book we can "read" and which "expresses" the astral reality. Moreover, what we have just established for man and the universe is everywhere, for each part of the universe reproduces and reflects the initial structure of all things. Thus, in all these bodies—even the inert ones, the elements, stones, metals—we must admit the existence of an invisible "soul" which is expressed by the material bodies. Moreover, it is evident that all bodies, like the entire universe, are constructed and maintained by powers whose material bodies and exterior phenomena are only "bodies," "dwellings," "expressions."

But it is not necessary in this doctrine in which everything exterior is an image *(Gleichniss)* to see in the material world only an image,[31] only a symbol without its own reality, without power and real existence. The world and the bodies in it are not pure symbols or images. Paracelsus is no idealist. Very much to the contrary, the relation of the bodily expression to the power or essence expressed necessarily exposes the reality of both terms. It is true that this implies and entails a new complication in the conception of the Paracelsist world. The action of the stars on earth and on us operates in two ways: first,

there are the stars—bodies which act on our bodies as they act on
all bodies of the universe. Then there is the human soul which,
insofar as it can be, is influenced by the *Astrum,* i.e. by the "soul" of
the stars, by the incorporeal *Gestirn.*

This influence is exerted in a double sense. On one side, the human
soul sustains the influence of the *Astrum* and, when it frees itself a
little from the bonds of the body, it proceeds to "create fictions"
with the world soul and through marvelous dreams,[32] which occur
especially, though not uniquely, during sleep. There is, on the other
side, the inverse influence of the human soul, which in its own
activity can influence the world soul, can "suggest" to it ideas and
dreams. The world soul then thinks and imagines them itself, and
in thinking and imagining them, realizes them in the world. In this
way, the human soul can command the stars, direct events, and can,
with assistance, produce or cause to be produced new beings.[33]

We have just said that Paracelsus is no idealist. So little is he an
idealist that, for him, this relation of the soul to its body or "house," [34]
the exterior habitation of an interior power (principle), is an absolutely general relation. There is no exterior without an interior,
no body without soul, but also, no soul without a body, no interior
without an exterior. There is no expression without sense, but also
no sense or thought without expression. The notion of an incorporeal
mind, of a disembodied mind, seems absurd to him and, in fact,
the double perspective of Paracelsus—that of vital dynamism like
that of expression *(signatura)* [35]—makes embodiment appear an absolute necessity. In fact, the soul, being at once a magical power and
a thought, a center of power and a center of conscience, or rather a
center of "power-conscience," evidently cannot *not* produce itself,
cannot *not* act, cannot *not* express itself. A center of power evidently
cannot not possess a "point which is itself," a region where it exercises itself freely and where it would be at home. This home, this
region of domination *(Haus),* this domain where the "being-power"
lives, serves at the same time as a point of departure, as a means of
action *ad extra,* and as the "stuff" in and by which the soul is expressed—*this* is the body, the first "product" of the soul.

These are the considerations or analogues which lead Paracelsus
once again to divide the three "essences" [36] which comprise his
world.[37] The material body is perishable; it disappears. But, at least,
the human soul endures; it needs a body—an astral body, of course.
And how could the mind, which is eternal, be without a spiritual
body? [38] On the contrary, the animated body, the human body, no

longer is content to have a soul as its dynamic center. It receives its spiritual double: the corporeal mind. And so the Paracelsist world becomes more and more complex, and the old fantasies, the old popular stories, the experiences—do not forget that in the sixteenth century magic was a science and apparitions were experiences—still come to enrich it. One must explain it all; one must give an account of prophetic dreams and of houses haunted by apparitions of the magical action of the will, of the fact that one can communicate at a distance, and that roses covered with dew, freshly cut in Valence, have been brought to Berne in full winter.

Paracelsus does not embarrass himself for so little. Nor did anyone in his generation, Porta or Telesio no more than Agrippa or Trithemius. Actually, all is possible, for nothing can surpass the creative and productive power of nature. So how could one doubt the possibility of a fact? [39]

Very seriously—and quoting well-known examples—he explains to us that things happen in a very simple way, that there is no reason to be astonished and to believe in a miracle or in a diabolical act. The physical body disintegrates in the tomb. But, even for the physical body, it is still necessary that its elements return unto chaos. In the same way, the corporeal mind [40] endures for a certain length of time after death, and it is completely natural that this mind, which was in a sense the motor of the body (subordinated to the soul), continues to operate for some time, but by inertia, by habit. Therefore it haunts the places where its body had lived, carries out semblances of gestures that it executed during its life, and returns to the treasure that it kept secret. But it is not necessary to believe that this shadow *(Schatten)* possesses anything other than the shadow of life. The *larvae* are only semblances, only floating images of past life, a habit which took on a body, or, to be more exact, which preserved a semblance of body. The soul is no longer there, and thus, these semblances have neither power nor will nor conscience. Everything else, on the other hand, is the *evestrum*—the astral body of the soul, or the soul provided with its astral body. This being, as a power and a center of action and thought, can act, determine physical actions, and also act directly on souls (without using the physical mode). And this *evestrum* brings news and allows the true *magi* to communicate with one another. We know that Agrippa of Nettesheim taught something similar.

Moreover, the *magi* have other means at their disposal. Indeed, let us not forget that all elements are inhabited and, in fact, there is no reason why life could not create subordinate centers elsewhere than on the earth's surface or in the depths of the waters. There is no reason why beings, evidently less perfect than man,[41] could not build their bodies with elements other than those which constitute men and animals. If Paracelsus said otherwise it would be absolutely contrary to the philosophy he accepted. In fact, visible elements such as the earth, water, and fire, are not elements, properly speaking. They are only, as we have already said, the bodies of the true elements; not their materials but their dynamics.[42] Now since the four elements come from one, why is it that what is possible in one would not be possible in another? Moreover, experience itself proves it: everyone knows that there are nymphs in the water and gnomes on land, just as there are elves in the element air. True science should not deny the established facts; it should explain them.[43] Sound philosophy then, shows that gnomes, salamanders, and elves are not beings comparable to man, as too often they are believed to be. They are mono-elemental beings. There are others which are embodied in two elements, that is, whose body is made up of two physical elements. The magicians, then, use these spirits or elementary beings, which one must be careful not to confuse with demons. Demons are fallen angels, while natural spirits have, as we have just seen, a wholly different nature. They have not sinned; they are not therefore damned. But they will not be saved and will have no part in immortality. It is unnecessary to fear them like demons, but one must mistrust them. They like to play tricks on men. They can, on the other hand, reveal important secrets, for the most elevated ones, at least, thoroughly know the properties of their element. But it is complete foolishness to want to use necromancy and, among other things, to seek to receive revelations about the world beyond the grave from the spirits of the dead. We have already seen that the *larvae,* those who come back, know nothing. They do not even think but respond mechanically, except in the case where a demon takes possession of their body-semblance in order to ensnare those who indulge in these deplorable practices.

Of all these "spirits" one must carefully distinguish among those that man himself—or rather his will and faith (or what is approximately the same thing, his imagination) [44]—creates and produces. In fact, we already know that the soul is a center of life, a magical power (an ardent fire, says Paracelsus).[45] It is also a center of conscience, thought, and particularly of will.

The will of the soul, which is a power, acts first on its own body.

It creates and forms it; it also commands and moves it. Let us study its mode of action more closely. We see that there is a double movement determined by the double nature of the soul: power and conscience at the same time. Indeed, *the soul is a source of power that directs itself by proposing, through its imagination, an end for it to realize.* The soul thinks something, attaches itself to this thought in the form of an image, desires it, tends toward it, wishes it. Its plastic and creative power then introduces itself therein as in a mold, informs itself, and impresses in the body the image conceived by the imagination. Thus, when we imagine a movement, the soul, by printing this image on the body, realizes it. When we imagine a sound, which reveal the form the soul imprints upon them by the imagination we will be able to change completely the aspect and exterior form of our bodies, as we change the aspect and expression of our faces, which reveal the form the soul imprints upon them by the imagination and will, or by the will of the imagination, or again, by the imagination of the will. Note well that we must not confuse imagination and fantasy. The latter has no power; its images float in our mind without any deep connection with one another, or with us. The fantasy is without any basis in nature.[46] Actually, it is purely of the intellect, a game of thought. If one took its creations seriously, it would give rise to errors and could even lead to madness. Everything else is the imagination. And, as the term indicates, it is the magical production of an image. More exactly, it is the expression by an image of a tendency of the will; and, if we pay attention to it, we will see that the imagination is the magical power par excellence,[47] and that it offers us the essential type of magical action. Now all action is magical —creative or productive action before everything. The image produced by the imagination expresses a tendency, a powerful tension of the will. It is born in us, in our soul, in an organic manner. It is ourselves, and so it is ourselves that we express in it. The image is the body of our thought and desire. In it, our thought and desire are embodied.

Once formed, the image, as we have just said, serves as a mold for the plastic power of the soul which seeks to be cast therein, in order to realize the image and realize itself in it. In the same way pregnant women realize, produce, create, and bring into the world the children on whom their soul prints the imagined form. In this way the birth of monsters [48] is explained, as is the well-known case of resemblance where there is no empirical kinship. The same organic process which expresses its desires and tendencies in the astral material of the soul uses the matter of the body in order to print an imagined form on the malleable matter of the child.

Now one must go even further in the comparison and the assimilation of the birth of the image to the birth of the child. The image produced by the soul is not a simple modification of the soul. It is much more than that. It is a natural organic product of the astral body of the soul. We said above that it was a body which embodied thought. This expression must be taken literally. The image is a body in which the thought and will of the soul are incarnate. The soul, which gives birth to these thoughts, ideas, and desires, gives them a being *sui generis* through the imagination. It is not yet the real being, for the soul does not create in the actual sense of the term. It confers immediately a sort of magical existence on the image, which, to a certain degree, is independent even of the will of the soul which engendered it. Like children who acquire their own being from the very moment of their conception, although they are products of our organic being, the ideas that we conceive [49] become centers of power which can act and can exercise an influence of their own. In the *Gestirn* of little centers of action, these are little magic beings. Evidently they have more power than the imagination and the will which engendered them and are the stronger. Also by this personal dynamism of the products, effects, or children of our imagination, the action of one will on another can be explained. Speaking plainly, these are the spirits that the will sends forth to ensnare an alien soul, and, if the initial impetus was sufficiently powerful, i.e. if our imagination was able to endow this *Willengeist,* this "mind-will," with a sufficiently plastic power, it will act on the alien soul, on the astral body of the person to whom we send it, and make him carry out our will in place of his own. And this is how wills battle against one another, and how one explains the fact that one can communicate one's thoughts across space. The mechanism—more exactly the dynamism—of the imagination allows us also to understand the case of mental contagion, as well as certain illnesses. For example, rabies is in fact produced by the very powerful imagination of a mad dog, which somehow manages to impregnate his saliva so that it becomes a physical vehicle of illness. When the dog bites you, his imagination traps your will which is already weakened by fear. The same mechanism ultimately explains not only the birth of monsters but normal births as well. The "will-imagination" of parents, by mixing together, produces conception by creating a tincture (*tinctur*) which then forms the body.

Exactly in the same manner—by "imagining" it—God created the universe.[50] By conceiving things in his imagination and then exterior-izing his will, his *fiat,* God created the world; He produced and drew it from his own being, essences, and eternal uncreated powers. This is why the world and the beings in it can be envisioned in two differ-ent ways. First, they are seen in themselves, existing separately, and expressing their individual essence by their exterior configuration. Each thing carries in its exterior, in its body, the "signature" by which we can judge the powers and qualities it conceals. This allows us, when we look at a plant or a crystal, for example, to know its medical properties in advance by its signature.[51]

Second, one can also envision the entire world as a single whole, as a single signature of the Creator. (Paracelsus cannot think in any other way than through psychological or organic analogies.) The Creator produced a world like his own body when he engendered it. Things will, then, be "members" of the body of the universe, and this explains their harmony and their agreement. The God of Para-celsus is, therefore, the soul and father of the world and of all creation, as well as the Father of man and of Jesus.[52]

Now let us look at the Paracelsist cosmology. We will see it unfold (one can easily know this in advance) in the same analogical, biological categories, always putting into operation the same dominant principles of his thought—biomagical dynamism and the concept of signature.

Since the world, for Paracelsus, is an expression and an organic embodiment of divinity, it is evident that the term "to create" does not have the same sense for him that it can have in a philosophy of a different type. The God of Paracelsus is, at the same time, an eternal mind and an eternal center of power—a *Mysterium Magnum* [53] —who develops, exteriorizes, expresses, and extends himself in the world, or, to be more exact, who creates the world by extending him-self—by pouring forth, by allowing to issue from his own breast in a cascade, in a dynamic river, the whole mass of partial powers which, in becoming more and more diversified, finally give birth to the physical world.[54] His God is eternal, and consequently nature, con-sidered as life, is also eternal. Equally eternal is the prime matter from which the world is made.

One does not have to identify God and nature. The latter is not God in the proper sense of the term. However, nature pertains to *divine* being as much as the soul and the body pertain to human being. One can distinguish them abstractly. One can, in fact one must, distinguish nature and God just as one distinguishes the soul from the mind and from the body. But, even in placing them in opposition, one must not lose sight of their essential relationship. One must be careful, on the other hand, not to confuse nature in general with the physical world. Indeed, God has always produced a world and has never been uncreative. Concrete nature, however, is perishable; this physical world is only temporal. Created, it will disappear; and there will be another, but it will no longer be the same one. This real world, therefore, is only a secondary product of God's eternal action.

Faithful to the principle of the progressive development of indistinct and intensive unity in an extensive multitude of individual forms, Paracelsus suggests as a base, source, and root of the world something that he calls by different names, the most common being *Chaos, Yliaster*,[55] and *Mysterium Magnum*.[56] The *Mysterium Magnum*[57] is the uncreated center of the world from which everything flows. It is the seed which conceals within itself all possibilities which will be realized later. In its power it already contains virtually (but in a hidden, undeveloped, and not apparent way) what its natural evolution—separation[58]—is going to make clear, reveal, and produce. The *Mysterium Magnum* is the egg from which the universe and every being are hatched and, in turn, become their own *Mysterium Magnum*. It is the seed from which everything grows and the active power which leads and directs evolution.

The *Yliaster* or *Yliader* is the first realization, or better,[59] the first concrete materialization of the *Mysterium Magnum* of life, the stuff, if one likes, from which the universe will be formed. It is not yet the gross matter of the physical world; it is not yet even the astral matter of the *Gestirn*. The *Yliaster* contains all that, but in a manner not yet differentiated. It contains them potentially. It itself is too fine, too "tenuous and subtle," almost impalpable and invisible—absolutely impalpable and invisible for our coarse senses—but it is already on the way to the elements and can be considered a first condensation or coagulation. Already it is opposed to the mind, and we have only to condense this impalpable matter more and more, so to speak, in order to obtain in these coagulations and differentiations more and more materials: the astral matter, the firmament, and, finally, our own matter.[60]

The unique power of the *Mysterium Magnum*, which is a creative and materializing force, is also divided into partial powers. The great mystery of separation[61] causes three principal powers to appear, which construct the world and its elements: *Sulphur, Mercurius, Sal.*[62]

Another degree of separation, condensation, coagulation, and the unique element finally divides into the four classic elements of Aristotelian physics—earth and water, air and fire.[63] More and more the primitive unity becomes diversified. The four elements and the three primitive forces which form them are embodied in a multitude of beings and give birth to bodies, metals, living bodies, and finally to man. These powers battle among themselves, and it is their battle and the predominance of one over the other which explain the real diversity of creatures.[64]

But the primitive unity is not lost. It exists and is everywhere present; furthermore, it is precisely in this diversity that unity realizes and reveals itself. Unity is revealed in a double sense, for not only is the world a signature of God, but nature also reveals herself to man, and he in turn reveals the splendors of the divine power. Man "understands" them. Unity is realized again in his thought. Nature herself is found again in science. In fact, nature is only visible science and science is only invisible nature.

These are the same powers—as in the old doctrine of the *Tabula Smaragdina*—and the same elements which appear at each stage of world evolution, and everything that we find at an inferior level we will also find at a superior level, or, if one prefers, inversely. All that is divine in God and celestial in the heavens is found on earth in a terrestrial state as well. What is water on earth is *aquaster* in the superior region. The *aquaster* is not completely the soul of water but is, if one wishes, its dynamic soul, what corresponds to water on the astral plane.

In our analysis we have neglected an important point—that of the perennial nature of superior worlds and the temporal brevity of our world with respect to us. The temporal world as we see it is actually a fallen world. It has not preserved its primitive nature. From *yliastric* it has become *cagastric*.[65]

The actual world is due to a double creation or double movement: one of descent and one of ascension. First and foremost, it is the product of the fall, notably that of Lucifer and his angels;[66] it is as a prison for spirits that the world was created. Thus, it is the theater of divine action and power, which seeks to lead the world back to a superior level.[67] Now man, again, the *limbus minor,* offers us the exact image of the process and history of the *limbus major.* The human body, like that of the universe, is *cagastric,* the product of a fall, the issue of the *cagastric* person of Eve. Adam, on the other hand, had (before the fall) an *yliastric* body, which was an "extract" of the universe and "represented" it. Moreover, Adam was justly created by God in order to lead nature to a superior level and be his worker in the universe. The fall transformed him (it plunged him into the coarse world of separated elements that man now represents) to the same extent that he represented the primitive world. Before the fall, Adam's body was a dynamic body, not nourished as we are, for he did not eat. Although all beings need nourishment,[68] the superior beings—angels for example—do not eat with their mouths as do animals, and as we have done ever since the fall. Adam had neither intestines nor sexual parts. He was not subject to death. He would have had to reproduce magically, being an androgyne [69]

Actual man represents the actual universe. He is always a microcosm. As the universe is reproduced by the matrix of nature, by the firmament, man is produced by the matrix of his mother. He is a cast-off remnant, as is the material universe. He has only a limited time to live, and the material universe has only a limited time to exist. The human soul has only a given number of revolutions to make, after which its course is complete; it dies as the material universe will die and dissolve, when it completes its given number of revolutions. Gross matter resists the soul more than it expresses it; the soul cannot command it, nor completely vivify it, because the fallen material, the cagastric element, is simply too strong. It is the same for the bodies of the universe. They are impure, and although the vital force of nature is sufficient to enable them to combat their tendency gradually to deteriorate, it only rarely succeeds, and with much trouble and time expended. This is why metals, the most perfect bodies, are formed so slowly. Also this is why one so rarely finds precious metals, and, even when they are found, they are always in an impure state. To accomplish the work of nature or to permit nature to accomplish its work in a shorter time, it is necessary to proceed by means of numerous manipulations.

For all nature—and this is an important point—tends toward its primitive state and tends once again to enter into the unity of the celestial element. But it cannot do it itself. It needs help from above.

Man is the image of the universe. Created twofold [70] and in two times, he received his body from "below," [71] while from "above" the divine image, the mind, was impressed into him. He also received a tincture which transformed him, just as the tincture transforms the metallic matter on which it acts. Christ, Man-God, is our tincture. The new Adam transfigures us and gives us a spiritual body [72] just as the philosopher's stone transforms and transfigures metallic matter. Moreover, if one pays attention, the metallic process itself, the "great work," at least for Paracelsus and the alchemists of the Middle Ages, is only a "signature," a symbol of the more general process of transfiguration and return of the world to God.

We should stop here for a few moments in order to look at Paracelsus' philosophy from a new point of view: that of alchemy. Evidently we cannot recapitulate here the history of alchemy either with respect to science or to its philosophical bases. We will restrict ourselves to its role in Paracelsus. It forms an integral part of his doctrine and it was, to a much higher degree than is generally admitted, an element of the intellectual universe, a universally accepted belief, throughout the entire Renaissance.

The alchemical philosophy, as it is presented in the Paracelsist books, appears at first glance to be an organic dynamism, a kind of doctrine of evolution, if anything a monist doctrine. It is extremely curious, even disconcerting, because it is an *ascending* doctrine of evolution and not at all the descending evolution we have come to know.

The *mysterium*, the *prima materia elementorum*, the *limbus*, etc. (all these many terms often signify the same thing) appear as the undifferentiated *root* of the world. As a tree of life, it rises above the abyss, sprouts branches, fruits, flowers, and, in a natural progression, "evolves" from inanimate beings, from the roughest, crudest elements, into the purest and most perfect elements, which are organized, animated, and conscious. Material nature, bodies—all come from a single, same source-root.[73] They all represent different degrees of evolution and organization. They are transformed from one into the other. Natural evolution seeks to produce this transformation, which the artist, or alchemist, can only accelerate in his laboratory.

The transmutation of metals is only one particular aspect, certainly important, but not central to the alchemist doctrine. Even if, in practical terms, this were the particular work which occupied the studies and leisure of the alchemists, it is wrong to think, as even now one too often does, that alchemy was concerned entirely with research for making gold. Paracelsus, among others, was not at all preoccupied with this,[74] and the legends reported by Oporinus seem to be merely legends.

Moreover, there was nothing absurd in the belief in transmutation. Did not the daily practice of metallurgists show that by appropriate manipulation—we note especially by the action of fire [75]—one could transform metallic rocks found in the mines into brilliant and precious metals? Did one not see every day that the addition of a small quantity of metal could produce an alloy [76] with completely new qualities and properties? Did one not know, moreover, that metals "are formed" within mountains? So it was evident that, like every living thing, metals are transformed through aging. It was also evident that, by fire, one could activate this evolution, this "life" of metals. Let us not forget that the distinction between elements and composite chemicals only occurred recently and that the alchemical concept of the "mixed" substance does not correspond to it at all. [77] Natural evolution of metals tended to produce the most perfect metal: gold. Gold was thus the end toward which nature herself was directed, and one had only to suppress the "impediments" to allow nature to follow her course. One did this by a series of operations, all of which had as their goal to "purify" matter and to permit "nature," the "creator seed," the "tincture," the "leaven," to act freely.

Actually the "tangible" and "material" metals are only the products or expressions, materializations or incarnations of powers, "virtues," and dynamic forces. They are only inert "bodies" which express the essence or the metallic "quality" with more or less success or perfection. Tangible matter can oppose the action of the "quality," the generating principle, or form. It can oppose to its action the action of another principle or form. It can thus prevent evolution from attaining its goal.

Let us not forget that the world is full of diverse powers which mutually oppose one another. The powers and the seeds embodied in metals are in fact only outpourings of astral powers. They are astral powers plunged into matter, the same powers which are also embodied and expressed in the stars. This is why metals correspond to the stars; they are, so to speak, embodied stars. [78]

Moreover, the entire material universe is, as we have seen, an incarnation and a "coagulation" of the *elementum*. The entire material universe expresses the *astrum*. It expresses it badly, however, and this is why it evolves; the living seed of the universe successively realizes itself in time, permitting its diverse degrees to coexist, and this explains the multiplicity of metals or stages of metallic evolution. Indeed, the dynamic power cannot be realized in any way other than as embodied in a material substance. Now it can find matter to be more or less great in quantity, and its "virtue" is there embodied in a more or less adequate manner. The result will be either an imperfect metal, a perfect metal, or, finally, a "tincture." Here is the task of the alchemist: to free the principle of transformation, the essence, the concentrated *tinctur*. Added to a well-prepared material, one that is purified and liquefied, the *tinctur*, the *magisterium*, will act to transform it, just as the addition of a mere taste of poison transforms water into poison and a mere taste of vinegar transmutes wine into vinegar.

There is no reason to see in transmutation anything other than a curtailment of a normal process of nature. It is based on the *tendency* of all metallic matter to become gold, because its seed pushes it in this direction. The metals grow and tend toward gold, which is their perfection, because all being *tends* toward its perfection. One can make gold from them because, basically, virtually, and potentially, they are gold already. They evolve because they are not yet there. They do what all beings of the universe do. They evolve because they are living and because all living being, at the same time, is what it is not yet, and is not yet what essentially it is.

Moreover, the whole of life is but an alchemical process. Do we not employ alchemy in preparing food? Are we not natural alchemists in feeding ourselves? Is digestion anything but an act of the same genre as the production of gold? Is there not in a man's body a subtle alchemist who proceeds by means of all the operations required of this art—putrefaction, sublimation, transmutation—and evacuates the cagastric refuse? [79]

And is the process of spiritual rebirth anything other than the alchemical process? Is not the coarse body, by the *magisterium* of the mind, transformed into a spiritual body, and does not our soul pass through the same stages of liquefaction, purification, and transfiguration as do matter and the world?

We have underlined the analogy because, as the most characteristic analogy for this whole school of thought, it is completely animated by the belief that the processes of the exterior world, of the physical world, only cause those of the soul to be represented and symbolized. The alchemical books always speak in symbols—not in allegories or in cryptograms [80]—and they always speak of two things at once: nature and man, the world and God. The philosopher's stone is the Christ of nature, and Christ is the philosopher's stone of the spirit. Mercury, being the intermediary between the sun and the moon (the gold and silver, ☉ ☽ and ☿), *is* Christ in the world of matter, just as Christ, the mediator between God and the world, is the spiritual mercury of the universe. This is more than a simple allegory or comparison. The analogy is more profound. The same symbols are applied to the material and spiritual processes because, fundamentally, there is an identity between them. The identity of symbols is explained by the identity of these processes.

It certainly seems that Christian alchemy, which always admitted the same principles—organic evolution, analogy as a mode of reasoning, the doctrine of the microcosm—had always tried, in its symbols, either to make visible or to hide the identity of nature and spirit, of the world's evolution and that of man.

What makes the comprehension and the systematic presentation of the conception of the world in alchemical philosophy so difficult, both generally and particularly in its Paracelsist interpretation, is the fact that it must, so to speak, come at the same time from above and below; from God and from man, from "naturing nature" and from "natured nature." Somehow, one must adopt simultaneously the points of view of the Creator and of the creature, of action and passivity, of descent and ascent. This difficulty, moreover, is general enough. It is present wherever one finds the myth of the cycle, the myth of the return to the origin. The organic conception of the world and of evolution submits with difficulty to logical boundaries. The idea of the seed leads us into a vicious circle, a circle which the mind cannot understand but which life resolves as it plays itself out.

However, the question is posed: why *time?* Why evolution to attain an end given in advance, to arrive at a stage of perfection? And from the two things comes one: if perfection was in the beginning, in the uncreated,[81] why was it abandoned? And if, on the contrary, perfection is only at the end, why have it realized in succession? [82]

The descent, the emanation of things, and their return to God are not logically coordinated. They cannot be so for Paracelsus. If they were, man and God would have to express themselves freely and perfectly. But in fact they do not. Material nature would then have to have been gold, and hence it would not have been nature at all (at least nature as she is). But nature does exist. The ultimate irrationality of this fact remains irrational despite all the attempts at explanation, and Paracelsus, like Boehme later, saw it everywhere.[83]

Why the battle? We well understand, when reality is perceived from below, that the seed can only realize itself progressively, that nature evolves in time. We also understand, if reality is viewed from above, that God, desiring to express his nature in and by the world, in and by man,[84] and to reveal the *magnalia Dei*,[85] creates and forms an exterior expression, a book to read, and one to read it.[86] What we do not understand is why the expression is imperfect, why the book

is unreadable. We well understand that, in order to obtain a transformation, it is necessary first to destroy the form proper to concrete
matter. We well understand, therefore, that it must be made calcine,
putrefied, liquefied. We also understand that we must purify it,
sublimate it, etc. and that afterward it is necessary to act on it with
a "ferment," a *magisterium*, a tincture. But we do not understand
where the inferior forms come from, the origin of the stain and the
impurity. We well understand that man must die to himself, he must
repent (purify, liquefy, calcinate himself—let the interior fire consume
his sin). We understand that grace, the ferment of the supernatural
life, must act on his soul if it is to be regenerated. But, again, we
do not understand where sin and evil come from, the origin of the
necessity of repentance and purification.

Paracelsus was very much aware of the difficulty. We cannot reproach him for not having tried to resolve it and for not having
given it a solution. One would be more tempted to reproach him for
the variety and abundance of solutions offered. Indeed, he offers no
less than three.[87]

First, there is the solution of ignorance. Evil is everywhere visible.
All things are "based" in good and evil. There are good and bad or
wicked qualities. All things by their natures are good or evil—man,
plants, animals. There is evil and good in the heavens and in the
astra. But where did it all come from? Paracelsus does not know and
sadly he concludes: "But from wherever God has taken the bad and
the good, it is not given to man to know." [88] Everything was good
in the beginning. But time has worn out and split up the unity; it
has separated and opposed the good things to the bad.[89]

Then there was the solution which agreed most with the by no
means identical traditional theories of evil as negation. Even from
what we have just said, that *evil and good are everywhere, that there
is evil in each and every thing*, it is easy to see that evil is something
absolutely essential to the being of created things, that it forms a constitutive element of created and finite being. Now it seems evident
that the latter cannot be perfect, and would only be imperfect because
it is limited in its qualities as it is in its being. Moreover, the very
fact that the creatures are *created*, composed of being and nothingness,
implies that they are imperfect and perishable. One ought also to
mention that "nothing" is itself a constitutive element of creatures;
it is, so to speak, the material of creation, and that is why everything
containing nothingness within itself, tends toward nothingness. But
such a tendency, although necessary, is from all evidence contrary

to the tendency toward the good, which is the principle of being and of life. One, therefore, returns to the conclusion (which is not absolutely identical with the point from which we began) that all finite, limited, created being necessarily carries within itself a mischievous tendency toward evil,[90] that is, toward nothingness. Now if evil seems to be thus identified with nothing—which would confirm the initial premise that all things are composed of good and evil—it is comforting to know that evil bears in itself its remedy, since it is nothing. Its victory implies its own disappearance and so, in terms of time, evil will be nothing and only good will remain. All will return to order and everything will be as before. . . .[91]

But this is hardly a satisfying solution, since it implies either that everything is to begin again, or, on the contrary, that, in general, to begin was not the problem. So Paracelsus outlines a third solution, which has the advantage of agreeing with his medical doctrines, with his theories about illnesses.

What is evil, and can one speak of evil in general? What is bad for one is good for another. Fish die in air and man cannot live in water. The same poison that kills one man leaves another unharmed. Thus, it is known that serpents live with poison which, however, is not deadly for them. Therefore evil is not at all something in itself. Only by its connection with this or that being can one speak of it as something. A substance is good for one being when it is favorable to it, when it nourishes it. It is bad when, on the contrary, it poisons this being. Therefore it is not substances themselves—all of which are good—but their relationships with others, which give rise to evil. Evil is produced by a disagreement, by a disorder, by a disharmony. The different powers that constitute beings—good in themselves—battle among themselves and thereby produce illnesses, suffering, and death.

So sickness for the most part is only a battle between two life currents. In itself, illness is a being, an entity, a life. A parasitic life,[92] a life which develops to the detriment of the life of the sick individual. Consequently it is an evil for the latter. But in itself it is a life which is nourished on the life of a sick animal or man, as it draws its nourishment from these other lives, which it is obliged to destroy in order to maintain and affirm itself. The *Archeus* of the sick man fights the parasitic life; it is hostile toward the illness, and the doctor aids in combating it.[93] This battle, the disorder resulting from it, and the discord that it presupposes are the evil.

Hence evil is reduced to a disordered opposition of forces. In no way is it a being, and this is why one can conceive its destruction, once order is reestablished. Now if the disorder, the battle, is not something natural, necessary, and eternal, and if it is produced by an act which is contrary to order—e.g. the fall of Lucifer—then one has the explanation he has sought.[94] Lucifer's fall transforms the divine world into a hell. In place of the two-storied world of the visible and invisible, Paracelsus substitutes a three-storied image: hell, paradise, and our own world, which is an intermediary between the two. It is intermediary in being, not in space, of course, since the three worlds are strictly coextensive. To this triple world, then, corresponds a trinity (triplicity) in man—man's threefold life.

However, illnesses are not all of this nature; there are others, notably those which derive from the corruption of matter and from the hostile influence of astral forces, or those which have their source in the human organism itself. These are the tartaric illnesses *(tartarische, gagastrische)*.[95] No longer are there two lives which battle one another, but the life current battles the conditions of embodiment and existence. The humors which compose the body become corrupt, and the "powers" and "bodies," of which the living being is composed, deteriorate. That also is explained by disorder. The astral forces may be too strong or too weak; nourishment may be too abundant or insufficient; the contrary (hostile, poisonous) outpourings propagate, and cosmic disorder, a cosmic fall, explains it all.

Also there is the fact that matter is corrupt in general and is *cagastrum*.[96] For this reason, life can neither dominate nor totally penetrate it; so there is refuse, remains, tartars. These are the impurities which choke the organism and poison it. Life thus seems to fight with itself, to accumulate obstacles along its way. Here again, the fall explains it. The fall consists in separation, in the individual egoism of beings and powers. Each being, animal, metal, material, or power wants everything for itself, wishes to isolate itself, to preserve its being and its powers and seize for itself those things which originate from above. Here is the resistance of matter to the breath of the spirit which penetrates it; here, in general, is the resistance of all inferior forms of being to superior beings, the refusal to serve them as means of expression and embodiment. This is why life, the development of each "seed," finds in itself a resistance which it must combat. This is the real reason for evil: the fall, the separation, which is the source of the battle and combat, the suffering, evil, and illness in the world of vulgar, impenetrable, and egoistic bodies. But, happily, this "world" is temporal. It has death "as its center," and it will die just as all terrestrial life dies and disappears.[97]

Now Paracelsus cannot be resolved to see in creation and life only one basically absurd episode,[98] a circular rhythm leading everything back to where it began. No, whatever emanates from the mystery cannot come back internally such as it was "before." Transformed and transfigured, the creature eternally exists. Is not the mind eternal and is not man the child of God, a little god himself [99] and consequently indestructible and eternal? Has not man received as a commission the task of revealing the mysteries of God? [100] Is he not the Lord's worker? Would his task be given in vain? Would the world simply perish?

Once again the doctrine of the microcosm, the alchemical doctrine of identity, the ground of the process in nature and in man,[101] comes to our aid. Since man will be transfigured, the world will also be transfigured. It is inadmissible that God created it for nothing; the *magnalia Dei* cannot be once again cloaked in mystery. Nothing which is or has been can disappear; the flowers themselves, fragile and ephemeral, are going to exist eternally, revived and transfigured.[102] This transfiguration, this deification of the universe, has already begun. Christ is proof of it. He is revived, He has clothed himself with a spiritual body, the symbol of the world's transfiguration. Moreover, do we not see this mystery of transfiguration accomplished every day in the holy sacrament? And are we not nourished by the faith, when we approach the sacrament with faith? Do we not thereby participate in this resurrection and transfiguration? [103] Finally, when the world, having completed its cycle, collapses into the nothingness, when everything which came from the *prima materia elementorum* returns to it and the *materia sacramentorum* returns to God, the beings who here below are transfigured into a spiritual body will exist,[104] and by and in them, by and in man, the entire world will be eternally preserved. Only divisiveness will have disappeared along with everything that comes from nothingness.[105]

The theological doctrine of Paracelsus very well agrees with his general conception of the world. It culminates in his conception of man, the absolute center of the universe, the book which contains *ab aeterno* all the marvels and essences of creation, the worker whose just task is to reveal them and accomplish them. We can see that, conceived in this manner, Paracelsus' man is in a certain way uncreated. Is he not an essential expression of God and the world? We also understand that to "practice philosophy" is his great concern in this life. Philosophy is knowledge and revelation of nature, and as such, the work of natural illumination. It does not depend on so-called revelation. The Bible is not a manual of physics; the Hebrews never understood anything about it. The work of Christ alone pertains to theology.[106]

This decision seems much neater than it is in reality, for, on one side, natural illumination is itself divine and the work of Christ is cosmic.[107] One then understands that in proclaiming—like the spiritualists of his time—the necessity of a spiritual knowledge and of "inspiration," and in distinguishing between divine wisdom,[108] direct illumination of the mind by the Holy Spirit, and natural wisdom, Paracelsus is far from denigrating the latter.[109] One sees that he magnifies man when he proclaims him superior to nature because he has the power of thought.[110] It is clear at the same time that between God and man he wants no intermediary.

Grace, the divine tincture, acts directly on the soul by releasing its spiritual powers. And the spirit, faith—the power of faith, imagination—saves or damns man according to his belief in God, the devil, or even in nature.[111] Belief in God is belief in Christ, in the image seized by the imagination of faith, the image which nourishes it spiritually through the sacraments. This is "spiritual" nourishment, but real nourishment at the same time, since the body of Christ is very much a body, and the *materia sacramentorum,* the spiritual matter from which it is formed, although as spiritual as it can be, is yet material. It is faith which saves man, thinks Paracelsus. But his faith is far from the Lutheran faith, and his God is far from the Lutheran God.[112]

Faith is the center, so to speak, for spiritual being; it is the source of its power. It is that which engenders the new man, the spiritual man, and which nourishes and directs the magical matrix of the imagination.[113] And his God, the eternal creator, or, more exactly, the eternal source of the universe, is at the same time the just God, the God of justice, the God of truth. Father of the universe, he is especially father of man. And man, the child of God, is his image, a "little god," as we have already seen.[114]

This little god is free. Everything is within him: paradise, hell, evil, good, God, and Satan. His faith, his imagination, is the door to one or the other of these regions or stages of being which constitute the Paracelsist world. Hell is there; paradise also. There will be no "voyage" after death. There is descent or ascent in being, not in space.[115]

For man it is necessary to do his work as God does his. Man must fulfill his mission, permit himself to love and be enlightened by God, and allow himself to be guided by Christ, the Holy Spirit, the Paraclete. Man must grieve and seek; search himself, his innermost heart, his interior heaven. "Wer da sucht, der findet," repeats Paracelsus; "wer da sucht in dem innerein Himmel." [116]

This is a curious doctrine, certainly confusing—a mixture of mysticism, magic, and alchemy. Throughout it is very beautiful because it represents a sincere effort to see the world in God, God in the world, and man participating in both and "understanding" both. It was also a very influential doctrine. Through Boehme, Weigel, and others, it still remains the very basis of the theosophical movement of modern times, a movement, as we well know, whose importance cannot be underestimated by the historian of ideas.

NOTES

[Prof. Koyré frequently includes the full German quotation to which his notes refer. Since it is not practical in a volume such as this to reproduce these extensive citations, the interested reader is referred to the French original. The notes below are complete save for these citations.—ED.]

1. On the name of Paracelsus see the preface to vol. VIII of K. Sudhof's admirable edition of the *Oeuvres Complètes* of Paracelsus (*Th. Paracelsus, Gesammelte Werke*, Abt. I: *Medizinische Schriften*, 13 vols. in 8 (Munich, 1920–31).)

2. The biography of Paracelsus has not yet been written. Moreover, it is only now, after Sudhof's studies and discoveries, that one can think of writing one which would not be a romantic biography like all those done so far.

3. This is the opinion of B. Groethuysen in his remarkable *Philosophische Anthropologie, Handbuch der Philosophie*, Bd. III (Munich, 1931; French trans. Paris, 1954).

4. We will cite from the Huser edition, 4 vols. (Basel, 1589). As Sudhof established, Huser is completely reliable.

5. It would therefore be necessary to admit the principle of equivalence from the part to the whole, a principle whose importance for primitive thought has been established by L. Lévi-Bruhl and for metaphysics by Hegel.

6. It is incontestable that Paracelsus was a "precursor"—but a precursor of whom? Precisely here is the question which can be resolved only after a study of Paracelsus. The mania for researching precursors has very often irremediably falsified the history of philosophy.

7. To avoid misunderstandings, let us say that we by no means accept either the variability of forms of thought or the evolution of logic.

8. Paracelsus admitted the influence of the stars on illnesses and even the possibility of using the stars for evil spells. He objected only to providential astrology because he attributed general effects to the stars, individually diversi-

fied by the different receptivity of individuals, and attributed nothing to the effects individualized in themselves.

9. Belief in the growth of metals was widespread from antiquity until the 17th century. Cf. O. Lippmann, *Entstehung und Ausbreitung der Alchemie* (Leipzig, 1925).

10. Duhem has shown that astrology was a perfectly reasonable and rational system and that, before Copernicus, the belief in the influence of stars was inevitable for all those who studied and accepted a scientific determinism in nature. Aristotle's cosmology, to give only one example, necessarily leads to astrology. Cf. also F. Boll, *Sternglaube und Sterndeutung* (Leipzig, 1926 [3]).

11. *Ibid.*, as well as F. Cumont's *Astrology and Religion Among the Greeks and Romans* (New York, 1912).

12. What for a long time was doubted has now been definitely proved by Sudhof, who found the document for it in the Verona Archives. See Paracelsus, *Oeuvres* VIIII, p. xxxvii.

13. In the 13 volumes published by Sudhof only the course of study taught at Basel in 1527 is in Latin. See IV, 1–131.

14. All the popular stories are to be found again in Paracelsus. The *Evestra, Larvae, Leffas, Mumiae* come from folklore. They are ghosts, spirits of the dead, etc. The astral matter is basically what the spirits are "made" of. Paracelsus believes in amulets and the power of magical formulas. He knows how to act on serpents and how to obtain the influence of the moon. One would never finish if one tried to list all his beliefs. A good number of them are assembled in Adelung, *Die Geschichte der menschlichen Dummheit* (Berlin, 1784); Jensen, *Deutschland im Zeitalter der Reformation,* VI (Leipzig, 1905); Lehmann, *Geschichte des Aberglaubens* (Leipzig, 1906). To be sure, Paracelsus was not alone in believing them.

15. Paracelsus boasts that he is a "simpleton," raised in misery and owing his knowledge only to himself.

16. Paracelsus proclaims himself the *Monarcha* of the new science. Aristotle, Avicenna, and Rhasis are not worthy to touch his robes. This is a trait of the age. Giordano Bruno or Campanella shall sin no less with their excess of modesty.

17. Paracelsus was not absolutely wrong in his attacks. It is enough to open a medical book of the period to accept most of its critics. Pharmacy in the 15th and 16th centuries was a distasteful and unmentionable cuisine, which, in preparing its remedies, went to the point of using the powder of mummies *(mumia)*. As for the agreement among pharmacists, it seems that it was the rule. Paracelsus' remedies are relatively simple. He introduced into the practice certain metallic remedies and opium—the only real progress, it seems, that he made in medical science.

18. Paracelsus, *De Vita Rerum Naturalium*, lib. IV, *Oeuvres* VI, 276–277. Here one sees Paracelsus adopting the notion of "occult" qualities as opposed to "exterior" qualities. This union of contraries within the concrete being already was known in antiquity. See L. Thorndike, *A History of Magic and Experimental Science,* I (New York, 1923), 317ff.

19. Paracelsist "nature," like the "nature" of the philosophers of the Renaissance generally, is life and magic. J.-B. Porta, writing about it in his book on *Natural Magic,* only expressed the common sentiment: magic is natural because nature is magic. This is the reason why the Renaissance is an epoch of un-

bounded credulity. Indeed, how does one know what is possible and what is not? Is not everything possible for natural magic? How does one know what can produce the magical action of the stars or elements? How except by "experience," which becomes the surest basis of superstition?

20. No body without "spirit," but also no spirit without body.

21. That does not stop Paracelsus from recognizing that the soul and man are more difficult to know than exterior nature. Moreover, it is one of the advantages of the doctrine of the microcosm to allow the difficulty to result in studying the "big world" before the "little," and in explaining man by analogy with the universe. It is one of the reasons why astrology is necessary for medicine. This does not prevent man from remaining the basis and "type" of all knowledge. Did not St. Augustine say: *valde profundus est ipse homo?*

22. Paracelsus, *De generatione stultorum, Oeuvres* IX, 29.

23. Paracelsus, *Liber Azoth sive de ligno et linea vitae, Oeuvres* X, app. I, p. 3.

24. Paracelsus, *Philosophia Sagax,* lib. I, 2, *Oeuvres* X, 261.

25. "To understand" means "to take up, embrace."

26. Paracelsus, *Philosophia Sagax,* lib. II, 1, *Oeuvres* X, 263.

27. Paracelsus, *Philosophia Sagax, Oeuvres* X, 263.

28. Paracelsus explains that the interior *Astrum* of man is ruled like a watch. It has a determined number of revolutions to make and human life consequently has a natural duration, individually determined for each man. Moreover, the vitalistic conception of evolution implied a natural term to this evolution. When, according to Paracelsus, man dies before his term is ended, i.e. when the vital force is not yet totally employed *(verbraucht, abgelaufen),* the remainder "is embodied" in the astral body, and forms a *mumia,* which possesses vitalizing properties that one can utilize in medicine. Thus, on the one hand, the spirits of men executed haunt the places where they were hanged or beheaded. (Paracelsus had the experience himself; "all my students," he complains, "have been taken from me by the hangman.") On the other hand, the objects which have touched them and which are impregnated with an unused vital force, are powerful remedies. It is amusing to see how Paracelsus "explains" an accepted statement of popular superstition—like the medical use of mummy powder.

29. Paracelsus, *Paramirum, Oeuvres* I, 73. Cf. *Phil. Sagax, Oeuvres* X, 16.

30. Paracelsus, *Ein ander Erklärung der gantzen Astronomey, Oeuvres* X, 448.

31. We must carefully distinguish between the attitudes and conceptions of the world as the "natural revelation of God" put forth by the Christian rationalists of the 11th and 12th centuries, and those of the naturalistic mystics of the 16th and 17th centuries. The terms, very often identical, give rise to an easy confusion, and yet there is a very profound difference there. One can only say that for the philosopher-theologians of the 12th century the world was "unreal," while for the theosophists of the 16th century it had a reality independent of God. For one and the other, the world *quodammodo* reflects and reveals God. But it certainly seems that the *manner* was different. The world in the 16th century is not a "symbol," a "theophany," a "reflection" of the creator; it is a manifestation of the creator, an "organic expression." God is in the world not as "the author is in his work" but as "the spirit is in its body." He is not confused with the world, but becomes more "real," more *in se* if not more *a se.* The uniquely spiritual link (thought and will) is doubled by an organic link (soul and life).

32. Paracelsus, *Erklärung der gantzen Astronomey, Oeuvres* X, 418.

33. Paracelsus, *Liber Azoth sive de ligno et linea vitae, Oeuvres* X, 23.

34. Paracelsus, *Philosophia Magna,* IV, *Oeuvres* VIII, 124.

35. Paracelsus, *Philosophia Sagax,* lib. I c. 4, *Oeuvres* X, 38, 40. Cf. III, 40.

36. Paracelsus, *Philosophia Magna,* lib. I, *De Elemento aeris,* §6, *Oeuvres* VIII, 58.

37. Paracelsus, *De Virtute imaginativa, Oeuvres* IX, 298.

38. Paracelsus, *Philosophia Sagax,* I, c. 3, *Oeuvres* X, 45.

39. Criticism of the fact (historical and experiential criticism) has only been formulated on the basis of a new ontology, beginning at the moment when the notion of the impossible took on some meaning. One has reached the *non esse* having begun with the *non posse,* and not the reverse.

40. Cf. *supra:* the vital force incorporated in the *mumia.*

41. Man lives in all the four elements and is "inhabited" by these four elements. He expresses them all, and this is why he is the total and perfect expression of the entire universe in all its forms and in all its aspects.

42. Paracelsus, *Philosophia ad Athenienses,* lib. II, 6. *Oeuvres* VIII, 24.

43. One of the most curious and characteristic traits of the epoch is this complete absence of the category of the *impossible.* Everything is possible, and there results an unbridled and uncritical credulity.

44. Paracelsus, *Erklärung der gantzen Astronomey, Oeuvres* X, 29.

45. Paracelsus, *Liber Azoth sive de ligna et linea vitae,* c. I, *Oeuvres* X, app., 3.

46. Paracelsus, *Ein ander Erklärung der Gesammten Astronomey, Oeuvres* X, 474-475; *passim.*

47. The magical role of the imagination was accepted in antiquity and the high Middle Ages. Cf. Thorndike (note 18), I, 218.

48. Paracelsus has two additional explanations for the birth of "monsters." The astral influence determines them (which agrees very little with the doctrine he maintains elsewhere that the matrix of the woman *is* the *Gestirn,* the *Astrum* of the child), and, also, there are elemental spirits (inferior ones to be sure), who amuse themselves by performing "experiments." Cf. *De Generatione Stultorum.*

49. The term "to conceive" must be taken in its strongest sense, viz., "to engender." For Paracelsus, as for Boehme, there is an identification of organic conception with the conception of an idea.

50. The notion of the imagination, the magical intermediary between thought and being, the incarnation of thought in image, and the placement of the image in being, is a conception of the highest importance. It occupies the foreground in the philosophy of the Renaissance, and one can find it again in Romanticism. Cf. my book, *Philosophie de J. Boehme* (Paris, 1929), pp. 205ff.

51. The notion of the *signature* necessarily springs from the usage of the category of "expression." It dominates all Renaissance philosophy.

52. Paracelsus, *Philosophia Magna,* lib. I, *De Elemento aeris,* n. 2, *Oeuvres* VIII, 5ff.

53. Paracelsus, *De Vera influentia rerum, Prologus, Oeuvres* IX, 131; *ibid., tract.* I, 133.

54. Paracelsus, *Philosophia magna, De Elemento aeris,* lib. I, n. I, *Oeuvres* VIII, 55.

55. The doctrine of Paracelsus is not always the same with respect to the *Yliaster,* any more than with respect to the *Mysterium Magnum.* Sometimes the *Yliaster* is identified with the unique element, which, in dividing itself, gives us the four elements. Sometimes the *Mysterium* is identified with God; other times the *Mysterium Magnum* and the *prima materia* are a single thing. The *prima materia* is at times identified with the *Yliaster,* the *Gestirn,* and the *prima materia sacramentorum.* The terminology is so often inconsistent that, without a very close study, which would perhaps discover in the *Corpus Paracelsicus* works of diverse provenance, one cannot think of giving an absolutely exact exposition. One must be satisfied with the approximate.

56. Paracelsus, *Philosophia ad Athenienses, Oeuvres* VIII, 6. Cf. *Liber vexationum,* VI, 378.

57. Paracelsus, *Philosophia ad Athenienses, Oeuvres* VIII, 7 and 10.

58. *Ibid.,* p. 9. The separation—the procession of many from one—is sometimes entrusted to a special principle, the *Archeus.*

59. Paracelsus, *Philosophia de generationibus et fructibus elementorum, Oeuvres* VIII, 55.

60. Basically the *Yliaster* is none other than the ether, and it is under this name that it appears in the romantic *Naturphilosophies.*

61. Paracelsus occasionally introduces a special power of separation which he calls *Archeus* or *Separator.* The *Archeus* personified is the regent of the world, the world Spirit which governs its soul.

62. Paracelsus, *Philosophia Magna,* lib. I, *De Elemento Aeris,* 3, *Oeuvres* VIII, 56; 4, p. 57; 8, p. 60.

63. Paracelsus, *Liber meteorum, Oeuvres* VIII, 184–185.

64. Paracelsus, *Liber Paramirum,* II, *Oeuvres* I, 80. The connections among the four physical elements and the three chemical elements present enough difficulties. We have occasionally affirmed their simple juxtaposition in Paracelsus. Mme. H. Metzger, in her work on *l'Histoire de la théorie chimique en France* (Paris, 1923), glorifies the French Paracelsists for having put all this in order. But Paracelsus himself had already taken care of this, as is seen in the texts cited. The four "elements" are the four modes of being of matter, the four formative principles, and the four classes of material bodies. But in *each* real body to which one or the other of these elements pertains, one finds the three chemical elements, the formative powers of all corporeal being.

65. *Cagastrum* in Paracelsus' language designates the product of a fall, perversion, or corruption.

66. The cosmic disorder cannot be explained by Adam's fall, for he is too weak an agent. Boehme would take up this doctrine: "the world" had once been Lucifer's heaven.

67. Paracelsus, *Philosophia de Elemento Aeris, Das erste Buch Meteororum, Oeuvres* VIII, 288.

68. All created being, not existing from itself, needs an influx of power to replace what it uses; it needs a "restoring" influence. This is the sense of physical or spiritual "nourishment."

69. This doctrine is to flourish. Via Boehme it will enter into the general baggage of theosophy.

70. Paracelsus, *Philosophia Sagax, Oeuvres* X, 7.

71. Man had not been created from nothing but from the *limus terrae* which

is a quintessence, an extract, of all the material universe which is visible as well as invisible. God the Father has created man from matter. Christ has infused his spirit in him.

72. Paracelsus, *Philosophia Sagax, Oeuvres* x, 26.

73. Paracelsus, *Philosophia ad Athenienses,* I, *Oeuvres* VIII, I.

74. "Mach arkana," Paracelsus teaches his students, i.e. study the forces hidden in nature; learn to make "extracts" and "tinctures" which will be used in medications. Alchemy, for him, included the entire domain of actual and even chance chemistry. The baker is an alchemist because he prepares bread by transforming flour and employing leavening. The preparation of medical drugs is mainly the working of alchemy: it is a question of "drawing out" and "isolating" the "spirit" of different natural materials in order to make "tinctures" and "magisteria" from them. Expressions in language now current have preserved some of the old alchemical concepts. Do we not speak of the spirit in wood or wine, of the tincture of iodine, and the essence of clove?

75. Life being conceived as "fire," the action of fire was naturally related to the vital action.

76. Alloys were considered to be new materials, mixtures, products of the tincture. Indeed the tincture provided the classic example of the concentration of power, of the spirit, in a volume restricted by matter. One could stain glass. Why then could one not stain metal? Two different conceptions are expressed in the same alchemical terms. (1) One can conceive of metals having separable qualities (accidents); one changes the hardness and color of copper when one prepares bronze (one *tints* it), so why not in the same way change all the other qualities? This is an alchemy of separated qualities. One can also (2) conceive of a profound transformation of all the essence of the metal submitted to the influence of tincture which acts like a new form, like a seed or leavening.

77. The notion of an alchemical *mixtum,* which has played as great a role in the philosophy of the Renaissance as in Boehme, has nothing in common with the "composite" chemical. The *mixtum* is not a combination of substances but a mixed substance. The constituent parts do not exist *actu* in the *mixtum,* as atoms of composite chemicals exist. One cannot separate the *mixtum* by mechanical division. The quality of the *mixtum* is one, like the quality of elements, and yet the composing elements exist virtually in the mixture. The Aristotelian conception of the mixture is that of a new form which replaces the composing forms in the composite material. Thus the form of bronze replaces that of copper and of tin. One sees the difficulties in this interpretation and so it is not surprising that, for the most notorious alchemists, the forms of composing materials do not disappear at all. Thus, they admit a plurality of forms and an interior tension in the composite matter. The form of the "tincture" did not destroy that of the "tinted" body but subjugated it, so to speak, and the resulting form was a synthesis, a fusion or domination, according to each case. We can see how the chemical mixture could provide the example of a reconciliation of contraries in a synthetic body. On the notion of the mixture see P. Duhem, *Le mixte et le composé chimique* (Paris, 1902). Cf. also H. Kopp, *Geschichte der Chemie* (Braunschweig, 1843).

78. The correspondence of stars and metals is one of the oldest dogmas of alchemy and one of the bases of alchemical notation. Cf. M. Berthelot, *Les origines de l'alchemie* (Paris, 1885), *Introduction à l'étude de la chimie des anciens* (Paris, 1889).

79. There is within us, according to Paracelsus, a subtle alchemist, an *Archeus*, who separates foods, extracting from them all that is necessary for our nourishment.
80. Cf. Silberer, *Symbolismus der Alchemie* (Vienna, 1914). Silberer's book is extremely interesting for the analysis of alchemical symbolism. It is very regrettable that he submitted to the obsession of psychoanalytic explanations.
81. Paracelsus, *Philos. ad Athenienses, Oeuvres* VIII, p. 2 text. 4.
82. Of course, this difficulty is not peculiar to Paracelsus. It is found in all the theistic and idealistic systems where time "flows from eternity."
83. "Separation" is the greatest mystery of being, says Paracelsus.
84. Paracelsus, *Phil. Sagax, Oeuvres* X, 49, 51.
85. Paracelsus, *Phil. Sagax, Oeuvres* X, 46.
86. Paracelsus, *De Vera influent. rerum, Oeuvres* IX, 134–135.
87. The term "evil," *malum*, as equivocal as it is, still does not yield the multiple meanings of the German term *böse*, especially in its adjectival form. For Paracelsus, as later for Boehme, difficulties are only added to this. In fact, *böse* (the abstract term being not *das Böse* but *die Bösheit*) is something neatly "positive" and "active." It is not absolutely *wicked*, nor is it *mischievous*. Savage animals are *bös*, fire is *bös*, a fever is *bös*, hail and dryness, water and wind can be *bös*. This is not the quality of being harmful or destructive; it is a certain destructive ardor which pertains, with qualifications, to the thing or phenomenon itself. It is certainly understandable that, with the popular use of the term permitting it and after considering the "solvent" and "burning" acids to be *bös* (*aqua regia* for example), Paracelsus should come to see in the *Böse* evil as a cosmic power. After that it was easy to view the impenetrability and "egoistic" isolation of the body as a power that came from *evil*. One then comes to see within all concrete reality evil battling with good, evil vanquished by good "in the beginning," but, thanks to the fall, reappearing in its isolation and in its own being.
88. Paracelsus, *Philos. Sagax, Oeuvres* X, 373.
89. Paracelsus, *Philos. Sagax, Oeuvres* X, 372.
90. Moreover, life is *böse* in itself. It is ardor, fire, then destruction. Boehme will draw from this idea the notion of the anger and wrath *(Zorn)* of God.
91. Paracelsus, *Liber de Origine morborum invisibilium, Oeuvres,* I, 222.
92. One could consider this conception of illness as one of the most beautiful and most profound intuitions of Paracelsus. An illness is a dynamic, vital being, which is developed according to its own nature and which "follows its course." If one wants to see in Paracelsus the precursor of modern medicine, it is there that one would be able to find a prevision or a presentiment of the microbe theories. But it is evident that we do not want in any way to make Paracelsus a precursor of Pasteur. Paracelsus had no idea of microorganisms, and he laughed at antiseptics.
93. We see here the real reason for Paracelsus' opposition to the medicine of his day, the medicine of symptoms. To Paracelsus it seemed as ridiculous to combat the symptoms of an illness with its opposites as to combat them with likenesses. The two medical rules, *similia similibus* and *similia contraribus,* seemed equally inept and void of sense to him. In fact, the medicine of symptoms only acts on the *exterior expression* of illnesses without attacking the *center.* What sense can there be in combating fever with exterior cold? None—except to aggravate the case by causing the fever which escaped to "reenter" the

organism. The true doctor must recognize in and through the symptom-signatures the true essence of the illness, and act to reinforce the current of the organism's own life, his *Archeus*, by *poisoning* the illness. This, indeed, would be a medication of causes, not of effects.

94. Paracelsus, *Secreta creationis, Oeuvres* III, 115. The created being is therefore a mixture of *güt* and *bös*, where goodness first predominated. Lucifer's fall set free the wicked forces, giving them a "separate" being.

95. Even the term is characteristic. *Tartaric* (*tartarische*) illnesses are not, as was often believed, sicknesses of the Tartar peoples, but those illnesses which came from *Tartaros* [Hell]. These are, for example, stones and scleroses. This was an idea which played a great role later on; the notion of the self-poisoning of an organism derives from it.

96. Paracelsus, *Secretum Magicum von dreien gebenedeiten Steinen, Oeuvres* (ed. Strasbourg, 1603) II, 677.

97. Paracelsus, *Oeuvres* III, 97.

98. The *separatio*, which is the reason why the *element* (*Yliaster, Mysterium Magnum*, etc.) is transformed into a multitude of elements, is something negative. The process then is negative in itself, *cagastric*, and one can say that it is the addition of nothingness to being; creation is a fall.

99. Paracelsus, *Philos. Sagax,* lib. I, *Oeuvres* X, 375.

100. Paracelsus, *Liber de Imaginibus, Oeuvres* IX, 389.

101. Paracelsus, *Philos. Sagax, Oeuvres* X, 27.

102. Paracelsus, *Philos. ad Athenienses* XXI, *Oeuvres* VIII, 14.

104. Faith is an "imagination" and transforms the being of the believer.

104. Paracelsus, *Philos. ad Athenienses,* lib. II, text. 11, *Oeuvres* VIII, 29.

105. Paracelsus, *idem.,* VI, 315 and 328.

106. Paracelsus, *Liber Meteorum, Oeuvres* VIII, 201.

107. Paracelsus, *Philosophia Magna,* lib. I. *De Elemento Aeris,* 5, *Oeuvres* VIII, 58.

108. Paracelsus, *Philos. Sagax,* lib. I, *Oeuvres* X, 5.

109. Paracelsus, *Philos. Sagax, Oeuvres* X, 24.

110. Paracelsus, *Philos. Sagax, Oeuvres* X, 161–162.

111. Paracelsus, *Eine ander Erklärung der ganzen Astronomey, Oeuvres* X, 475.

112. Paracelsus, *De Origine morbuum invisibilium,* lib. I, 185.

113. Paracelsus, *Liber Azoth, sive de ligno et linea vitae, Oeuvres* X, app. 61.

114. Paracelsus, *Vom Fundament der Weisheit und Kunsten, Oeuvres* IX, 426.

115. Paracelsus, *Liber Meteorum, Oeuvres* VIII, 295. Cf. Weigel, *Vom Orth der Welt,* c. 15, and *Drey Teile einer Anweisung* (Newenstatt, 1618), p. 72.

116. Paracelsus, *Philos. Sagax,* Liber II, Preface, *Oeuvres* X, 247.

9

HEIKO A. OBERMAN

Simul Gemitus et Raptus:
Luther and Mysticism *

In his second contribution to the volume, Simul Gemitus et Raptus: *"Luther and Mysticism," Oberman critically assesses popular definitions of mysticism, especially the influential typology of the German Luther scholar, Erich Vogelsang. Vogelsang distinguished three basic types of medieval mysticism: Dionysian, Latin, and German. According to Vogelsang, Luther rendered a clear "No" to Dionysian mysticism; a "Yes" and "No" to Latin mysticism; and an enthusiastic "Yes" to German mysticism. Oberman points out the difficulties involved in locating various mystical thinkers consistently within these categories, especially when they are seen through Luther's eyes. He argues that the role of mysticism in Luther's thought can only be accurately measured when prefabricated definitions and typologies are put aside and Luther's de facto use of mystical terms is studied sentence by sentence and word by word. Following this method, Oberman deals with mystical concepts clearly rejected by Luther, especially those which inflate human possibilities and detract from the unique mediatorial role of Christ. Then, more constructively, he presents a case*

* This article is the heretofore unpublished original English version of Prof. Oberman's address to the Third International Congress for Luther Research (Summer, 1966). It has appeared in German translation in *Kirche, Mystik, Heiligung und das Natürliche bei Luther. Vorträge des Dritten Internationalen Kongresses für Lutherforschung* (Göttingen, 1967), pp. 20–59.

study of Luther's use of three major mystical terms: excessus, raptus, *and* gemitus. *Oberman shows how each is appropriated by Luther and made to subserve his new theology. Indeed, so skillfully does Luther take over and define these terms that the scholastic summary of his Reformation theology, "simul iustus et peccator," can, without surrender of meaning, find its spiritual equivalent in the mystical formula, "simul gemitus et raptus."*

"We will deal with that material than which none is more sublime, none more divine, and none more difficult to attain. . . ." Jean Gerson [1]

"That [mystical] rapture is not the passageway [to God]." Martin Luther [2]

INTRODUCTION

I T CANNOT BE our task to determine whether Luther is to be regarded as a mystic. For an empathic biographer it is interesting that Luther himself testifies to the highest degree of mystical experience when he writes: "once I was carried away *(raptus fui)* to the third heaven." [3] Yet, in complete accordance with a widespread concern and hesitancy almost monotonously expressed in late medieval pastoral literature, he also states in 1516 that this "negotium absconditum" is a rare event.[4] Furthermore there are grave dangers in the pursuit of the *suavitas* which "is rather the fruit and reward of love than love itself." [5] Luther never based his authority on special revelations or high mystical experiences, nor does he write for the "aristocrats of the Spirit" who are granted a special foretaste of the glory to come. Rather it is our task to investigate the relation between Luther and medieval mystical theology and its possible significance for the formation and understanding of Luther's theology.

The fact that *mysticism* is a form or degree of religious experience, and hence to some extent individually determined, makes this topic highly elusive. We have to turn, therefore, to mystical theology, which is the effort of those who may or may not have had these experiences themselves to report, order, or teach the methods and goals of "the mystical way." Even so we shall find that there is a considerable variety of views both as to the method and goal germane to Christian mysticism. Furthermore, in the particular case of Luther, I believe that a consensus can be reached among scholars in the field that it is highly precarious to separate the mystical tissue from the living organism of Luther's spirituality. The tissue of mysticism cannot be treated as one aspect of Luther's theology, such as his relation to certain historical events, men, or movements (e.g. the Black Death, Karlstadt, or the Hussites) but it is part and parcel of his overall understanding of the Gospel itself and therefore pervades his understanding of faith, justification, hermeneutics, ecclesiology, and pneumatology.

I. METHODOLOGICAL CONSIDERATIONS

In view of the complexity of the question before us it is not my intention to offer any final solutions, but rather to indicate a series of desiderata for research and suggest the direction in which the problem might be fruitfully pursued in the years ahead.

Centuries of controversy are reflected in the varying views presented on Luther's relation to mysticism: the tension between Philippism and Pietism; the differing views on the relation of the young Luther to the mature or—more descriptively—the old Luther; the evaluation of the thesis of "the Reformers before the Reformation"; the Holl–Ritschl debate on justification as impartation *(sanatio)* versus imputation; the intimate interplay of politico-nationalistic and theological factors in the clash of *Deutsche Christen* and the *Bekennende Kirche* reflected in the confrontation of Luther as the spokesman of an endemic "Deutsche" or "Germanische Mystik" (Eckhart-Luther-Nietzsche!) versus an appeal to Luther as the witness to the God who is *totaliter aliter,* without a natural point of contact *(Seelengrund,* etc.) in man; the unclarity regarding the relation of the *Via moderna* to the *Devotio moderna*—and more generally of nominalism to mysticism. It will prove to be impossible to bypass these battlefields, but we will have to approach them with appropriate caution.

Yet the greatest obstacle methodologically is doubtless the fact that the terms "mysticism" and "mystical theology" themselves shift in meaning from author to author. The preliminary question is therefore: what is mysticism and with what structure of thought do we compare Luther?

1. On first sight the most obvious procedure for answering this question, which has indeed recently been suggested, is: "What is common to mystics, and where do we find these common elements in Luther?" [6] On two scores we cannot accept this solution. In the first place there is no guarantee that the common denominator gathers in much more than a general structure such as *purgatio, illuminatio, unio,* or the contrast between scholastic theology and mystical theology

as *sapientia doctrinalis* versus *sapientia experimentalis*. Perhaps more important, the search for the common mystical denominator presupposes that one knows what authors are to be regarded as mystics and therefore the proper subject of investigation.

2. The alternative approach is a dogmatic answer. Protestant theologians are not too helpful for our purposes because they have by and large chosen the *via negativa* in their evaluation of mysticism, inclined to regard the *Christus pro nobis* and *extra nos* as alternatives to the *Christus in nobis*.

A clearer answer can be garnered from Roman Catholic manuals and encyclopedias. In Thomistically oriented works one frequently encounters the name of Philipp of the Holy Trinity, well known as interpreter of St. Thomas and famous for his *Summa Theologiae Mysticae*, first published in Lyon in 1656. His influential definition is: "mystical and heavenly theology is a kind of knowledge of God drawn forth or produced by divinely infused light through the union of the will with God." [7] We are fortunate in that there is a recent and learned example of the application of this standard to a topic similar to ours: Augustine's relation to mysticism. [8]

Without explicitly mentioning the definition quoted above, the author relies on Philipp for the corresponding description of the stages leading to mysticism in the strict sense of the word. In a few words we report his outline to clarify both his final conclusion and the technical terms we shall use later on. The first stage is ascetics or mysticism in the general sense of the word. It starts with oral prayer and meditation characterized by "discursive, decisional thinking." [9] Not study as such but love is the goal, and the more love is elicited the more an irrational element characteristic of love is introduced so that finally in persistent meditation the intuitive mode replaces the discursive mode of thought. From the resulting affective prayer, "the state of meditation, in which purification and inner unification is achieved, transforms itself, with the aid of God's grace, into an acquired state of contemplation." [10] The ensuing peace of soul and enjoyment of divine truth should not be confused with mysticism proper. What is important is that "the acquired state of contemplation is a habit and a fully controllable act which is accessible to every individual soul, given the assistance of ordinary grace." [11]

It is only from here onward that one embarks upon the *via mystica* proper—to which I shall refer as "high mysticism"—when the soul suffers in sheer receptivity and passivity the divinely infused contemplation, is transformed in spiritual marriage, and finally absorbed into God, gazing upon God Himself or upon the Holy Trinity. Applying this definition to the thought of St. Augustine, Hendrikx argues that Augustine teaches merely the achievement of *sapientia* with the aid of ordinary grace, typical of acquired and not of infused contemplation; therefore "in the closed system of Augustinian convictions there is no place for mystical knowledge of God in the genuine sense of the word." [12]

Since the two stages of acquired and infused contemplation are alien to Luther's thought, acceptance of Hendrikx' definition of mysticism would mark the end of this essay. Furthermore, this scholastic understanding of mysticism—which is anachronistic with regard to Augustine—excludes with St. Augustine a large group of eastern and western theologians from the realm of mystical theology "in the genuine sense of the word," since it presupposes the thirteenth century secularization of Neoplatonic and Augustinian epistemology.

3. In addition to the phenomenological and dogmatic solutions, there is still a third option, namely, the historical-genetic approach. Again in the year 1936 Erich Vogelsang made a significant contribution by no longer operating with the general and usually vague concept of mysticism. After first enumerating the mystical authors said to be known to Luther—Dionysius Areopagita, Hugh and Richard of St. Victor, Bernard, Bonaventure, Gerson, Brigit of Sweden, Tauler, and "the Frankfurter"—Vogelsang distinguished between "Dionysian mysticism" *(areopagitische Mystik)*, "Latin mysticism" *(romanische Mystik)*, and "German mysticism" *(Deutsche Mystik)*. With this more differentiated view of mysticism, Vogelsang could give a more refined answer to our question: (1) From 1516 onward Luther renders the clear verdict of "No" to "Dionysian mysticism" as a speculative bypassing of the incarnate and crucified Christ; [13] (2) *re* "Latin mysticism" both a "Yes" to its emphasis on the earthly Christ and on mysticism as experience rather than doctrine, and a "No" to its bypassing spiritual *Anfechtung,* to its erotic marriage mysticism, and to its ultimate goal of ecstatic union with the uncreated word; [14] (3) an enthusiastic "Yes" characterizes Luther's evaluation of the third type of mysticism, "German mysticism," in which Luther found what he hailed in "Latin mysticism," but beyond that a spiritual understanding of purgatory as self-despair characteristic of the Christian life, and the idea of the *resignatio ad infernum,*[15] both presented in his German mother tongue and representative of a nearly forgotten, submerged, genuinely German theological tradition.

II. TOWARD A NEW CLASSIFICATION: "SIC ET NON"

1. Insofar as Erich Vogelsang works here with concepts and categories which have been operative and influential in Luther research until this present day, it is appropriate to raise some fundamental questions which lead us, I believe, in medias res.

The medieval use of authorities is seldom characterized by a total endorsement of an earlier theologian as such; rather it is an effort to establish support on a particular point under discussion, while leaving ample room for overt criticism in another context. The relation of Thomas Aquinas to Augustine, of Jean Gerson to Bernard of Clairvaux, and of John Eck to Gregory of Rimini may serve here as three well-known examples drawn from the traditions of the *theologia speculativa* and the *theologia affectiva*. The same "sic et non" procedure can be amply documented with regard to Luther's attitude toward many preceding theologians, including Augustine, Bernard, Thomas, and Scotus.[16]

Hence it is inappropriate to chart on the basis of one or two references, whether positive or negative, reliable lines of relationship and dependence. When Luther refers to or praises a medieval doctor whose thoughts on other accounts prove to be completely alien to his own theology, it is often suggested that Luther "misunderstood" him, or—as it is sometimes put more nicely—that Luther is led into a "productive misunderstanding." If one collects these kinds of statements from a wide range of Luther studies, one cannot but conclude that Luther is uniquely naïve and ignorant!

In the case of Pseudo-Dionysius we have the very positive statement by Luther in 1514 that the *via negativa* is the most perfect. "Hence we find with Dionysius often the word 'hyper,' because one should transcend all thought and enter darkness." [17] Luther seizes here upon an aspect of the theology of Dionysius [18] which in the *Disputation Against Scholastic Theology* in 1517 will be formulated as "the whole of Aristotle relates to theology as shadow to light." [19] I am inclined to classify this theme with the earliest statement on this matter in 1510: "Theology is heaven, yes even the kingdom of heaven; man however is earth and his speculations are smoke. . . ." [20] It is the "hyper" element which Luther approves and by no means the anagogical *facere quod in se est* of man which would bypass God's revelation in Christ.[20a]

In 1514 it is already clear that "darkness,"—*tenebrae, umbra,* or *caligo*—shares in the double meaning of *abscondere* and *absconditus:*

not only apart from faith is God obscured in our speculations, but even in faith the faithful live "in umbraculo," in God's protective custody,[21] as friends of God on earth. If one turns for comparison to a passage from the hand of such a true disciple of Pseudo-Dionysius as Dionysius the Carthusian († 1471), where he discusses the *unio mystica* in terms of the most intimate sons of God *(secretissimi filii Dei)*, elevated halfway between the blessed and the average believers and through love and rapture absorbed in the ocean of God's infinity,[22] one sees immediately that it would be misleading to overlook the "sic et non" character of this and other asides Luther makes to Dionysius in the early years.[23] When from 1519–1520 onward Luther attacks "Dionysian speculations" there is no reason to base on this finding a theory of development, let alone of reversal. Rather, he now associates explicitly the name of Dionysius with a theological position which had never been his own, a phenomenon perhaps not unrelated to the fact that his earliest opponents had started immediately to make use of Pseudo-Dionysius to defend the validity of the papal hierarchy.[24]

2. Turning now to the second category of "Latin mysticism," we begin by stating that it makes exceedingly good sense to establish a separate category for medieval authors from Bernard to Gerson who, in contrast to the tradition characterized by the *Doctor Ecstaticus* [Meister Eckhart], do not allow for the absorption of the believer into the abyss of the Godhead. As Etienne Gilson has shown clearly for Bernard, the Christian has to lose his *proprium* in the process of union with God through love, but this *proprium* is not the individuality of the *viator*, but rather the distortion of his image by the impact of sin.[25]

In Bernard's influential *De diligendo Deo* there is an acute awareness of the limits and limitations of man's bond with God on this earth. After distinguishing four degrees of love—of oneself for one's own sake *(se propter se)*, of God for one's own sake *(Deum propter se)*, of God for God's sake *(Deum propter Deum)*, of oneself for God's sake *(se propter Deum)*—of which the first three are familiar to us from late medieval scholastic debates as *amor sui*, *amor concupiscentiae*, and *amor amicitiae*, Bernard confesses that he is not certain that anyone can attain to the fourth degree in this life: "I for one confess that it seems impossible to me. But without doubt this will come about when the good and faithful servant will have entered into the joy of his master, exhilarated by the abundance of God's house."[26]

3. It is not without good reason that in so many fifteenth century

meditations and sermons Bernard and Gerson constitute the two major authorities, often mentioned in one breath and interchangeably. Without denying Gerson's independent synthesis in his *Theologia mystica speculativa,* it is, e.g., at such a climax in his work as the description of the several interpretations of transformation and union with God that Gerson falls back on *De diligendo Deo.* In a fascinating sermon preached on the Feast of St. Bernard, dated August 20, 1402, he appropriates Bernard's heritage, and extols the *Doctor Mellifluus* by having Bernard speak autobiographically.[27] Here three stages of contrition, meditation, and contemplation are described as the way to peace and union with Christ with the usual reference to Gal. 2:20: "it is no longer I who live, but Christ who lives in me."[28] Gerson selects two points which the young Luther would also associate with Bernard: (1) not to progress is to regress *(non progredi, regredi est),*[29] and (2) the hermeneutical principle that for a proper interpretation one has to clothe oneself in the affective state of the writer *(affectus induere scribentis).*[30] In my opinion the most revealing index of the intimate relation between Gerson and Bernard is the fact that on the one point at which Gerson warns his listeners against Bernard, he refers to a Pseudo-Bernardian work. Not yet five months before the exuberant encomium and completely in accord with the "sic et non" tradition, Gerson expresses his disapproval of a too intimate and proleptic description of the union of love in Bernard's *Epistola ad fratres de Monte Dei,* which actually is from the hand of William of St. Thierry.[31]

I am not convinced that Bonaventure should be mentioned in the same breath with Bernard and Gerson. Though one can interpret Gerson's theological program as an effort to reestablish in the Parisian theological faculty the balance of mind and heart which had characterized Bonaventure's *opus* a century and a half before, and though Gerson regrets that the Franciscan *moderni* abandoned the great tradition of Bonaventure,[32] it is questionable whether Bonaventure would have reciprocated this admiration and whether he would have sided with the Parisian Chancellor in his critique of Ruysbroeck's transformation (eucharistic) mysticism, or would have appreciated Gerson's insistence on the "conformitas voluntatis" as the axis of mystical theology.[33]

Furthermore, when Bonaventure develops his own typology[34] in accordance with the threefold spiritual sense of Scripture, and hence distinguishes between *doctores (fides), praedicatores (mores),* and *contemplativi (finis utriusque),* Bernard of Clairvaux is classified as a preacher rather than with Dionysius and Richard of St. Victor as one concerned with the *studium contemplativorum.* Whereas Hugh of St. Victor [35] forms the apex of Bonaventure's typology, embracing the offices of doctor, preacher, and contemplative, we find in a parallel typology from Luther's later opponent, Kaspar Schatzgeyer, that Bonaventure has replaced Hugh of St. Victor. In his *De perfecta et contemplativa vita,* a hitherto hardly noticed work dating from 1501,[36] Schatzgeyer distinguishes—according to a psychological instead of an exegetical scheme—between doctors who have special gifts "in vi rationali" (Augustine, Ambrose), "in vi irascibili" (Jerome), and "in vi concupiscibili" (Gregory the Great, Bernard). While Jerome does not seem to have any intellectual progeny, Thomas, Alexander, Scotus, and the later commentators on Lombard stand in the succession of Augustine and Ambrose. Bonaventure, however, stands out as the appropriate guide for all those in orders, since he combines the characteristic gifts of both Augustine and Bernard.[37]

This classification finds its echo in Luther's evaluation. He can place Bernard before Augustine as the *preacher* of Christ [38] but refers to Bonaventure as "the highest among the scholastic *doctores.*" [39] It is exactly where Bonaventure straddles the two schools and combines the *theologia speculativa* with the *theologia affectiva* that Luther deviates from him and testifies: "he almost drove me out of my mind, because I wanted to feel the union of God with my soul, as a union of both the intellect and the will." [40]

4. From the point of view of Luther, it is not so obvious that Gerson should be classified under the rubric of "Latin mysticism" rather than with Tauler and the Frankfurter as "German mysticism." Conceding that Luther hails in Tauler a concept of spiritual temptation,[41] we note that it is exactly this aspect of Gerson's writing which leads Luther to say: "Gerson is the first who came to grips with the issue which concerns theology; he too experienced many temptations." [42] And: "Gerson is the only one who wrote about spiritual temptation." [43]

In 1516 Luther notes explicitly the anthropological parallel between Gerson and Tauler [44]—characteristically replacing their *apex mentis* and *syntheresis,* regarded as the highest part of the soul, by faith.[45] In view of the dramatic importance sometimes attached to the influence of Tauler upon Luther, it may be noted that this position of Luther can be traced back to a reference to Gerson in the earliest layer of the *Dictata,* more than two years before the discovery of Tauler.[46]

If the different classification of Gerson and Tauler is argued on the basis of Gerson's adherence—with Bernard and Bonaventure—to the mystical ascent by way of *(per christum)* rather than *to* the incarnate Christ *(in christum)*, we may recall that Luther noted in 1516 that Tauler preached one sermon on the basis of *theologia mystica*, which for Luther is characterized by its concern with the spiritual birth of the *uncreated* word, in contrast with theology in the normal sense *(theologia propria)*, which is concerned with the spiritual birth of the *incarnate* word.[47] Luther insists on the right relation between the two—"Leah [*theologia propria*] ought to precede *(prius . . . ducere oportet)* Rachel [*theologia mystica*]"[48]—but does not now or later deny the possibility or validity of "high mysticism" in the sense indicated above, however qualified it is as *difficile* and *rarum*. When the "old Luther" refers to Gerson in a most revealing comment on Genesis 19, probably sometime in 1538, he notes first that Caspar Schwenckfeld *cum suis* speculates about God as the monks used to when they bypassed Christ. Against this dangerous *commercium* with the *Deus nudus* Luther pits the true speculative life which concerns God's *potentia ordinata*, the incarnate and crucified Son.[49] It is quite clear, however, that Luther does not here condemn Gerson as the spiritual father or ally of Schwenckfeld.

Whereas it is often argued that the young Luther was a mystic until he saw the dangers of mysticism in the encounter with the left wing of the Reformation,[50] we note that Luther's reference to Gerson in 1538 reveals basically the same attitude as in his marginals to Tauler's sermons of 1516. High mysticism is not said to be out of the question or impossible, but "often extremely dangerous and a sheer trick of the Devil. . . . If one wants to be safe, one had best flee these speculations altogether. . . ."[51] Not even in this last stage of his development does Luther put Gerson on the Index. To the contrary, he exhorts his audience to study Gerson (and other authors of his genre), though with a restriction similar to that we noted with Gerson vis à vis Bernard: he should be read "cum iudicio."[52]

One could, of course, argue that beyond the earlier qualifications of the mystical union as "difficult" and "rare," the old Luther adds the warning "dangerous." However, we find this implicitly[53] stated in Luther's comment on Romans 5:2, dating from approximately the same time as his marginals on Tauler. Again, as in the example of Leah and Rachel, Luther insists on the priority of *accessus* to *raptus*, of justification by faith through the incarnate and crucified word to the *raptus* by the uncreated word. "But," Luther concludes this

passage, "who would consider himself so clean, that he would dare
to pursue this, unless he is called and, like the Apostle Paul, lifted
up by God (II Cor. 12:2). . . . In short, this 'raptus' cannot be
called 'accessus.' " [54]

There is here a transition from "rare" to "dare," from *rarum* to
periculose; yet this transition is not so unexpected and is understandable in the light of the fact that in the prologue of the most important nominalistic *Sentences* commentaries, the Apostle Paul is
introduced on the basis of II Cor. 12 as an exception to the rule
de potentia ordinata according to which the status of the *viator* is
contrasted with that of the *beatus* in that he is not yet a *comprehensor,*
not yet face to face with God, and hence without immediate knowledge of God.[55] Though Luther employs the concept of the *potentia
ordinata* of God, so characteristic for nominalistic theology, in his
commentary on Genesis, he gives it a Christological point instead
of its primary epistemological meaning: the *potentia ordinata* is here
not primarily the order established by the inscrutable free God who
could as well have established another order, but it is clearly the
order of redemption in Jesus Christ, established out of God's mercy
to provide sinful man with a refuge from danger. If we remind ourselves of the striking parallel with the *Dictata* passage (early 1515),
which insists, against those who want to be more immediately related
to God, on the protection (the *umbraculum*) which is necessary in
this life because we are not yet face to face with God,[56] we are
forced to conclude that there is a basic continuity throughout this
large span of years (1515–1538), notwithstanding Luther's encounter
with Tauler and the *Schwärmer.*

The fact remains that Tauler seems exempted from the "sic et non"
rule which generally applies to all Luther's authorities. This cannot
be due—as in the case of Wessel Gansfort [57] and Pupper of Goch [58]
or the author of "Beatus Vir" [59]—to temporary enthusiasm and later
disappearance from the sources. Bernd Moeller was able to compose
a list of twenty-six references to Tauler over the years 1515–1544
which remain positive to the very end.[60] We believe that Tauler and
the *Theologia Deutsch* [61] are and remain of vital importance for
Luther, among other things because they showed the growing Reformer how the mystical *affectus* could be retained while breaking
with both the synergistic elements in the *contemplatio acquisita* and
the speculative elements in the *contemplatio infusa.* Indeed, it is a
question whether it was not precisely this mystical *affectus,* with its
proximity to *sola* categories, which made it possible for Luther to

carry out this double break, or at least to formulate it theologically. It is important that we do not assume that all the so-called "mystical authors" listed by Vogelsang have been read by Luther as *mystical* authors. In the first place and more generally one can point to the democratization of mysticism [62] in late medieval devotional literature: what is retained of such an author as Bernard of Clairvaux or Hugh of St. Victor is often his piety, not his mysticism.[63] There is still a margin left for the "aristocrats of the Spirit," but the traditional mystical terminology is appropriated for the description of the Christian life of the average believer.[64] The *Via moderna* and the *Devotio moderna* share a common concern for the *theologia affectiva* rather than for the *theologia speculativa,* for ascetics rather than for mysticism, for the *contemplatio acquisita* rather than for the *contemplatio infusa*.[65]

In the second place, and more specifically with regard to Tauler: the very fact that Luther comes to the conclusion that Tauler develops one particular sermon on the basis of mystical theology [66] alerts us to the fact that Luther apparently does not assume this always to be the case. It is a daring step to build around Tauler—and the *Theologia Deutsch* [67] mentioned by Luther in the same breath—a whole category of so-called "German mysticism," especially if this is to include, as it usually does, an author such as Meister Eckhart to whom Luther has not related himself in any sense. Granted the generally acknowledged proximity of Eckhart and Tauler, there are noticeable differences which, when seen from the vantage point of Luther, are too formidable to overlook.[68] At any rate, the main conclusion drawn by Luther from the *Theologia Deutsch* is certainly not mystical: ". . . man should not confide in anything else but in Jesus Christ alone, not in his prayers, not in his merits or his works. Since it is not due to our efforts that we are to be saved but due to the mercy of God." [69] As appears from the final words of the 1518 preface to "Eyn deutsch Theologia" Luther regards it as a representative of the category "German Theology" rather than that of "German Mysticism": "hence we will find that the German theologians are without doubt the best theologians. Amen!" [70]

III. CHRIST'S EMBRACE: DEATH AND HELL [71]

1. Although we seemed to remain within the realm of methodological issues when we discussed the problems involved in extracting from Luther a "Yes" or "No" with respect to schools of mystical theology which did not present themselves as such to him, we have

already moved beyond the state of formal considerations. The only viable method open to us is to study and define mysticism on the basis of Luther's description and evaluation, hence, at least initially, bypassing the issue of the appropriate definition of mysticism as such and of the classification of its several schools.

On the basis of the foregoing discussion we can come to the following preliminary conclusions:

a) There is as yet no reason to assume that Luther rejected mystical theology as such.[72] Rather he opposes the dangers of what we called "high mysticism."

b) The first characteristic of this form of mysticism is for Luther the union of soul and body ("unio animae et corporis"). So far as I know, this is not a standard expression. Altenstaig brings in his *Vocabularius theologie* a definition of "beatitude" which includes both soul and body.[73] It may be that Luther hints at this form of final beatitude to expose the proleptic nature of this high mysticism as a presumptuous *theologia gloriae*. More specifically, however, the context of his remarks indicates that he has in mind a psychosomatic experience through which the human senses experience the object of speculation,[74] i.e. the union of the soul with Christ.[75]

Luther's stance is not due to the fact that he rejects the idea of union as such or that he holds that spiritual realities cannot be experienced. On the contrary, while they cannot always be formulated, they can be experienced, and on the basis of experience they can be learned. The point is, however, that true negative theology is "theology of the cross" and, as we shall see, its corresponding experience is the crying and groaning of the soul, the "gemitus inenarrabiles" (Rom. 8:26).[76]

c) The second characteristic of the kind of mysticism rejected by Luther is the bypassing of Christ in order to rest *in Deo nudo*. In his comment on Romans 5:2 Luther had insisted on the double requirement "per fidem" and "per Christum." [77] The single requirement "per Christum" could still be—and indeed was generally—understood as the necessary preparation for union and contemplation since it axiomatically presupposed the earlier and now transcended stage of faith. Especially the meditation upon the passion of Christ as the basis of all merits is advocated as the most useful means to generate intense devotion.[78]

A treatise by Schatzgeyer, in time (1501) close to Luther and filled with that monastic spirituality which was to evoke Luther's wrath, has by no means slighted Christ. The "pro nobis"—in this warm treatise put as "pro te"—establishes the intimate bond between Christ and the believer.[79] Furthermore the treatise insists that "there is but one way to heaven, through the cross of Christ." This proves, however, to evoke love and lead to the sweet embrace of Christ.[80] The true Christian turns away from the bitterness of this valley of tears to the beauty and splendor of Christ. Over against this *per Christum (et charitatem)* Luther places *per Christum* in the abiding context of faith *(per fidem)*.[81] For Luther the embrace with Christ is not sweet but death and hell: [82] "God wants us to be trained (by the cross), not absorbed." [83] The Christian does not turn away from the bitterness of this world but is in that very valley of tears identified with the cross of Christ.[84]

d) At this point one may wonder whether the question as to Luther's relation to mysticism has not already been answered. If, indeed, the *contemplatio acquisita* is ruled out because it presupposes man's strenuous cooperation with grace,[85] and if *contemplatio infusa* is ruled out as presumptuous *theologia gloriae*,[86] it seems that no latitude is left. Yet the contrast of *accessus* and *raptus* is not the last word. If Luther, on the one hand, rejects the *raptus*, he indicates, on the other hand, that the *accessus* takes on a number of traits which are usually characteristic of the *raptus* itself. Although the embrace and union cannot be experienced through the senses and the *gemitus* continues to characterize the human crying need for the full manifestation of God (Rom. 8:26),[87] still the embrace and union are not ruled out but grasped by faith. As appears from the third Galatians commentary, the confrontation with the left wing of the Reformation does not force Luther to break with his alleged mystical past. The amazing thing is that he does not criticize the *Schwärmer* for being too radical, but for not being radical enough. They separate faith in the heart and Christ in heaven, whereas, for Luther, these are inseparably intertwined. As regards this identification of Christ and the Christian Luther says concisely: "Es geht nicht speculative sed realiter zu"—it is not an imagined but a real matter.[88] It is important for us that this "realiter" is interpreted—undoubtedly expressing Luther's intention precisely—as the Christ in us who works "realiter," clarified by the eloquent adverbs "most present" *(praesentissime)* and "most efficaciously" *(efficacissime)*.

In the concluding section we want to probe Luther's use of typical mystical terminology in a series of thesis-like short paragraphs. To collect Luther's explicit statements *re* mystical theologians and their theology would prove to be an illegitimate short-cut. We have to take here the same seemingly unexciting or at least unspectacular way as in the study of other aspects of Luther's theology: patient comparison with the preceding tradition, with a special emphasis on the devotional tradition immediately before him.

IV. THE MYSTICAL CONTEXT: FUNDAMENTAL CONCEPTS

1. *Exegetical mysticism.* When one consults such a source as Altenstaig's *Vocabularius theologie*—published in the same year that Luther published his 95 theses—for the contemporary understanding of such technical mystical terms as "excessus," "extasis," and "raptus," one notices that the article on "extasis" is drawn up on the basis of two authorities. The first witness is the late medieval Church father, Gerson; [89] but in second place we find the Augustinian bishop and biblical exegete Jacobus Perez de Valencia. [90]

In the Prologue to the Psalms Commentary (1484) of Perez, we read that the *excessus* is the gift of vision to all prophets, a supernatural illumination which transcends the capacity of human knowledge. *Extasis* is a higher stage in which one is alienated from one's inner senses, as if he were outside himself *(quasi extra seipsum)*. The third and final *elevatio* is called *raptus,* which is granted to but a few. [91] Perez, just like Luther half a century later, could and probably did find this description dispersed throughout the works of Augustine. [92]

In the exegetical application, however, Perez does not retain the indicated distinctions. In commenting upon Psalm 115:11, Vulgate: "I said in my *excessus:* every man is a liar"—"excessus" is identified with "extasis" and interpreted by the verb "rapi" to describe the transition of David from "fides sola" to "contemplatio." Thus David is able to foresee the mysteries of the New Testament as prefigured in the law of Moses. [93] More important for the hermeneutical implications, exactly the same applies to the Apostles. First they have an implicit faith in Christ; but after Pentecost their minds are brought into ecstasy so that they grasp the mysteries of faith. [94] One may use here the term "exegetical mysticism" since it is the elevated state of mind, *excessus* or *extasis,* which allows the Apostles to understand Scripture. [95] The humiliation of which the preceding verse 10 speaks ("I am completely humiliated") is understood by Perez as the "sacrificium intellectus," the preparatory pre-Pentecostal state of mind. Thus, in a second stage, the "excessus" takes place in which David, the interpreter, comes to understand that only the divine law is reliable in the sense revealed by the Spirit. [96]

When we turn now to Luther's exposition of this text, we find that in his first comment on the *Psalterium* of Faber Stapulensis, the "excessus" is related to self-knowledge: elevated above himself man sees himself as he is, full of clouds and darkness.[97] Luther refers back to his exposition of Ps. 30 (:21) where he had said even more explicitly that *humiliation* is the result of the "excessus" or "extasis."[98] In contrast to Perez, humiliation is not the preparation for but the result of the "extasis."

In the interlinear gloss on the words "in my excessus," Luther notes the two meanings of "excessus" as either "raptus" or fear,[99] as he charts the four possible meanings of *extasis*.[100] Apart from this second connotation of fear, Luther interprets the term "excessus" ("extasis") in its mystical sense first as related to the "raptus" and the clear knowledge of faith; second, it stands for the understanding of faith *(sensus fidei)* which exceeds the literal understanding *(sensus litere)*. This first understanding is the *true* literal sense;[101] the "sensus litere" is the interpretation on which the unbelievers stubbornly insist. The understanding of faith is the understanding of Scripture, the Gospel itself, the "face" of God, elsewhere distinguished from the eschatological vision of God's face in heaven.[102]

In his comments Luther makes three successive attempts to interpret this text. He is especially concerned to bring together the "excessus" as (1) the transition of the sinful man *(homo mendax)* to the man who is spiritual through faith *(homo spiritualis per fidem)*, and (2) as the state of man stricken by fear (particularly the fear due to persecution),[103] in which the believer experiences his complete dependence upon God.[104] "In my excessus" proves to become a synonym for both "in faith" and "in struggle"; it designates man's place "coram Deo" where the demarcation between "verax" and "mendax" is revealed.[105] This "excessus" does not imply the transcendence of this valley of tears and a rest in the peace of God, but the "demasque" of the enemies of truth (i.e. the flesh and the world) and marks the beginning rather than the end of the battle.[106] There is definitely an elevation involved in the "excessus," an elevation which gives the believer a true perspective on the "futura bona" and produces the humiliating acknowledgment that he has no claim to these.[107]

Though the exegetical tradition concerning Ps. 115:11 will have to be explored in more detail, we suggest that four conclusions can be drawn from the preceding exposition.

a) The mystical term *excessus* is related by Luther to the idea of battle or struggle typical for the life of the *viator*, the soldier of Christ.[108] As such this is by no means unusual; ever since Augustine it had been noted that *excessus* refers to an extraordinary state of mind either due to fear and suffering or to revelation. It would remain for Luther characteristic that the *excessus* through which the *homo mendax* becomes the *homo spiritualis* continues to be seen in the context of *pugna, tribulatio, Anfechtung*. What must have fascinated Luther most in Tauler is the idea that man *suffers* the birth of God.[109] This is what Luther means when he contrasts "realiter" with "speculative."

b) There is another aspect to this very same contrast. The "realiter" also means that one does not leave Scripture behind as a mere starting motor for the *affectus*.[110] Against the usual monastic order of *lectio (oratio), meditatio, contemplatio*, Luther prescribes a *lectio* initiated by *oratio* and leading toward *relectio*. When compared with the preceding tradition, it is striking that Luther no longer regards *lectio* (letter) and *meditatio* (spirit) as two *successive* stages. In 1539, dealing explicitly with the proper order, it is stated that true *meditatio* is *lectio* and *relectio*.[111] The axis of this Scripture-oriented meditation is not speculation *(prudentia—intellectus)* but the affective state *(affectus)* which prepares man's intellectual powers for the sudden insights and breakthroughs which we should not limit to a once and for all *Turmerlebnis*.[112] The scope of the *affectus* is exactly the reality *coram Deo* which, as we saw, is revealed *in excessu mentis*,[113] when the knowledge of *futura bona* and the self-knowledge that *omnis homo mendax* coincide.[114] Luther can refer here to the believers exactly because it is to them, as the *spirituales* or the *mystici*,[115] that the mysteries of redemption and Incarnation are revealed.

c) Just as Luther rejects a false Christological mysticism—which, as we saw, speculates on the uncreated word and is not satisfied with the "homo abscondens divinitatem"—so also he rejects a false exegetical mysticism which forces access to the Father "through the mysteries of Scripture." Either way makes for pride or desperation, *superbi* or *desperati*, a traditional allusion to the two erring groups on the left and the right of the *via media* of the Church militant.[116]

d) The dual aspects of the *excessus mentis* as faith and tribulation may help us to explain why, in the first lectures on the Psalms (1513–1515), Luther repeatedly slights the fourth sense of Scripture, the anagogical interpretation.[117] It is certainly not completely absent; but when it occurs it stands increasingly for the horizontal perseverance of the faithful and not for the vertical ascent of the aristocrats of the Spirit. Accordingly, in one central passage the anagogical work of God is not mystical elevation but the goal of God's work in history, either in heaven or in hell.[118] The deviation from the principles of Bonaventure [119] and from the practice of men like Dionysius the Carthusian and Kaspar Schatzgeyer cannot escape our attention. I am inclined to find here support for the conclusion of Gerhard Ebeling, accepted by the editors of *WA* 55, that the reduction of the fourfold sense is to be related to another hermeneutical schema: head–body–members.[120] Just as its head, Jesus Christ, so does the body, the *ecclesia militans*, march toward history's goal through the same valley of tears as its suffering Lord: [121] "Therefore if you look for a sign of the grace of God or wonder whether Christ himself is in you: no other sign is given to you but the sign of Jona. Therefore if you were to be in hell for three days, *that* is the sign that Christ is with you and you in Christ." [122]

2. *Raptus*. Not only *excessus* but also *raptus* and *rapi* function in Luther's theological vocabulary. The well-known sharp contrast between the *temporalia* and the *aeterna*, etc., referring to the difference between existence *coram hominibus* and *coram Deo*, can be summarized by Luther on the inside of the title-page of his Psalter with the words: "In Holy Scripture the most important thing is to distinguish the Spirit from the letter; this is what truly makes one a theologian." [123] In a significant parallel in early 1514, Luther had noted that a true theologian is born "in rapture and ecstasy; this is what makes a true theologian" *(in raptu et extasi, et hec facit verum theologum)*.[124] After we have seen that *excessus* or *extasis* is at once *fides* and *pugna*, we are no longer tempted to oppose without far-reaching qualifications the mystical Luther of 1514 to the mature one of 1520 who states in the *Operationes in Psalmos:* "By living, indeed by dying and being damned, one becomes a theologian, not by thinking and reading and speculating" *(Vivendo, immo moriendo et damnando fit theologus, non intelligendo, legendo aut speculando)*.[125]

Raptus is the reliance on the righteousness of Christ outside ourselves *(extra nos)* and can be described as a complete transformation into Christ *(in Christum plane transformari)*.[126] Again, as we noted with *excessus*, *raptus* does not mean an ontological transformation but a transformation of *affectus* and *fiducia*, of our love and trust. Hence we do not argue that Luther is a mystical theologian because of his use of these terms. Rather we stress that their new function cannot be understood without a thorough grasp of their original mystical context. If future research confirms my suggestion that Luther's concept "extra nos" is related to *raptus*, one of the major arguments for a forensic interpretation of Luther's doctrine of justification has been preempted.[127] Though we have no claim to the *iustitia Christi* which is not our "property" *(proprietas)*, it is granted to us as a present possession *(possessio)*.[128] *Extra nos* and *raptus* indicate that the *iustitia Christi*—and not our own powers—is the source and resource for *our* righteousness.[129] Epithets such as "external" and "forensic" righteousness cannot do justice to Luther's doctrine of justification. Luther can use the *raptus* not only because of its connotation of "extra nos" but also because of its implication of absolute passivity. According to what we called "high mysticism," sheer passivity is typical of the last stage of true mysticism experienced by the elect few. Luther takes this term and applies it to the life of faith as such and hence to *all* true believers. Parallel to his deletion of the wall of separation between the *praecepta* and the *consilia evangelica*—the shaking of the foundations of monasticism—Luther's particular kind of democratization of mysticism robs high mysticism of one of its main characteristics. At the same time, its original context alerts us to the fact that when Luther uses *rapi* in one breath with *duci* and *pati*,[130] the sinner is not a dead instrument of the omnipotent God, and justification by faith is not quietism.

3. *Gemitus.* Both *excessus* and *raptus* imply that faith and justification are not the harmonious realization of man's capacities and desires. In his Romans commentary Luther uses a term which he could have read in Gerson's *De mystica theologia*, the "juxtaposition of opposites" *(antiperistasis)*, synonymous with "sub contrario," in the transcript rendered as "in abscondito." [131] Here we are in the immediate proximity of Luther's own use of the word mystical: all wisdom and love are hidden in the suffering and dying Christ— "hidden because visible to mystical and spiritual eyes *(mysticis et spiritualibus oculis visibiles)*." [132]

At this point we should at least mention the term *gemitus*, though its absence in the relevant literature and the limits of this paper do not allow for more than some introductory observations. In the light of the preceding tradition with regard to *gemitus*, two points are particularly noteworthy in Luther's earlier works. In the first place the parallel between *fides* and *gemitus*. Justification, and more precisely the nonimputation of sin, takes place "on account of faith and groaning" *(propter fidem et gemitum)*, and culpable sin is not found "in those who believe and cry out [to God]" *(in credentibus et gementibus)*.[133] *Gemitus* is not another word for *facere quod in se est* or *humilitas* as some kind of condition for justification; rather it characterizes the life of the *sancti,* whose righteousness is hidden.[134] It describes the state of complete identification with Christ.[135] Whereas in the connection between *gemitus* and true penitence there is a basis for comparison with Abelard,[136] Bernard and Gerson refer to *gemitus* as part of the preparatory stage in the triad "purgation–illumination–contemplation" [137] or as initiation of the birth of God in the soul.[138]

The real significance of the fact that Luther can combine *gemitus* and *fides* appears, however, when we realize that the use made of *gemitus* by both Bernard and Gerson as a stage on the mystical way is by no means a coincidence. According to an influential gloss by Jerome *gemitus* refers to *synderesis,* which means that the gloss attributes to the human spirit what Romans 8:26 describes as the operation of the Holy Spirit: "the Spirit petitions for us with unutterable groanings." [139] This combination of *gemitus* and *synderesis* functions in scholasticism in such a way that we are not allowed to study the one concept without the other. For Bonaventure the *synderesis* is the affective power in man which intercedes with God with "unutterable groanings," [140] since it makes man desire the good. Since this *synderesis* is an inalienable part of man, Geiler can exhort his readers to self-purgation by going "diligently into the inner ground [of the soul]." [141] It is this same virginal part of man which, according to Dionysius the Carthusian, is kindled by love until the soul is completely absorbed in God.[142] And it is in a call for the full exploitation of these divine resources in man that Schatzgeyer's 1501 treatise on the spiritual life culminates in the Epilogue.[143]

As is well known, there is a marked interest with the young Luther in the *synderesis,*[144] which I am inclined to relate to his early defense of the *facere quod in se est* and the *merita de congruo.*[145] Yet in the most explicit statement in this period it is quite clear that the *synderesis* points man to the proper *goal* but does not show him the *way* to that goal.[146] Even here the *gemitus* is not the emotional expression of the *synderesis* but the mark of its impotence and hence of man's absolute dependence on God. The *synderesis* characterizes man's *esse,* not his *bene esse.*[147] Schatzgeyer had—in accordance with the tradition—based his high expectations of man's innate *synderesis* on Ps. 4:7: "the light of your face is manifest to us, O God." In the *Dictata* (1516) and again emphatically in the *Operationes in Psalmos* Luther says explicitly that this interpretation is false: "The first principle of all good works is faith." [148] *Gemitus* (just as much as *oratio*) presupposes faith and does not refer to a stage of preparation or to a virginal sinproof part in man, but to the life of faith itself: "Prayer is his desire for Christ; the cry is for Christ to transfigure his wretchedness." [149]

Reviewing our conclusions it can be said that Luther has gathered in terms characteristic of the extremes of the *via mystica* to clarify its center and axis. On the one hand *excessus* and *raptus,* on the other *gemitus* have been put to the service of clarifying the Christian life. It is exactly in the balance of these ideas that I discern the genius of Luther's theology of the Christian life. The *gemitus* aspect neutralizes the dangers of the *theologia gloriae* of the mystical *raptus.* The *excessus* and *raptus* aspect neutralizes the synergistic elements in the traditional scholastic combination of *synderesis* and *gemitus.* The test for this conclusion can be carried out in a separate discussion of Luther's use of bridal imagery and his view of the *unio fidei,* which we cannot execute here. Searching our way among the many pitfalls inherent in the theme "Luther and Mysticism," we hope to have shown that this crucial area cannot be regarded as a side issue in the rich world of thought of the Reformer.

One can designate the theology of Luther with the generally recognized summarizing formula, "simul iustus et peccator"—simultaneously righteous and sinful. The very same reality which is summarized by this formula can be expressed in the language of mystical spirituality, and that means for Luther in the language of the personal experience of faith, by the formula, "simul gemitus et raptus." [150] For both formulas it is characteristic that they do not indicate a *via media,* but a *simul* which reveals a *coincidentia oppositorum.*

NOTES

[In the printed German edition from which I have translated these notes, Prof. Oberman includes the citations from the primary sources to which his notes refer. Since it is not practical in a volume of this nature to reproduce these extensive Latin and German quotations, the interested student is referred to the apparatus of the German version. The notes below are complete save for these quotations.—ED.]

1. *De mystica theologia, Tractatus primus speculativus. Prologus,* ed. André Combes (Lucani, 1958), cons. 2, pp. 27–29.

2. *WA* 56,300.7f.; Cl. (=*Luthers Werke in Auswahl,* I–VIII, hrsg. von Otto Clemen), 5,248.16f (to Rom. 5:2; 1516).

3. *WA* 11,117.35f. (1523); cf. 2 Cor. 12:2. Thomas Aquinas relates the "third heaven" to the *contemplatio intellectus,* and he understands the rapture of Paul as a higher level "quod pertinet ad affectum." (S. Th. II/II, q. 175, a. 2, c.a.)

4. *WA* 9,98.19 (Marginal Notes on Tauler's Sermons, 1516). See Johannes

Ficker, "Zu den Bemerkungen Luthers in Taulers Sermones (Augsburg, 1508)." *Theol. St. u. Kritiken* 107 (1936), 46–64.

5. *WA* 9,100.38f.; Cl. 5,308.11f. (1516).

6. Artur Rühl, *Der Einfluss der Mystik auf Denken und Entwicklung des jungen Luther* (Theol. Diss. Marburg, 1960), p. 6.

7. "Theologia mystica coelestis est quaedam Dei notitia per unionem voluntatis Dei adhaerentis elicita vel lumine coelitus immisso producta." So reported by Thomas de Vallgornera O.P., *Mystica theologia divi Thomae* (Barcelona, 1662). Philipp and Thomas were both dependent upon the commentary of John of St. Thomas († 1644) on Thomas of Aquinas, *S.Th.*, 1/11, q. 67–70. Cf. *Les dons du Saint Esprit,* trans. R. Maritain (Juvisy, 1950²).

8. Ephraem Hendrikx O.E.S.A., *Augustins Verhältnis zur Mystik* (Theol. Diss. Würzburg, 1936); in abbreviated form in *Zum Augustin-Gespräch der Gegenwart,* ed. Carl Andresen (Darmstadt, 1962), pp. 271–364.

9. *Ibid.,* p. 272.

10. *Ibid.,* p. 274. L. G. Mack points out: "Above all the humanity of Christ should be meditated upon, for man is more deeply impressed by visible objects. . . . As to the acquired contemplation, Domenichi seems to admit a contemplation, inferior to the infused, it is true, yet genuine contemplation, which can be reached by human efforts." The *'Liber de contemplatione Dei' by Dominicus de Dominicis, 1416–1478* (Rome, 1959), pp. 14, 16f. In the Thomistic mystical tradition it is unthinkable that the higher levels of mysticism should be subject to the efforts of man. Marie Louise von Franz suggests that this Commentary could be a transcript of the last words which Thomas Aquinas spoke in his ecstasy on his deathbed. *Aurora consurgens: A Document Attributed to Thomas Aquinas on the Problem of Opposites in Alchemy* (New York, 1966), pp. 430f. On the other hand, the identity of the soul with God, which in one place even looks to such union from the side of man (*ibid.,* p. 363), suggests the opposite conclusion.

11. Hendrikx (note 8), p. 275.

12. *Ibid.,* p. 346. It may be noted that a generally respected authority on mystical theology, writing in the same year as Hendrikx and working with a different definition of mysticism, came to the opposite conclusion about Augustine. Joseph Maréchal, *Etudes sur la psychologie des mystiques* II (Brussels, 1937), 180ff.; cf. 250, 255. A more balanced judgment is made by Ernst Dassmann in regard to Ambrosius: "Ein wie auch immer akzentuierter *moderner* Begriff von Mystik kann nun aber wiederum nicht als Maszstab an die Aussagen des Ambrosius gelegt werden." *Die Frömmigkeit des Kirchenvaters Ambrosius von Mailand* (Münster, 1965), 181.

13. "Luther und die Mystik," *Luther-Jb.* 19 (1937), 32–54, esp. 35. Vogelsang was not the first to go beyond an often unrewarding general definition of mysticism. He acknowledges the merits of Hermann Hering, *Die Mystik Luthers* (Leipzig, 1879). Cf. also W. Köhler, *Luther und die Kirchengeschichte* I (Erlangen, 1900), 368, where an "areopagitische und germanisch-bernhardinische Mystik" are described.

14. Vogelsang (note 13), pp. 40f. In his later essay, "Die unio mystica bei Luther," *ARG* 35 (1938), 63–80, Vogelsang focuses his earlier exposition as he now expressly applies the "yes" and "no" to bridal and union mysticism; see especially the reference (p. 70, n. 4) to Luther's emphasis on faith as "copula." Cf. further Friedrich Th. Ruhland, *Luther und die Brautmystik nach Luthers Schrifttum bis 1521* (Giessen, 1938), pp. 54ff., 142f. Vogelsang could

still write in 1937 that Luther preferred Tauler to Bernard because, among other things, the bridal mysticism "bei Tauler ganz zurücktrat" (42). Cf. however Ruhland, pp. 59ff., and Vogelsang, *ARG* 35 (1938), 78ff.

15. On the spiritual nature of temptation (*Anfechtung*) and the *resignatio ad infernum* in Jean Gerson, cf. Walter Dress, *Die Theologie Gersons. Eine Untersuchung zur Verbindung von Nominalismus und Mystik im Spätmittelalter* (Gütersloh, 1931), pp. 167, 180ff.

16. For Augustine see *WA Tr.* 1,140.5; Cl. 8,45.36 (Nr. 347); cf. *WA* 54,186.16. For Bernard esp. *WA Tr.* 3,295.6 (Nr. 3370b). For Thomas: *WA Tr.* 1,135.12 (Nr. 329). For Scotus: *WA Tr.* 3,564.3; Cl. 8,150.4 (Nr. 3722).

17. *Schol.* to Ps. 64 (65):2 (*WA* 3,372.13–27; early 1514). Martin Elze has warned that one cannot interpret this passage as a positive reference to Dionysius; see his important article, "Züge spätmittelalterlicher Frömmigkeit in Luthers Theologie," *ZThK* 62 (1965), 381–402, 395, n. 51. If one examines this text as a whole, one finds that in the "attamen"-sentence Luther indeed says that the text of Dionysius should not be understood in an anagogical sense. In the sentence which begins "Nam ut dixi . . . ," however, it is necessary to understand the words "unde nimis temerarii sunt nostri theologi" as a reference to the "hyper" of Dionysius. Cf. also the *Schol.* to Ps. 17 (18):12 (*WA* 3,124.29–39; Cl. 5,94.14–25).

18. Soon thereafter, perhaps in the summer of 1514, Luther emphasizes in the *scholion* to Ps. 79 (80):3 the "supra rationem" of faith. This passage shows that by "contemplativi" Luther can mean not the spiritually privileged among the faithful, but the faithful as such: "Christi fides non potest esse nisi in iis, qui supra rationem contemplativi sint. Apparet enim, quando in eum creditur. Sed credere nequent, nisi filii Rachel, elevate mentis." *WA* 3,607.22–24. On the significance of "in eum credere" in place of "eum credere" or "eo credere" cf. my book, *The Harvest of Medieval Theology* (Cambridge, Mass., 1963), pp. 229, 119. I fully agree with the important observation of Bernhard Lohse that "positiv . . . die contemplatio letztlich mit dem Glauben identisch gesetzt (wird)" and that Luther "zumindest der Sache nach die contemplatio mit dem Glauben gleichsetzt oder doch auf die entscheidende Bedeutung des Glaubens hinweist." *Mönchtum und Reformation. Luthers Auseinandersetzung mit dem Mönchsideal des Mittelalters* (Göttingen, 1963), pp. 230f. To be sure, to the extent to which *contemplatio* = *elevatio mentis* = *excessus mentis*, Luther's interpretation is not completely without precedent; cf. infra, n. 93. But in the *Dictata* for the most part "contemplativi" refer to a peculiar group in the Church and is often connected with the "doctores." For further documentation of this point see Joseph Vercruysse, *Fidelis Populus. Een onderzoek van de ecclesiologie in Martin Luthers Dictata super Psalterium (1513–15)* (Diss. Gregoriana, Rome, 1966), typed ms., pp. 176–182.

19. *WA* 1,226,26; Cl. 5,324.8.

20. *WA* 9,65.14–16; Cl. 5,9.29–31 (Marginal Notes to Lombard, *Sent.* 1, d. 12, c. 2). In regard to Luther's rejection of the "facere quod in se est" between reason and revelation, cf. my essay "Robert Holcot O.P. and the Beginnings of Luther's Theology," *HThR* 55 (1962), 317–342, esp. 330ff. [Chap. V in this book.—ED.]. On sinful blindness as "caligo" in the later years, cf. the commentary on Gen. 42, *WA* 44,472.38; 473.42 (1535–45).

20a. See Luther's later statement in the *Operationes in Psalmos,* Ps. 5:12 (*WA* 5,176.29–33).

21. *Schol.* to Ps. 90 (91):1 (perhaps early 1515; *WA* 4.64.24–65.6; cf.

65.28–31). In Ps. 121 (122):3, another aspect of this theme is touched upon. Here Luther warns: be careful with the idea of participating in Christ! In this life, he writes, not even the most perfect of the saints have the whole Christ (". . . nunquam habet aliquis sanctorum totum Christum, sed quilibet partem eius, etiam perfectissimi"). *WA* 4,401.25–30. The significance of this passage has been noted by L. Pinomaa, "Die Heiligen in Luthers Frühtheologie," *St Theol.* 13 (1959), 1–47, 6f., and by B. Lohse (note 18), p. 230, n. 15, who quotes the second half of the citation. It is precisely the first half of the citation, however, that shows that Luther consciously sets forth this theme as a major and not a minor motif. Luther's conclusion, the Bernardian "stare est regredi," harkens back to the "in hac vita": in this life the *activi* and the *contemplativi* remain *viatores*.

22. Dionysius the Carthusian, *Enarratio in canticum canticorum Salomonis* in D. *Dionysii Cartusiani Enarrationes piae ac eruditae in quinque libros sapientiales* (Coloniae, 1533), *Opera omnia* VII (Monstrolii, 1898), 386 B–387 B.

23. Although I do not believe that John Eck was in any way decisively indebted to the Areopagite, Eck still makes reference in a completely understandable way to the *via negativa* of Dionysius as representative of the tradition of the Church. *Chrysopassus, Centuria* IV, 44 (Augsburg, 1514). Cf. *WA Tr.* 1, Nr. 257.

24. See in regard to Eck, *WA* 2,55.34–56.1 (1519). Ambrosius Catharinus Politus († 1552) writes: "As the great theologian Dionysius says," the ecclesiastical hierarchy is as much like the heavenly hierarchy as possible." *Apologia pro veritate . . . adversus impia ac valde pestifera Martini Lutheri Dogmata* (1520), ed. Josef Schweizer, *Corpus Catholicorum* 27 (1956), 2.7.18f. One finds this concept of the Church also with Sylvester Prierias, *De potestate papae dialogus* (1518) in Valentin Ernst Loescher, *Vollständige Reformations-Acta und Documenta,* II (Leipzig, 1723), 14. For the insistence upon the authenticity of the works of Dionysius as a disciple of Paul by Johannes Cochläus, see Martin Spahn, *Johannes Cochläus. Ein Lebensbild aus der Zeit der Kirchenspaltung* (Berlin, 1898; 2nd ed. Nieuwkoop, 1964), p. 234. For the high rating of Dionysius among northern humanists in the beginning of the sixteenth century we note, besides the well-known analyses by Nicolas Cusanus and the editorial work of Faber Stapulensis (cf. Eugene F. Rice, *Renaissance Studies* XI [1962], 126–160; 142), a letter by Konrad Peutinger (Augsburg, June 13, 1513), where Dionysius heads the list of the Greek and Latin Church fathers. *Briefwechsel des Beatus Rhenanus,* ed. Adalbert Horawitz and Karl Hartfelder (Leipzig, 1886; Hildesheim 1966²), pp. 57f. In a letter of Dec. 1, 1508, Beatus Rhenanus ranks him even with Paul and John as an instrument of revelation (*ibid.,* p. 18). Shortly before (Oct. 10, 1508), Rhenanus had already indicated as the most important reading "altissimam Dionysianae theologiae lectionem," "sublimem Cusani de sacris philosophiam," "Bonaventurae commentarios"—"the other theologians are not worth your time"—and the *Quincuplex Psalterium* of Faber. *Ibid.,* pp. 576f. In the later letters Dionysius is no longer mentioned!

25. *La théologie mystique de Saint Bernard* (Paris, 1947), pp. 21, 138, 155. The destruction of the false *proprium* means "reformatio": "transformamur cum conformamur." *Cant. Cant.* 62.5, as cited by Friedrich Ohly, *Hohelied-Studien. Grundzüge einer Geschichte der Hoheliedauslegung des Abendlandes bis um 1200* (Wiesbaden, 1958), p. 152.

26. *De dilig. Deo* 15.39 (*PL* 182, 998 D).

27. Jean Gerson, *Oeuvres complètes*, v: *L'Oeuvre oratoire*, ed. P. Glorieux (Paris, 1963), 326.

28. *Ibid.*, p. 329.

29. *Ibid.*, p. 335. Cf. Luther, *WA* 9,69.36f.; 107.23. See also the *scholion* to Ps. 4:2 in the Vatican Fragment: *Unbekannte Fragmente aus Luthers zweiter Psalmenvorlesung 1518*, ed. Erich Vogelsang (Berlin, 1940), p. 41. On Bernard, *Ep.* 91,3 (*PL* 182, 224).

30. Gerson (note 27), p. 334. Cf. *WA* 3,549.27–37.

31. Sermon "A Deo exivit" (Mar. 23, 1402), 14. Cf. *PL* 184, 337.

32. *Opera omnia*, ed. L. Du Pin, 1 (Antwerp, 1706), 91 D.

33. Cf. my book, *The Harvest of Medieval Theology*, pp. 338f.

34. *De reductione artium ad theologiam*, cap. 5, ed. Julian Kaup (Munich, 1961), 246.

35. On the relation between Hugo of St. Victor and the Pseudo-Dionysius, see Roger Baron, *Etudes sur Hugues de Saint-Victor* (Angers, 1963). Baron, who edits Hugo's commentaries, regards them as late works, ca. 1130–40 (*ibid.*, p. 88).

36. Otfried Müller cites from this work without calling attention to its early date. *Die Rechtfertigungslehre nominalistischer Reformationsgegner: Bartholomäus Arnoldi von Usingen O.E.S.A. und Kaspar Schatzgeyer O.F.M.* (Breslau, 1939). The same is true for another work on Schatzgeyer by Heinrich Klomps, *Freiheit und Gesetz bei dem Franziskanertheologen Kaspar Schatzgeyer* (Münster, 1959). Together with the equally neglected yet quite significant *Apologia status fratrum ordinis minorum de observantia* (1516), *De Perfecta et contemplativa vita* forms the main source of our knowledge of Schatzgeyer before 1517, and hence it permits us by way of comparison with the *Scrutinium* and other later works to measure the influence of the *causa Lutheri* on the development of Schatzgeyer's thinking. The pre-Reformation writings of Counter-Reformation authors deserve our special attention. Cf. the conclusion of Ernst Walter Zeeden: "Der Protestantismus hatte Augen, Herzen und Sinne auch der Katholiken geöffnet für das Wirken der Gnade." "Aspekte der Katholischen Frömmigkeit in Deutschland in 16. Jahrhundert," in *Reformata Reformanda. Festgabe für Hubert Jedin*, ed. Erwin Iserloh and Konrad Repgen, ii (Münster i. W. 1965), 1–18; 12.

37. Kaspar Schatzgeyer, *De perfecta atque contemplativa vita* (Conventus Monarchiensis, 1501) in *Opera omnia* (Ingolstadt, 1534²), fol. 318r–333v; directio 20, fol. 325.

38. *WA Tr.* 1,435.32f. (Nr. 872); *WA Tr.* 3,295.6–8 (Nr. 3370b); *WA* 40/3,354.17.

39. *WA Tr.* 1,330.1 (Nr. 683).

40. *WA Tr.* 1,302.30–34; Cl. 8,80.17–22 (Nr. 644). Cf. *WA* 40/3,199.32–35 (Ps. 126:6—1532–33, pub. 1540).

41. In the *Dictata* Luther breaks consciously with medieval tradition in the *scholion* to Ps. 90 (91):6 (*WA* 4,69.6–22—probably early 1515), in that he interprets the text not in the sense of "tentationes corporales," but as "tentationes fidei."

42. *WA Tr.* 2,114.1–3 (Nr. 1492); cf. *WA Tr.* 5,213.16 (Nr. 5523).

43. *WA Tr.* 1,496.7 (Nr. 979). Vogelsang notes "Gersons Sonderstellung" and refers to his earlier book, *Der angefochtene Christus bei Luther* (Berlin,

1932), p. 15, n. 56. Nevertheless, he finds with Gerson the same bypassing of the incarnate Christ as with Bernard and Bonaventure, "wenn auch auf dem methodisch gestuften Umweg über den Menschgewordenen, Gekreuzigten." *Luther-Jb.* (1937), p. 41 and n. 1.

44. *WA* 9,44.38–39; Cl. 5,307.22 (Marginal Notes to Tauler's Sermons).

45. *WA* 9,103.41; Cl. 5,310.27. I do not pursue this further pending the study by S. E. Ozment of the influence of Gerson and Tauler on the anthropology of the young Luther (a Harvard Ph.D. dissertation). [Now in print: *Homo Spiritualis: A Comparative Study of the Anthropology of Johannes Tauler, Jean Gerson and Martin Luther (1509–16)* (Leiden, 1969).—ED.] On the solidarity of Thomas and Tauler vis à vis Luther who "misunderstood" Tauler, cf. Heinrich Denifle, *Luther und Luthertum* I/1 (Mainz, 1904²), pp. 150ff. Cf. also A. M. Walz, "Denifles Verdienst um die Taulerforschung," in *Johannes Tauler. Ein deutscher Mystiker: Gedenkschrift zum 600. Todestag,* ed. E. Filthaut O.P. (1961), pp. 8–18. For Protestant assessments of the independent nature of Luther's appropriation of mysticism see Reinhold Seeberg, *Die religiösen Grundgedanken des jungen Luther und ihr Verhältnis zu dem Ockhamismus und der deutschen Mystik* (Berlin, 1931), p. 30; Wilhelm Thimme, "Die 'Deutsche Theologie' und Luthers 'Freiheit eines Christenmenschen,'" *ZThK* NF 13 (1932), 193–222, esp. 222; and Hering (note 13), p. 27.

46. *WA* 3,151.5–13 (*schol.* to Ps. 26 [27]:9—ca. Autumn, 1513). Cf. Gerson, *De mystica theologia* (note 1) 28.42–29.47; 34.24–35.31; 97.35f.

47. *WA* 9,98.20–25; Cl. 5,306.28–307.3.

48. *WA* 9,98.34; Cl. 5,307.13. For a parallel to this in a sermon from Aug. 15,1517 (according to Vogelsang it is from 1520—see *ZKG* 50 [1931], 132, 143), see *WA* 4,650.5–15; Cl. 5,434.19–30. To my knowledge the earliest treatment of this matter is in Luther's use of "deinde" with reference to the transition from the *vita activa* to the *vita contemplativa* in the *scholion* on Ps. 52 (53):7 (*WA* 3,298.31). Cf. the almost hymnic development in the *scholion* on Ps. 113 (114):9 (*WA* 4,94.40–95.11), where an attack on the "prius" is already considered dangerous. Cf. the striking parallel to this "prius" in John Geiler of Kaysersberg, in L. Dacheux, *Die ältesten Schriften Geilers von Kaysersberg* (Freiburg i. Br., 1882), pp. 215f. Cf. also the letter written a century earlier by Geert Groote, "Ad curatim Zwollensem" (1382), which warns of the importance of the "prius" by calling on the authority of the Pseudo-Dionysius, *Geraldi Magni Epistolae,* ed. W. Mulder, S.J. (Antwerp, 1933), p. 135. On Groote cf. K. L. C. M. de Beer, *Studie over de Spiritualiteit van Geert Groote* (Brussels, 1938), pp. 84–187. Groote warns of the serious danger of a mystical contemplation which is not preceded by ascetic purification (*ibid.,* pp. 186f.). While he has praise for Heinrich Seuse, Groote is very critical of Meister Eckhart and speaks in a qualified way about Jan van Ruysbroeck. It is noteworthy that Luther warns us not "festinari ad opera . . . antequam credimus." (*WA* 57,143.5f.—Hebr. 3:7, 1517).

49. Cf. *WA* 43,72.9–14, 22–28 (to Gen. 19:14).

50. More cautious is Johannes von Walter, *Mystik und Rechtfertigung beim jungen Luther* (Gütersloh, 1937), p. 21. Horst Quiring presents a representative view when he argues that Luther's (negative) relation to mysticism after 1520 is determined by his "Antithese zum Schwärmertum." "Luther und die Mystik," *ZSTh* 13 (1936), 150–174, 179–240, 234. Over against this view cf. Karin Bornkamm's instructive juxtaposition of Luther's exposition of Gal. 2:20 ("Vivo

autem non iam ego, sed vivit in me Christus") in 1519 and in 1531. *Luthers Auslegungen des Galaterbriefs von 1519 und 1531. Ein Vergleich* (Berlin, 1963), p. 98. In 1531 the intimacy of the union between Christ and the believer is described in stronger terms ". . . multo arctiore vinculo quam masculus et femina" (*WA* 40/1,286.1). Despite our emphasis on continuity, we do not deny a certain fluctuation and noteworthy parallels in the lectures on Romans and especially in the lectures on Hebrews. Cf. J. P. Boendermaker's study which comes to the conclusion that Luther's lectures on Hebrews are concerned "die neuen Erkenntnisse in alten, grösstenteils von der deutschen Mystik geprägten Begriffen auszudrücken." *Luthers commentaar op de brief aan de Hebreeën 1517–18* (Assen, 1965), p. 119; cf. p. 101. As we are trying to demonstrate, such was Luther's effort to depict the "*vera* vita contemplativa" from the very beginning.

51. *WA* 43,73.11–13, 21–29.

52. *WA* 43,72.31–73.9.

53. More explicit is the comment on Tauler at *WA* 9,100.28–30. Cf. Luther's Aug. 1517 (?) sermon, *WA* 4,647.19–25, 35–40; 648.13–16.

54. *WA* 56,299.17–300.8. Cf. *WA* 57,168.18–22; 167.17f.; *WA* 56,298.1f. On the basis of Luther's contrast between *raptus* and *accessus* Otto Scheel concludes: "So verliert die mystische Theologie ihre Bedeutung für die Praxis des religiösen Lebens . . ." "Taulers Mystik und Luthers reformatorische Entdeckung," in *Festgabe für Julius Kaftan* (Tübingen, 1920), pp. 298–318, esp. 318.

55. Cf. my *Harvest of Medieval Theology*, p. 41. On the debate between Ockham, d'Ailly, and Biel, cf. Altenstaig, under article "Viator," fol. 263ʳᵇ–264ᵛᵃ.

56. *WA* 4,64.24–65.6.

57. Cf. the preface to Gansfort's *Epistolae*, *WA* 10/2,316f. (1522); 317.3.

58. Cf. *WA* 10/2 329f. (1522). R. R. Post, the *connoisseur* of the *Devotio moderna*, has recently established that Pupper is a typical late medieval theologian. "Johann Pupper van Goch," *Nederlandsch Archief voor Kerkgeschiedenis* 47 (1965–66), 71–97, esp. 93.

59. Luther declares that he has nowhere found a better (i.e. nonphilosophical) treatment of original sin than in the "Beatus vir" (i.e. "De Spiritualibus ascensionibus") of Gerhard Groote (i.e. Gerhard Zerbolt von Zütphen). *WA* 56,313.13–16; Cl. 5,252.23–26. Cf. the Cologne ed. (1539), chap. 3. J. van Rooij considers Luther's praise a misunderstanding, since Zerbolt did not represent a "Protestant" doctrine of the total corruption of man. *Gerhard Zerbolt van Zütphen* (Nijmegen, 1936), p. 254.

60. "Tauler und Luther" in *La mystique Rhénane* (Paris, 1963), pp. 157–168, esp. 158, n. 3.

61. See the preface to the first, incomplete edition of the *Theologia Deutsch* (1516), *WA* 1,153: ". . . ist die matery fasst nach der art des erleuchten doctors Tauleri, prediger ordens." Henri Strohl points out that Tauler by comparison is more Thomistic (Dominican), whereas the *Theologia Deutsch* is more Scotist. *Luther* (Paris, 1962), p. 191.

62. Cf. *Harvest of Medieval Theology*, pp. 341ff.

63. Cf. Elze (note 17), esp. pp. 391ff. Cf. Jean Chatillon, "La devotio dans la langue chrétienne," in *Dic. de Spiritualité, ascétique et mystique*, III (Paris, 1957), 705–716, esp. 714.

64. François Vanderbroucke characterizes this era as marked by "le divorce entre théologie et mystique," *La Spiritualité du Moyen Age* (Paris, 1961), p. 533. Indeed, a general upsurge of affective theology can be noted, usually critical of the debates "in scholis." If theology is understood in this latter academic sense, Vandenbroucke's conclusion can be amply validated. Late medieval affective theology, however, with its elaborate use of mystical terminology, can perhaps better be assessed as a protection against such a divorce. This upsurge of affective theology and what I have called the democratization of mysticism are two sides of the same coin.

65. I am planning to deal elsewhere more extensively with the relation between the Observant movement and the *Devotio moderna.*

66. *WA* 9,98.20; Cl. 5,306.28.

67. On Luther's description of the *Theologia Deutsch,* see the title page of the second (and first complete) edition (1518), *WA* 1,376.A. Cf. the exposition of Ps. 51:3 in 1517, *WA* 1,186.25–29. Finally, cf. *Eine Deutsche Theologie,* cap. 42, modernized by Joseph Bernhart (Munich, 1946), p. 229.

68. On the distinction between Eckhart and Tauler see Käte Grunewald, *Studien zu Johannes Taulers Frömmigkeit* (Berlin, 1930), p. 41: "Statt einer Schaumystik also eine in diesem neuen Sinne wirklich voluntaristische Mystik." We do not, of course, deny that there are parallels between Eckhart and Luther; it is a more complex matter than mere "Verbindungslinien," as Rühl argues (note 6), p. 91. If Rühl is justified in describing as *the* point of distinction between scholasticism and mysticism the "Denkform" of the latter which "von einem Begriff ausgeht, andere anschliesst und wieder zum Ausgangsbegriff zurückkehrt" (38), and hence "die essentielle Einheit von diametral entgegengesetzten Konzeptionen enthüllt" (45), then the question must be raised: is not a minimal interpretation of just this "Denkform" encountered in every affective theology and hence no further typical for "high mysticism" in the described sense of the word? To the extent that one seeks an interpretation which would embrace "high mysticism," the "Denkform" rests then upon a "Denkinhalt" which presupposes a thoroughgoing monism in which opposites are present only in appearance. Further, Rühl's effort to distinguish Luther and mysticism generally on the basis of anthropology is unclear and does not take account of the fact that the anthropologies of Eckhart and Tauler are different. Cf. Grunewald, p. 8. Finally, there is a decisive difference between Luther's and Eckhart's understanding of creation. While for Eckhart creation is alienation (cf. *Harvest of Medieval Theology,* p. 326), it is for Luther "gnad und wohltat." *Tagebuch über Dr. Martin Luther,* ed. H. Wrampelmayer (Halle, 1885), p. 1559.

69. *WA Br.* 1,160.10–12; Cl. 6,10.15–18.

70. *WA* 1,379.11f.

71. *WA* 5,165.23. See note 82.

72. Cf. the discussion of Luther's use of the concept of bridal mysticism in my article, " 'Iustitia Dei' and 'Iustitia Christi': Luther and the Scholastic Doctrines of Justification," *HThR* 59 (1966), 1–26, esp. 25f. On the use of the expression, "du bist min, ich bin din," among German mystical authors, see the register assembled by Grete Lüers, *Die Sprache der deutschen Mystik des Mittelalters im Werke der Mechthild von Magdeburg* (Munich, 1926), pp. 309f. On the use of the expression, "minnende Seele," cf. Romuald Banz, *Christus und die minnende Seele. Zwei spätmittelhochdeutsche mystische Gedichte* (Breslau, 1908), p. 119.

73. "Illa autem unio animae et corporis . . ." (*WA* 43,73.11). Altenstaig writes in the article on "beatitudo," fol. 25ʳᵃ: "Beatitudo est duplex (ut scriptis reliquit Richardus di. XLIX ar. v, q. 2, li. IV), sc. anime et corporis." Under the article on "unio" (fol. 269ᵛᵃ) he writes: "unio quedam est corporalis, quedam spiritualis," although it is only in regard to the latter that mystical experience is discussed.

74. Bonaventure writes of such an experience: *Itinerarium mentis in Deum*, ed. Julian Kaup (Munich, 1961), IV.3, 112–114.

75. Cf. *WA* 40/3,199.5–10.

76. *Enarratio* Ps. 90:7 (1534–35, pub. 1541), *WA* 40/3,542.27–31; 543.8–13. A similar point is made in *WA Tr.* 1,108.1–11 (Nr. 257; 1532), where Luther writes against Eck as a disciple of Plato.

77. See note 54.

78. See Schatzgeyer (note 37), fol. 329ᵇ, Dir. 32. Cf. John Geiler of Kaysersberg in Dacheux (note 48), p. 247, and Jane Dempsey Douglass, *Justification in Late Medieval Preaching* (Leiden, 1966), pp. 180ff. In this connection we refer the reader to Gerson's "Ars bene vivendi," which appeared in Wittenberg in 1513 "apud Augustinianos" with Luther's publisher Johannes Grunenberg. It is inconceivable that Luther should not have known this edition, and it increases the number of Gerson's works which Luther probably had read.

79. Schatzgeyer (note 37), fol. 325ᵇ, Dir. 21.

80. *Ibid.*, fol. 329, Dir. 29.

81. Compare by way of contrast Dionysius the Carthusian, *Opera* VII, 301 D–302 A.

82. *Operationes in psalmos*, Ps. 5:2 (1519–20), *WA* 5,165.21ff.: "Sicut et filii patrem carnis dulcius amant post virgam, qua verberati sunt, Ita carni contraria voluptate sponsus sponsam suam afficit Christus, Nempe post amplexus. Amplexus vero ipsi mors et infernus sunt."

83. Cf. note 75. For both parallel and contrast cf. the emphasis on *exercitium* in Gerhard Zerbolt, note 59.

84. See the *scholion* to Hebr. 2:14 (1517), *WA* 57³,129.20–25.

85. *WA Br.* 1,160.

86. Cf. the exposition of Hebr. 9:5, *WA* 57³,201.15–202.6. Cf. the earliest exposition of Ps. 17:11 ("Ascendit et volavit super pennas ventorum") in *WA* 3,114.15; 124.16ff. On the two theologies which Luther contrasts in his exposition of Hebr. 9:5—"sapientia Christi gloriosi" and "sapientia Christi crucifixi"—cf. *WA* 39¹,389.10ff.

87. As we hope to show, this "gemitus" is closely related to the "syntheresis." On Luther's assessment and use of the concept "syntheresis," see Emanuel Hirsch, *Lutherstudien* I (Gütersloh, 1954), pp. 109–128. Without connecting "gemitus" and "syntheresis" with one another, M. A. H. Stomps collects a series of citations under the viewpoint "expectatio"—a term which is central for Luther's *theological* anthropology. *Die Anthropologie Martin Luthers. Eine philosophische Untersuchung* (Frankfurt a. M., 1935), esp. pp. 14ff.

88. Commentary on Galatians 3:28 (1531), *WA* 40¹,546.3–8, and the printed text of 1535, *WA* 40¹.546.25–28.

89. Luther speaks of "Gerson et ceteri patres" (*WA Tr.* 2.27.6f. [Nr. 1288] —1531). On the pulpit of the Amanduskirche in Urach, which was constructed in the last third of the 15th century, Gerson is depicted together with the four

fathers of the Church. Cf. Georg Dehio, *Handbuch der Deutschen Kunstdenkmäler*, III (Berlin, 1925³), 548.

90. See Altenstaig, *Vocabularius theologie* under article on "extasis" (fol. 83va); cf. the article on "raptus" (fol. 213^{va-b}). Cf. also the earlier *Vocabularius* (Tübingen, 1508; 2nd ed., Basel, 1514) under article on "ecstasis" (fol. 25³⁻⁴). As the epigram of Heinrich Bebel put it, this Latin schoolbook was considered an "antidote" to such little-valued books as the "Catholicon." The "Catholicon," a comprehensive book completed in March, 1286, and often published (there is a Cologne, 1497, edition), was a lexicon compiled by Joannes Balbus de Janua (Giovanni Balbi), and it was still used as an authority by Luther in 1509–10. Cf. *WA* 9,68.14. In 1524 Luther considered it (along with the *Florista, Grecista, Labyrinthus*, and *Dormi secure*) typical of the "tollen, unnützen, schedlichen, Müniche bücher," which glutted the libraries. *An die Ratherren aller Städte deutsches Lands*, *WA* 15,50.9f.; Cl. 2,461.10f. Humanists north of the Alps probably followed the variegated judgment of the work by Erasmus; *Opus Epistolarum* I, 115.89 (1489); 133.85 (1494); 172.32 (1497). At the time he wrote his first lectures on the Psalms (1513–15), Luther still considered the "Catholicon" authoritative.

91. *Prologus in Psalterium, tract.* II, a.2 (Venetiis, 1581), 16 F–17 B. For the larger context cf. Wilfrid Werbeck, *Jacobus Perez von Valencia. Untersuchungen zu seinem Psalmenkommentar* (Tübingen, 1959), pp. 81f. Cf. Luther *WA* 3,185.26f.: "in spiritu raptus intellexit in eo facto quid mystice significaret."

92. Cf. the by no means dated work of A. W. Hunzinger, *Lutherstudien*, I, *Luthers Neuplatonismus in der Psalmenvorlesung von 1513–1516* (Leipzig, 1906), pp. 105ff., esp. p. 106, n. 1. Cf. p. 74, where Hunzinger argues that Luther's Neoplatonism is not that of the Pseudo-Dionysius. For a necessary clarification of the basic differences, cf. the characterization by J. Koch, "Augustinischer und dionysischer Neuplatonismus und das Mittelalter," *KantSt.* 58 (1956–57), 117–133. I owe this reference to F. Edward Cranz, "The Transmutation of Platonism in the Development of Nicolaus Cusanus and of Martin Luther," which appears as part of the reports of the Cusa Congress of 1964.

93. Perez (note 91), fol. 837 F–838 A.

94. *Ibid.*, fol. 838 B.

95. *Ibid.*, fol. 838 D/E.

96. *Ibid.*, fol. 383 E/F.

97. *WA* 4,519.26–29. Cf. Augustine, *Enarr.* in Ps. 115, n. 3; Gl. ord., *PL* 113, 1038A; Peter Lombard, *PL* 191, 1030B.

98. *WA* 3,171.19–24.

99. *WA* 4,265.22 (Spring, 1515). Cf. Altenstaig, *Vocabularius* (1508), fol. 253–254.

100. *WA* 4,265.30–36. With Cassiodorus the connection between *excessus* and martyrdom is given prominence. See his exposition of Ps. 115:10f., *Corpus Christianorum* 98, col. 1042, lines 9–16.

101. Cf. *WA* 4,492.5–8 (Ps. 40, Faber). Luther's comments here are an exact mirroring of Faber's prologue to his Psalter. This important text is discussed in my book, *Forerunners of the Reformation* (New York, 1966), pp. 281–296.

102. *WA* 4,482.25–483.4. On this usage of "face" (*vultus/facies*), cf. John

Staupitz, *Tübinger Predigten*, ed. G. Buchwald and E. Wolf (1927), pp. 239.13–15. Cf. also the study by David C. Steinmetz, *Misericordia Dei: The Theology of Johannes von Staupitz in its Late Medieval Setting* (Leiden, 1968).
103. *WA* 4,267.16–33; Cl. 5,196.16–197.2. Compare Augustine's interpretation, *Enarr.* in Ps. 115, n. 3; *Corpus Christianorum* 40, col. 1654, lines 1–27.
104. *WA* 4,268.29–35.
105. *WA* 4,269.3–15.
106. *WA* 4,269.15–20.
107. *WA* 4,273.14–22.
108. Cf. Olavi Tarvainen, "Der Gedanke der Conformitas Christi in Luthers Theologie," *ZSTh* 22 (1953), 26–43, esp. 40. See also the *Operationes in Psalmos*, Ps. 5:12 (*WA* 5,167.36–168.7). Cf *WA* 5,188.30–32.
109. *Schol.* to Ps. 4:2 (Autumn, 1516), *WA* 55²,57.3–58.11. On Tauler's view of passivity as spiritual self-elevation, cf. Bengt Hägglund, "The Background of Luther's Doctrine of Justification in Late Medieval Theology," *Lutheran World* 8 (1961), 24–36, esp. 30f.
110. *WA* 4,467.24–26.
111. *WA* 50,659.22–24; cf. the discussion in " 'Iustitia Christi' and 'Iustitia Dei' " (cited in note 72), p. 12.
112. For a more exact analysis of the term "affectus" in the young Luther, cf. Günther Metzger, *Gelebter Glaube. Die Formierung reformatorischen Denkens in Luthers erster Psalmenvorlesung* (Göttingen, 1964). Metzger's definition of "extasis" in the excursus on "excessus" (*ibid.*, pp. 111f.) requires further work.
113. Cf. Reinhard Schwarz, *Fides, Spes und Caritas beim jungen Luther* (Berlin, 1962), p. 148, n. 213.
114. Cf. *WA* 1,342.37–343.8 (*Sermo de Passione*, 1518).
115. Comments on Rom. 8:6 as an explanation of Ps. 31(32):9; *WA* 3,176.14–24; Cl. 4,107.25–108.1.
116. *WA* 4,647.24f. (Sermon, Aug., 1517 [?]).
117. Cf. the discussion of this important discovery by Gerhard Ebeling, "Die Anfänge von Luthers Hermeneutik," *ZThK* 48 (1951), 172–230, esp. 226, and "Luthers Psalterdruck vom Jahre 1513," *ZThK* 50 (1953), 43–99, esp. 92ff. Cf. also the suggestion by Werbeck (note 91), p. 104, that in the medieval tradition the anagogical sense "weniger häufig . . . zum Zuge kam." Cf. Henri de Lubac, *Exégèse médiévale. Les quatre sens de l'Ecriture*, 1 (Paris, 1959), 139.
118. *Schol.* to Ps. 76(77):13, *WA* 3,532.7f.; Cl. 5,160.28f.
119. Cf. above, pp. 226–229.
120. Ebeling (note 117), pp. 95ff.; cf. *WA* 55/1,9.28ff.
121. Although the early ecclesiology of Luther is not a topic for detailed discussion here, I believe that the usual criticism by Roman Catholic scholars, which spies in the first lectures on the psalms documentation for an individualistic interpretation of the "congregatio fidelium," must be corrected by Luther's conception of anagogy as the *common* history of the people of God, without foregoing individual exceptions. On the literature, cf. Gerhard Müller, "Ekklesiologie und Kirchenkritik beim jungen Luther," *Neue ZSTh* 7 (1965), 100–128.
122. *Schol.* to Ps. 68(69):17, *WA* 3,433.2–4; Cl. 5,147.7–10.
123. *WA* 55/1,4.25f.
124. *Schol.* to Ps. 64(65):2, *WA* 3,372.23–25; Cl. 5,130.11f. Cf. *WA* 1,336.10–12 (*Sermo de passione Christi*, 1518).

125. *WA* 5,163.28f.

126. *WA* 8,111.29–5 (1521).

127. Cf. Thomas M. McDonough O.P., *The Law and the Gospel in Luther: A Study of Martin Luther's Confessional Writings* (Oxford, 1963), p. 53: "Indisputably, Luther understands imputative righteousness as an extrinsic or forensic relation. . . ."

128. *WA* 39¹,109.1–3 (*Disputatio de iustificatione*, 1536). In the Roman legal tradition "possessio" and "ususfructus" from the contrast to "proprietas" or "dominium." Cf. Max Kaser, *Eigentum und Besitz im älteren römischen Recht* (Weimar, 1943), pp. 310ff. and Ernst Levy, *West Roman Vulgar Law: The Law of Property* (Philadelphia, 1951), pp. 19ff.

129. One should concede that in one of its very earliest statements the "extra se (nos)" designates simply the contrast between God's aseity and the dependence of man on divine providence. *WA* 4,481.20f. (to Faber, *Quincuplex Psalterium*, Ps. 15(16):2). The "extra-dimension" is, therefore, not only applicable to fallen man and his justification, but also to man as a created being.

130. *WA* 5,144.34–36 (1519–21); *ibid.*, 176.12. *WA* 40¹,41.3–5. Cf. Karl Holl, *Ges. Aufs. zur KG*, I, 131. Cf. *WA* 56,386.24f., where it is clear that "rapi" need not necessarily mean an "excessus mentis" to God.

131. Gerson (note 1), pp. 190, 129f. Luther, *WA* 56,387.2–4; Cl. 5,270.14–16. Cf. the transcript, *WA* 57,199.6ff.

132. *WA* 1,340.35–341.3 (*Sermo de passione*, 1518).

133. *Schol.* to Rom. 4:7; *WA* 56,289.18–21; Cl. 5,245.11–15. *Ibid.*, 276.7ff; 289.29–31.

134. *WA* 56,290.18–22; Cl. 5,245.30–34.

135. *WA* 1,558.4f. (1518).

136. Peter Abelard, *Ethica* c. 19 (*MPL* 178, 664 D).

137. Bernard, *Tractatus de gradibus humilitatis et superbiae*, c. 6, n. 19 (*MPL* 182, 952).

138. Gerson, *In festo S. Bernardi* (Aug. 20, 1402), Glorieux, V, 336.

139. Commentary on Ezekiel 1:10 (*MPL* 25, 22); cf. Commentary on Malachi (*MPL* 25, 1563).

140. II *Sent.*, d. 39, a. 2, q. 1, ad 4; *ibid.*, ad 1. Cf. *ibid.*, a. 2, q. 3, ad 5. Cf. also Alexander of Hales, *Summa* I/II (*Ad Claras Aquas* II, Nr. 418); Scotus, *Ox.* II, d. 39, q. 1 (Vives, XIII, 409ff.); *Rep., ibid.* (Vives, XXIII, 203). For our purposes it is not important to discuss further the relation of *synderesis* and conscience or to distinguish *synderesis, apex mentis*, and *scintilla animae*. In this regard cf. Hirsch (note 87), pp. 11ff. An interesting variation of this concept appears in Wessel Gansfort, *De Providentia* in *Opera omnia* (Groningen, 1614), p. 722.

141. Geiler of Kaysersberg, fol. 6ᵇ (note 48), p. 222.

142. *Opera*, VII, 313 a/b.

143. Schatzgeyer (note 37), *Epilogus et conclusio*, 330ᵇ.

144. *WA* 1,32.1–16 (Sermon, Dec. 26, 1514).

145. Cf. my "Facientibus quod in se est Deus non denegat gratiam," *HThR* 55 (1962), 317–342, esp. 333ff.

146. *WA* 1,32.33–40 (Sermon, Dec. 26, 1514); *ibid.*, 33.36f.; 34.4–7.

147. *Ibid.*, 36.37–37.1. See the connection between *gemitus* and *homo vetus, Operationes in Psalmos*, Ps. 5:12; *WA* 5,164.22–31. For a more detailed

analysis of the texts which deal with the *synderesis* and *fides,* see S. E. Ozment (note 45).

148. *WA* 5,119.12–18 (1519–21); cf. *WA* 55²,80.29–81.2 (1516) and the detailed annotations in *WA* 55¹,22.34–25.9. Cf. the thesis of Arnold of Heisterbach in Gerhard Ritter, *Via Antiqua und Via Moderna* (Heidelberg, 1922; Darmstadt, 1963), 155.16ff.; cf. 63f.

149. *WA* 1,196.25f. *(Die sieben Busspsalmen,* 1517).

150. *Operationes in Psalmos,* Ps. 5:12; *WA* 5,176.11–22.

BIBLIOGRAPHICAL SOURCES
AND SURVEYS
OF THE REFORMATION

Alberigo, G. "The Council of Trent: New Views on the Occasion of its 4th Centenary," *Concilium* 7: *Historical Problems of Church Renewal* (Glen Rock, N.J., 1956), pp. 69ff.

Bainton, R. H. *Bibliography of the Continental Reformation* (Chicago, 1925).

————. "Interpretations of the Reformation," *The American Historical Review* 61 (1960), reprinted in *Studies on the Reformation* (Boston, 1963), pp. 104ff.

————. "The Left Wing of the Reformation," *Journal of Religion* 21 (1941), reprinted in *Studies on the Reformation* (Boston, 1963), pp. 119ff.

————. "The Present State of Servetus Studies, *Journal of Modern History* IV/1 (March, 1932).

————. "Survey of Periodical Literature in the United States, 1945–51," *ARG* 43 (1952).

Clebsch, W. A. "New Perspectives on the Reformation," *Religion in Life* 35 (1965).

Dillenberger, J. "Major Volumes and Selected Periodical Literature in Luther Studies, 1950–55," *Church History* XXV (1956), 160ff.

————. "Major Volumes and Selected Periodical Literature in Luther Studies, 1956–59," *Church History* XXX (1961), 3ff.

Dowey, E. A. "Studies in Calvin and Calvinism Since 1948," *Church History* XXIV (1955), 360ff.; *Church History* XXIX (1960), 127–204.

Febvre, L. "Le Progrès récent des études sur Luther," *Revue d'histoire moderne,* 1 (1926).

Fraenkel, P., and M. Greschat, *Zwanzig Jahre Melanchthonstudium: Sechs Literaturberichte (1945–1965)* (Geneva, 1967).

Franz, G., ed. *Bibliographie de la Réforme, 1450–1648*, I–V (Leiden, 1961–65).

Friesen, A. "Thomas Müntzer in Marxist Thought," *Church History* XXXIV (1965), 306–327.

Grimm, H. J. "Luther Research Since 1920," *Journal of Modern History* XXXII (1960), 105ff.

Hagen, K. G. "Changes in the Understanding of Luther," *Theological Studies* 29 (1968), 472–496.

Hassinger, E. *Das Werden des neuzeitlichen Europas 1300–1600* (Braunschweig, 1966²), pp. 401ff.

Hillerbrand, H. J. *A Bibliography of Anabaptism* (Elkhart, Ind., 1962).

Huber, R. M. "Recent Important Literature Regarding the Catholic Church During the Late Renaissance Period (1500–1648)," *Church History* X (1941), 3ff.

Iserloh, E. "Zur Gestalt und Biographie Thomas Münzers," *Trierer Theologische Zeitschrift* 71 (1962), 248–253.

Kirchner, H. "Neue Müntzeriana," *ZKG* 72 (1961), 113–116.

Kohler, W. *Bibliographie Brentiana* (Berlin, 1904).

————. "Das Täufertum in der neueren Kirchenhistorischen Forschung. IV. "Die Spiritualisten," *ARG* 41 (1948), 164–171.

Kohls, E. W. "Zum Forschungsstand der Theologie des Erasmus Innerhalb der Erasmusliteratur," Introduction to *Die Theologie des Erasmus* I (Basel, 1966).

Krahn, C. "The Historiography of the Mennonites in the Netherlands," *Church History* XIII (1944), 182ff.

Lau, F. and E. Bizer, *Reformationsgeschichte Deutschlands bis 1555. Die Kirche in ihrer Geschichte* III/k (Göttingen, 1964).

Liebing, H. "Reformationsgeschichtliche Literatur (1945–54)," *Deutsche Vierteljahrsschrift für Literaturwissenschaft und Geistesgeschichte* X (1954), 516ff.

Locher, G. W. "Die Wandlung des Zwingli-Bildes in der neueren Forschung," *Zwingliana* XI/9 (1963), 560ff. English translation: "The Change of the Understanding of Zwingli in Recent Research," *Church History* XXXIV (1965), 3ff.

Margolin, J. C. *Douze Années de Bibliographie Erasmienne (1950–61)* (Paris, 1963).

McNeill, J. T. "Thirty Years of Calvin Study," *Church History* XVII (1948), 207–240.

Metzger, W. "Müntzeriana," *Thüringisch-Sächsische Zeitschrift für Geschichte und Kunst* 16 (1927), 59–78.

Moeller, B. *Spätmittelalter. Die Kirche in ihrer Geschichte* 2/H/I (Göttingen, 1966).

Müller, G. "Neuere Literatur zur Theologie des jungen Luther," *Kerygma und Dogma* (1965), 325ff.

von Muralt, L. "Zum Problem: Reformation und Taüfertum," *Zwingliana* 6 (1934), 65–85.

Niesel, W. *Calvin Bibliographie 1901–59* (Munich, 1961).

Oberman, H. A. "From Occam to Luther: A Survey of Recent Historical Studies on the Religious Thought of the 14th and 15th Centuries," *Concilium* 17: *Historical Investigations* (New York, 1966), pp. 126ff.

O'Malley, J. W. "Recent Studies in Church History, 1300–1600," *The Catholic Historical Review* 55 (1969), 394–437.

Parker, T. H. L. "A Bibliography and Survey of the British Study of Calvin, 1900–1940," *Evangelical Quarterly* (1946), pp. 123ff.

Pauck, W. "The Historiography of the German Reformation During the Past Twenty Years: Research in the History of the Anabaptists," *Church History* IX (1940), 305ff.

Pesch, O. H. "Twenty Years of Catholic Luther Research," *Lutheran World* 13 (1966), 303–316.

————. "Zur Frage nach Luthers reformatorischer Wende: Ergebnisse und Probleme der Diskussion um Ernst Bizer, *Fides ex auditu*," *Der Durchbruch der reformatorischen Erkenntnis bei Luther*, ed. B. Lohse (Darmstadt, 1968), pp. 445–505.

Pollet, J. V.-M. "Erasmiana," *Revue des Sciences Religieuses* 17 (1952).

Read, C., ed. *Bibliography of British History: Tudor Period* (Oxford, 1959²).

Robbert, G. S. "A Checklist of Luther's Writings in English," *Concordia Theological Monthly* 36 (1965), 772ff.

Rupp, E. G. "Luther: The Contemporary Image," *Kirche, Mystik, Heiligung und das Natürliche bei Luther. Vorträge des Dritten Internationalen Kongresses für Lutherforschung* (Göttingen, 1967), pp. 9–19.

Schmid, R. "Thomas Müntzer im Geschichtsbild des Dialektischen Materialismus," *Deutsches Pfarrerblatt* 65 (1965), 258–262.

Schottenloher, K., ed. *Bibliographie zur deutschen Geschichte im Zeitalter der Glaubensspaltung*, I–VIII (1962–).

Spitz, L. W. "Current Accents in Luther Study: 1960–67," *Theological Studies* 28 (1967), 549–573.

————. "Reformation and Humanity in Marxist Historical Research," *Lutheran World* 16/2 (1969), 124–139.

Stupperich, R. "Stand und Aufgabe der Butzerforschung," *ARG* 42 (1951), 244ff.

————. "Buceriana," *ARG* 43 (1952), 106ff.

———— and E. Steinborn, "Bibliographia Bucerana," *Schriften des Vereins für Reformationsgeschichte* 169 (1952), 37–96.

Tavard, G. "The Catholic Reform in the 16th Century," *Church History* XXVI (1957), 275ff.

Teufel, E. "Die 'Deutsche Theologie' und Sebastian Franck im Lichte der neueren Forschung," *Theologische Rundschau* N.F. 11 (1939), 304–319.

Thompson, B. "Bucer Study Since 1918," *Church History* XXV (1956), 63ff.

———. "Zwingli Study Since 1918," *Church History* XIX (1950), 116ff.

Vajta, V., ed. *Luther and Melanchthon in the History and Theology of the Reformation* (Philadelphia, 1961).

Valkoff, M. "Chronique Castellionienne," *Neophilologus* 42 (Groningen, 1958), 277–288.

Wicks, J. "Luther on the Person Before God," *Theological Studies* 30 (1969), 289–311.

Williams, G. H. "Studies in the Radical Reformation (1517–1618): A Bibliographical Survey of Research Since 1939," *Church History* XXVII/1 (1958), 46ff.; *Church History* XXVII/2 (1958), 124ff.

———. "Bibliography of Material in English Translation Written by Representatives of the Radical Reformation," *Spiritual and Anabaptist Writers* (Philadelphia, 1957), pp. 285ff.

Wolf, G. *Quellenkunde der deutschen Reformationsgeschichte,* I–III (Gotha, 1915–33).

INDEX

Abelard, 238
Abraham, 122
Absil, J., 74
Acceptatio divina, in Ockhamism, 114
Acquoy, J. G. R., 183
Adam, Paracelsus' interpretation of, 200–201
Adam, Alfred, 138
Adolf, duke of Geldern, 55
Adrian VI (pope, 1522–1523), 179
Agricola, Rudolf, 42, 49, 61, 164
Agrippa of Nettesheim, 75, 190, 194
Albert the Great, 173
Albrecht of Brandenburg, 55
Alchemy, Paracelsus' view of, 187–188, 202–205, 211, 216, 217
Alexander the Great, 171
Alexander of Hales, 138, 227, 250
Alexander de Villa Dei, 163
Altenstaig, Johann, 231, 233, 248
Ambrose, 165, 173, 175, 227
Amon, K., 66, 74
Andreas, Willy, 64
Andrelini, Faustus, 175
Anne, Saint, 42

Anselm of Canterbury, 121, 127, 165, 167
Appel, Heinrich, 70
Aquinas, Thomas, 3, 21, 25, 36, 69, 125, 127, 166, 173, 222, 227, 239, 244; authority of, in Erfurt, 30; and *facere quod in se est,* 139; and Luther, 151, 153
Aristocracy, 28, 87; in Bohemia, 95–97
Aristotelianism, 89
Aristotle, 26, 41, 122, 123, 138, 212; Luther's view of, 130
Arnold of Heisterbach, 251
Astrology, 187–188
Auer, A., 69
Augustine, 26, 36, 42, 49, 122, 124, 128, 165, 173, 175, 213, 224, 227; criticism of, by John of Wesel, 31; ecclesiology of, 32; and mysticism, 222–223; rule of, 182
Aurelius, Cornelius. See Gerard, Cornelius.
Avicenna, 189, 212
Axters, S., 69

Bach, A., 68
Bainton, Roland, 137

257